COMPANY LAW

To Rita, Dawn and Catherine

COMPANY LAW

Colin Thomas

LL.B. (Honours), Dip Ed, Barrister-at-Law
Senior Lecturer at Liverpool Polytechnic

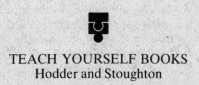

TEACH YOURSELF BOOKS
Hodder and Stoughton

First printed 1982

Copyright © 1982
Colin Thomas

British Library Cataloguing in Publication Data

Thomas, Colin
Company law.—(Teach yourself books)
1. Corporation law—England
I. Title
344.206′66   KD2079
ISBN 0 340 26820 4

Printed and bound in Great Britain for
Hodder and Stoughton Educational,
a division of Hodder and Stoughton Ltd,
Mill Road, Dunton Green, Sevenoaks, Kent,
by Richard Clay (The Chaucer Press) Ltd,
Bungay, Suffolk. Photoset by
Rowland Phototypesetting Ltd,
Bury St Edmunds, Suffolk.

Contents

Preface

I have often told my students that the study of company law is similar to completing a jigsaw puzzle. Although each piece is looked at separately, at the end of the course the pieces fit into place and the overall picture can be seen. So it is with company law.

My aim in writing this book is to show in as concise a manner as possible how companies are formed, financed, controlled and liquidated. I have quoted many cases, as these illustrate the many facets of company law.

My thanks are due to the Department of Trade for permission to reproduce their synopses of the Companies Acts 1980 and 1981.

My thanks also to my wife, Rita, for her encouragement, patience, and for being such a good listener.

Colin Thomas

1

The History and Development of Company Law

The medieval guild was one of the earliest forms of business association. The guilds sought to preserve a monopoly of trade in a particular
area by regulating the activities of their members, and were therefore
monopolistic and restrictive in character.

With the growth of trade in the Middle Ages traders found it
advantageous to combine with one another in trading ventures. They
were able to bring together large amounts of capital and they would
share in the profits of such ventures. This form of partnership had no
legal existence apart from the individual partners, as the property and
debts of the partnership were regarded as the property and debts of the
individual partnership. Such a partnership ceased to exist on the death
of any one partner.

Although the Crown had granted charters to individual companies
since the fourteenth century, it was only when the Tudor monarchs
granted charters of incorporation to trading companies in the sixteenth
century that the movement towards merchant investment and capital-
ism gained momentum. Companies sought Royal charters in order to
obtain a monopoly of trade in certain areas of the world, for example,
in Africa and the Indies. The Crown also benefited in that it was able to
control trade in these areas.

The emergence of the joint stock company

Two types of overseas trading companies emerged during this period –
the regulated company and the joint stock company.

The earliest form of company was the regulated company, which
was a loose association of traders and merchants who traded with their
own stock on their own account, for example, the Baltic and the

Levant companies. They were, however, subject to the discipline of the governing bodies of these companies.

At a later date there evolved the joint stock company, such as the East India Company and the African Company. Traders operated on a joint stock and each contributed to the merchandise to be sold at the end of the voyage (i.e. the stock) and would share rateably in the profits at the conclusion of the venture.

A considerable amount of capital was raised for financing these ventures. The East India Company, formed to trade with the Indies, attracted £1 500 000 by public subscription for its voyages in 1617.

The incorporated company was seen to possess certain characteristics and advantages. The company's property was under the control of the board of governors or directors; it had a common seal; it was capable of existing in perpetuity; and an individual member was not liable for the debts of the company.

The end of the seventeenth century marked a decline in the number of companies formed for foreign trade, but the number of domestic companies increased. These companies had a permanent fixed capital and encouraged investment by having shares which could be freely sold and transferred. Many of these companies were formed without being incorporated by Royal Charter or Acts of Parliament but merely by executing deeds of settlement. The provisions contained in those deeds were similar to the provisions of incorporated companies.

Other companies purchased the charters of moribund companies and engaged in any venture or trade which appeared profitable – for example, a banking company acquired the charter of the Sword Blade Company which had been incorporated in 1690 to manufacture hollow sword blades.

Another form of enterprise which appeared at the end of the seventeenth century was that of lending money at interest to the State. The Bank of England was formed in 1694 when the government incorporated a group of its creditors.

The South Sea Bubble and its effect

In 1719 the Bank of England was outbid by the South Sea Company which offered £7 500 000 to acquire the whole of the national debt of £31 000 000. The South Sea Company considered that a loan which carried interest, owned by the State, would enable it to raise large sums of money to work its monopoly of the South American trade. In 1720 Parliament passed the Bubble Act which prohibited unincorporated trading companies from acting or presuming to act as corporations. It also prohibited the use of charters other than for the purposes for which they were originally granted. The Act was passed for the benefit of the South Sea Company. It was expected that the prosecution of the four other companies operating with obsolete charters, who were trespassing on the South Sea Company's preserves, would result in more capital being invested in the South Sea Company. These prosecutions led to widespread panic and loss of public confidence. South Sea stock fell in six months from 1000 per cent to 125 per cent. The company was then rescued by government intervention and remained in existence until 1807.

The combined effect of the loss of public confidence and the restrictions contained in the Bubble Act made it almost impossible for companies to raise further capital by public subscription for the next 100 years. During that time capital was obtained almost exclusively from affluent private investors. A few companies were incorporated by special Acts of Parliament from 1760 onwards to finance the construction of canals, and later the construction of railways – between 1758 and 1802 £13 000 000 was subscribed for canal construction.

As the Bubble Act had made the privilege of incorporation too costly or impractical, businessmen had to devise a new form of business association. They formed unincorporated companies which were associations formed by deeds of settlement, under which members agreed to take shares and abide by the regulations. The management of the company was entrusted to directors, and provision was made for the transfer of shares. Although the undertaking thereby had perpetual succession, the Courts treated it as a partnership and its members were liable for its debts. It would appear that there was little litigation relating to these companies in the eighteenth century and that most of the disputes were submitted to arbitration.

The Bubble Act was repealed in 1825, and although it was a purely negative measure it was soon established that unincorporated associations were lawful at common law.

The emergence of company legislation

In 1841 a committee, under the chairmanship of W. E. Gladstone, was set up to consider company law reform. Its recommendations led to the passing of the Joint Stock Companies Act 1844, which provided a simple method of incorporation for a joint stock company.

Certain documents giving details of the company's organisation and membership had to be registered with the Register of Joint Stock Companies and were open to public inspection. Although the company could hold property and take legal proceedings in its own name, its members remained personally liable for the company's debts. The

1844 Act provided that a 'full and fair' balance sheet should be presented at the annual general meeting; that an auditor should be appointed to report on the balance sheet; and that an audited balance sheet should be filed with the Registrar.

The Joint Stock Companies Act 1855 introduced the principle of limited liability, despite warnings that such a change would encourage fraud and reckless conduct by promoters and directors. Three-quarters of the company's capital had to have been subscribed, and the company could not continue in business if it lost three-quarters of its capital.

A further Joint Stock Companies Act was passed in 1856, which consolidated the Acts of 1844 and 1855, and thenceforward made company formation simple and inexpensive. A mere seven signatures were required for a document called *the memorandum*, and a company no longer required a deed of settlement. It could register its own articles or adopt a model set of articles which were attached to the Act. Once registered, a certificate of incorporation would be granted and the company could then commence business.

Five other Acts were passed between 1856 and 1862, when the first Companies Act was passed which consolidated the previous Acts relating to companies. Provision was made for guarantee and un-limited companies, and the provisions relating to the winding up of companies were extended. The model set of articles attached to the Act was called Table A.

This remained the principal Act until the Companies Act 1908 which consolidated previous company legislation. Some eighteen Companies Acts had been passed since the Act of 1862, and had introduced various new concepts such as the private company, the auditing and publication of company accounts, the registration of mortgages and requirements dealing with prospectuses.

The next landmark in company legislation is to be found in the 1929 Companies Act. This consolidated previous company legislation and introduced certain modern innovations including the emergence of the redeemable preference share, minority protection rights and account-ing provisions dealing with holding and subsidiary companies.

The 1948 Companies Act and subsequent legislation

The 1948 Companies Act adopted most of the recommendations of the Cohen Committee on company law amendment, which recommended that information should be readily available to a company's share-holders and creditors, and to the public, and suggested that means should be found to make it easier for shareholders to exercise a greater degree of control over the company's management. Provision was made for greater disclosure in balance sheet and profit and loss accounts, and for group accounts. The Board of Trade was given wider powers for company investigation, whilst minority rights were also extended.

The 1948 Companies Act remains the principal Act dealing with company legislation and, like its predecessor in 1929, is a consolidating Act, although major changes have been made in company legislation by the subsequent Companies Acts of 1967, 1976, 1980 and 1981.

The 1967 Companies Act gave effect to some of the recommendations of the Jenkins Committee on company reform which presented its report in 1962. The exempt private company was abolished, and important new provisions were introduced in connection with company accounts, directors' reports, re-registration of companies, and Department of Trade investigations and inspections.

The 1976 Companies Act amended various accounting provisions and made new provisions for the appointment, qualifications and powers of auditors. It also required a greater degree of disclosure of interests in a company's shares.

The Companies Act 1980 amended certain aspects of company law and introduced far-reaching changes in connection with the classification and registration of companies. New definitions were introduced for public and private companies, and provision made for the registration and re-registration of companies. New requirements were set out for the issue, payment and maintenance of capital. New pre-emption rights were given to shareholders, and provision was made for variation of certain classes of shares. Restrictions were imposed on the distribution of profits and assets, while numerous sections dealt with directors' duties and conflict of interests. 'Insider dealing' became a criminal offence, while new safeguards were introduced to protect the interests of employees and members.

The Companies Act 1981 included provisions dealing with company accounts, thus implementing the European Community's fourth directive. In particular it reduced the amount of information required from small and medium-sized companies when filing their accounts. The arrangements for the approval of company names were simplified. Companies were permitted to purchase their own shares, 'management buyouts' were facilitated, and restrictions on the use of the share premium account were relaxed, while the law on the disclosure of interests in shares was strengthened. The powers of investigation and enquiry of company inspectors was strengthened and further restrictions imposed on the activities of fraudulent directors.

Company law and community law

As a result of becoming a member of the European Community, the United Kingdom has become subject to the provisions of community law which consist of original and amending treaties and secondary legislation.

The most important sources of secondary legislation are regulations, which are binding on the member states 'without further enactment'; and directives which are binding in principle, although the member states have to legislate to bring them into operation.

The Council of Ministers of the European Economic Community has approved five directives on the harmonisation of company law within the European Community, and four other draft directives are under consideration.

The first directive deals with disclosure of information and the validity of obligations entered into by the company. Section 9 of the European Communities Act 1972 gives effect to most of the proposals of the first directive and has introduced changes giving protection to third parties dealing with the company and its directors; it also provides for the disclosure of certain documents and information, and regulates pre-incorporation contracts.

The second directive deals with the formation of companies, and maintenance of capital and the increase and reduction of capital. The Companies Act 1980 implements the second directive.

The third directive deals with the internal mergers of companies. This includes takeovers, mergers by forming a new company, and the takeover of a company by another which is its sole shareholder.

The fourth directive deals with the contents of the annual accounts, with particular reference to the balance sheet and profit and loss account. It also deals with the disclosure of financial information. This directive has been implemented by the Companies Act 1981.

The fifth draft directive deals with the structure of the limited liability company, with some form of employee participation.

The sixth directive deals with the co-ordination of prospectuses and the requirements for listed securities.

The remaining three directives deal with group accounts, the role and qualifications of auditors, and company re-organisation when a company is dissolved without a winding up and its undertaking transferred to others.

The European Company

The European Commission has published proposals for the creation of a new form of business organisation within the European Community – the European Company.

The aim of the proposals is to provide national companies, already operating within several member countries, with a single unified legal framework. Such a company would have the status of a national company in every member state.

It is envisaged that such a company could only be formed when two or more existing companies, registered in different member states, either amalgamate or form a holding company or a joint subsidiary. The company would be registered in the European Commercial Register kept at the European Court in Luxembourg.

The minimum share capital required by a European Company will be expressed in European Units of Account (E U A) and will be 250000 E U A in the case of a merger or the formation of a holding company, and 100000 E U A in the case of a formation of a joint subsidiary.

There are proposals for the creation of management and supervisory boards with employee representatives on the supervisory boards. The day-to-day management of the company will be exercised by the management board, but will be subject to general supervision by the supervisory board. The management may not close or transfer the company's undertaking, or expand or curtail the company's activities without the previous authorisation of the supervisory board. Substantial provisions are also made for consultation with a works council representing the interest of the employees in such matters as recruitment, promotion and dismissal of personnel, provision of holidays and social facilities.

2

Incorporation

The formation of a company

A company is formed by delivering certain documents to the Registrar of Companies and paying certain fees and stamp duties.

The documents which must be delivered are:

 (i)   a memorandum of association;
 (ii) the articles of association (unless the company intends to adopt Table A as the company's articles);
 (iii) a statement in a form prescribed by the Inland Revenue for the purpose of assessing capital duty;
 (iv) a statutory declaration by either a solicitor engaged in the formation of the company, or by a director or secretary of the company that requirements as to registration have been complied with;
 (v)   a statement of the intended situation of the company's registered office;
 (vi) a statement containing the names and particulars of the first directors and first secretaries of the company.

If a company is formed as a public company it must deposit further documents to satisfy the Registrar that it meets the new capital requirements of public companies, that is that the amount of share capital stated in its memorandum is not less than the authorised minimum – an allotted share capital of £50 000.

The Registrar will sign and issue a certificate of incorporation if he is satisfied that the documents are in order. He must also publish in the *London Gazette* a notice of the issue of a certificate of incorporation. The issue of this certificate is conclusive evidence that the requirements in respect of registration have been complied with, and that a company is duly registered under the Act. If the certificate contains a statement that the company is a public company, this is conclusive evidence of that fact.

A private company can commence business immediately upon receipt of a certificate of incorporation.

A public company is prohibited from doing business or exercising any borrowing powers unless the Registrar has issued an additional certificate that the company's allotted share capital is not less than the authorised minimum, and the company has received at least one quarter of the nominal value of each issued share, plus the whole of any premium payable on such a share (1980 Companies Act, section 4).

The consequences of incorporation
From the date of incorporation a company becomes a body corporate or corporation. It is an artificial legal person with rights and duties distinct from its members or shareholders. This was established in the nineteenth century in the case of *Salomon v. Salomon*. Salomon was a prosperous leather merchant living in Leicester who sold his business to a limited company, formed for the purpose, for £39000. Salomon was given 20000 £1 shares, debentures to the value of £10000 and the balance in cash. His wife and five children were given one share each. A year later the business foundered with assets of £6000 and liabilities of £17500, of which £10000 was owed to Salomon for the debentures. (In a winding up, a debenture holder is paid in priority to unsecured creditors.) The unsecured creditors claimed that as Salomon Ltd was in reality the same person as Salomon, their debts should be paid first. It was held that Salomon was entitled to the £6000, as the company had been validly formed and was therefore an independent legal person. The business belonged to the company, i.e. to Salomon Ltd and not to Salomon.

In *Lee v. Lee's Air Farming Ltd*, Lee held 2999 of the company's 3000 shares. He was the company's governing director and was also employed as the company's chief pilot at a salary to be determined by himself. He was killed in an air crash and it was held that his widow was entitled to compensation as her husband was employed by the company.

In *Macaura v. Northern Assurance Company*, Macaura formed a company and sold his timber estate to the company, receiving shares as payment for the sale. However, he insured the timber in his own name. A fire destroyed most of the timber and it was held that he could not claim under his policy as the timber was owned by the company.

A corporation also has perpetual succession in that its existence is maintained by new members who replace those who have died or transferred their interests. Should the membership fall below the statutory minimum of two, the company continues in existence. In such a case application may be made to the Court to convene a meeting of the company.

Certain consequences follow from this legal fiction of the legal personality of a company. A company may enter into contracts in the same way as a natural person, provided that it is not acting *ultra vires* (i.e. beyond its powers). If a contract is required to be under seal, that is in the form of a deed, a company's seal has to be affixed. If a contract is required to be in writing, a person acting under the company's authority may sign the contract. Should it be an oral contract, a duly authorised person may contract on the company's behalf.

A company may be a founder member, shareholder, director, secretary or manager of another company, but it cannot be an auditor of another company. It may also be a partner in a partnership, and a partnership may be formed where all the partners are companies.

A company has the capacity to commit torts, or civil wrongs, and is liable for the torts of its employees or agents as long as they are acting in the course of their employment (i.e. vicarious liability). In *Limpus v. London General Omnibus Co. Ltd*, the drivers of the horse drawn buses had been expressly forbidden by their employer, the company, to race against buses of other companies. In one race, a bus overturned and Limpus and other passengers were injured. Nevertheless, the company was liable.

It is uncertain if a company is liable for the torts of an employee whose acts are *ultra vires* the company. This can only arise if the company has expressly authorised those acts. A widely held view is that the company is not liable as it cannot authorise an act which is beyond its powers. A company may also be prosecuted for the crimes of its employees, if the statute imposes liability on the employer as well as on the employees, despite the fact that the offences have required *mens rea* (i.e. a guilty mind) which the company, as an abstract personality, could not have and which the board of directors did not have. Nevertheless, in recent cases, the Courts have held that an act cannot impose criminal liability on a company unless the person or persons who manage its affairs are directly participating in the criminal act. In *Tesco Supermarkets Ltd v. Nattrass* a shop manager charged an old age pensioner the full price for a box of washing powder, despite the fact that the company had advertised the powder at a lower price. The company was held not liable under the Trade Descriptions Act, as the manager, according to Lord Denning, was one of the hands of the company and not part of its brain.

There are obviously certain crimes which a company *cannot* commit, such as perjury, bigamy, and offences for which the only punishment is imprisonment. A company *can* be charged with a variety of offences such as conspiracy to defraud, using a motor vehicle on a road contrary to the Road Traffic Act 1972, and offences under the Unsolicited Goods and Services Act 1971.

Lifting the veil of incorporation

A result of incorporation is that a veil is drawn between the persons dealing with a company and its members. Proceedings may not be taken against the members by third parties, as a company is 'a legal person just as much as an individual'.

However, the Courts have not hesitated to lift the veil of incorporation and examine the realities of a company's ownership and control if the need should arise. It has been lifted in the following cases:

If the number of members of a company falls below two, and the company carries on business for more than six months, the remaining member (if aware of it) is liable for the payment of the company's debts contracted after the six month period (section 31).

If control of a company registered in England is believed to be in enemy hands, it may be necessary to examine the reality of the situation. In *Daimler Co. Ltd v. Continental Tyre and Rubber Co.*, the members of the company were a company incorporated in Germany, and five other individuals. Four of the individuals were German and the other, a British subject, held one share out of the total 25 000. It was held that the company would be regarded as an enemy company.

Where one company is a holding company and it has a subsidiary or subsidiaries, the Court may decide that the subsidiary is an agent for the holding company. In *Smith, Stone and Knight Ltd v. Birmingham Corporation* certain premises were owned by a subsidiary of the parent company. The parent company had complete control of the subsidiary and kept its books and accounts. Only the holders of annual tenancies were entitled to compensation if their property was compulsorily acquired. Although it was the subsidiary that had the annual tenancy, it was nevertheless held that the parent company was entitled to compensation.

The Courts will lift the veil to determine whether one company is a subsidiary of another. Section 154 stipulates that a company is a subsidiary if another company is a member of it and controls the composition of the board of directors, or holds half of its equity share capital. It will also be regarded as a subsidiary if its holding company is a subsidiary of another holding company. The relationship of a holding company and its subsidiary is of importance in certain instances. As a general rule a subsidiary may not hold shares in its holding company. If a company has a subsidiary or subsidiaries, it must lay group accounts before the general meeting together with its own balance sheet and profit and loss accounts. An inspector appointed by the Department of Trade to investigate a company's affairs may, if he thinks necessary, investigate the affairs of a related company, that is its subsidiary or holding company as the case may be.

The Courts will lift the veil in some revenue cases in order to establish in what country a company is resident, and where its management lies. In *Unit Construction Co. Ltd v. Bullock*, a United Kingdom company had three Kenyan subsidiaries which were, in theory, completely separate from the parent company. The parent company nevertheless controlled their activities, although it had no constitutional right to do so. It was held that, for tax purposes, the Kenyan subsidiaries were resident in the United Kingdom where their control and management were located.

The veil of incorporation is lifted if a proposed merger has to be examined by the Courts. Under the Fair Trading Act a merger arises if two or more enterprises cease to be distinct enterprises in that they are brought under common ownership or common control, or one of them ceases to be carried on at all, as a result of an agreement to prevent competition between the enterprises. Although the E E C Treaty does not expressly provide for a system of merger control, the Commission and the Court of Justice have taken the view that Article 86 may in certain circumstances be used to control mergers. Article 86 prohibits any abuse by any undertaking of its dominant position within the Common Market in so far as it may affect trade between member states. Secondary legislation has also decreed that a holding company and its subsidiary should be treated as an economic unit.

Occasionally the device of incorporation has been used for some improper or illegal purpose, and the courts have lifted the veil in these instances. In *Merchandise Transport Ltd v. British Transport Commission*, a transport company applied for licences through its subsidiary company as it was unlikely to obtain these licences if it applied in its own name. It intended transferring its vehicles to its subsidiary. The Court refused to treat the application as one by the subsidiary, as it regarded the subsidiary and its holding company as one commercial entity. In *Gilford Motor Co. Ltd v. Horne*, an employee covenanted that after leaving the firm he would not solicit his previous employer's customers. Shortly after leaving his employment he formed a company with his wife and one other person, and this company sent out circulars to his previous employer's customers. The Court granted an injunction against the ex-employee and his company.

The Courts will prevent an abuse of section 209, by prohibiting the formation of a new company by members holding 90 per cent of the shares in the existing company, if the new company is formed solely to expropriate the shares of minority shareholders (*Re Bugle Press*).

The Courts will also, in certain instances, have regard to the substance of an association rather than its particular form. This applies especially to small private companies which are founded on a personal relationship between their members. Some are to all intents 'partnerships' which are formed as companies. The Court may, if the personal relationship between members has foundered or soured, order such a company to be wound up under the just and equitable clause of section 222 (*Re Yenidje Tobacco Co*).

Companies and partnerships

The characteristics and attributes of a company can be conveniently compared with an alternative form of business association, the partnership.

A company is a corporation, a separate legal person, while a partnership is no more than the sum of its members. Although a partnership can sue and be sued in its own name, it is the partners who are liable for the firm's debts and contracts. The debts and contracts of a company are those of the company, and not its members.

The members of a company are not its agents and may not enter into contracts on a company's behalf, although its directors are limited agents. A partner is normally an agent for the partnership and may bind the firm by his acts. A member of a company may enter into a contract with a company, but a partner is not permitted to make a contract with the firm.

Shares in a company are freely transferable, unless a company's articles decree otherwise. A partner cannot transfer his shares in a firm without the consent of the other partners. A partner may assign his share in a firm, but the assignee does not become a partner and is merely entitled to the assigning partner's share of the profits. Different rights can also be attached to different classes of shares issued by companies. This degree of flexibility is not found in partnerships, although certain partners may be given certain rights and powers in a partnership agreement, for example to purchase a deceased partner's share. A company may now purchase the shares of its members (Companies Act 1981).

A company, apart from an unlimited company, is subject to rules regarding the raising and maintenance of its share capital, which can only be increased or reduced in accordance with the provisions of the Companies Acts. Partners may alter the amount of capital in a partnership without any such restrictions.

The property of a company is vested in the company. Partnership property belongs to the partners and any change in the constitution of the partnership, such as on death or retirement of a partner, is a change in the ownership of the partnership property.

The liability of a member of a company may be limited either by shares or by guarantee. The liability of a partner for the partnership debts is unlimited, with the exception of a limited partner under the Limited Partnerships Act 1907.

A company's powers are determined by the objects clause in its memorandum of association and by the Companies Acts in general. The doctrine of *ultra vires* does not apply to partners, who may carry on any activity which the partners have agreed to enter into, as long as it is legal.

A company must have a minimum of two members. There is no maximum. Partnerships may not consist of more than twenty partners, with the exception of partnerships of certain groups of professional men, such as solicitors, accountants, consulting engineers, stockbrokers and surveyors.

A company has perpetual succession so that any circumstance affecting a member – insanity, death, bankruptcy – does not directly affect the life of a company. On the death or bankruptcy of a partner the partnership is automatically dissolved. A partnership may also be dissolved at any time by a partner, unless entered into for a fixed time, but no one member of a company may wind up a company.

If an insolvent company is wound up, this does not make its members bankrupt; but the bankruptcy of a partnership means the bankruptcy of every partner (except for a limited partner).

A company's accounts are open to inspection by the general public, with the exception of the accounts of an unlimited company; partnership accounts are never subject to public scrutiny.

There are fewer formalities to be observed with partnerships, as a partnership agreement may be in the form of a deed, in writing, oral or even implied by conduct. In forming a company, certain documents must be delivered to the Registrar, and stamp duty, registration fees and legal costs are payable.

3

The Classification of Companies

The modern company is a form of business organisation which has proved attractive to businessmen and investors seeking the benefits of incorporation and limited liability. The present statutes governing companies are the Companies Acts of 1948, 1967, 1976, 1980 and 1981. The main Act is the 1948 Act and references in this book to the Act and to sections are references to the 1948 Companies Act and its respective sections. References to the other Acts are stated as such.

The Act recognises five main types of companies:

The chartered company;
The statutory company;
The cost book company;
The registered company;
The oversea company.

1 Chartered companies

Chartered companies are incorporated by the grant of a charter from the Crown. In previous centuries trading concerns were granted royal charters and some of these companies are still in existence at the present time – for example, the Hudson Bay Company was granted a charter by Charles II in 1670, while the Bank of England was granted a charter in 1694. The Stock Exchange Year Book lists seven chartered companies. Charters are now used to incorporate non-commercial bodies, universities and colleges.

There is no restriction on the number of members in this type of company, and unless otherwise stated the members are not personally liable for the company's contracts. The creditors' remedy lies against the company.

2   Statutory companies

These companies are formed by special Acts of Parliament. This method of company formation was frequently used in the past for the formation of public utilities such as railway, gas, canals, electricity and water companies. These companies often required special powers, such as compulsory purchase of land, and were usually granted a monopoly in a particular locality. As a result of nationalisation most statutory companies have been taken over by Public Boards, and by Corporations set up by Public Acts. Of the fifty-two remaining statutory companies quoted on the Stock Exchange, twenty-eight are water companies.

A statutory company must have a minimum of two members. A member whose shares are not fully paid up may be liable for the company's debts if the company has insufficient assets to satisfy its creditors.

3   Cost book companies

This is a special type of company governing tin mining, and is found mainly in Devon and Cornwall; it is basically a partnership. Its members are known as adventurers; the manager is known as the purser or secretary; and the officer supervising the mining operations is known as the captain of the mine. Its shares are known as 'doles' and the adventurers have unlimited liability for all the company's debts.

The Stannaries Courts formerly exercised jurisdiction over these companies, but this is now exercised by the County Courts of Cornwall. Although this type of company is mentioned in the Act, it is a rarity.

4   Registered companies

These are companies formed under the Act or one of the earlier Companies Acts. A registered company may or may not have a share capital, for although a share capital is essential for a trading company it may not be required by other companies.

The Act provides for three basic types of registered companies – companies limited by guarantee, unlimited companies, companies limited by shares – and two forms of companies – public and private companies.

(a)   Companies limited by guarantee
A company limited by guarantee has 'the liability of its members limited by the memorandum to such amount as the members may . . .

undertake to contribute to the assets of the company in the event of its being wound up'. It may be either a private or a public company.

It is usually formed by trade associations, professional associations, clubs and societies who wish to obtain the advantages of incorporation without incurring personal liability. A large number of guarantee companies obtain dispensation from the Department of Trade to register their name without the addition of the word 'limited'.

It is similar to a share company in that it has legal personality, and that the liability of its members is limited. It differs in that a member of a share company may be called upon at any time during the existence of the company to pay the amount outstanding on his share, while a member in a guarantee company may only be called upon to honour his guarantee if the company is wound up and is unable to meet its debts.

A past member may be liable if he ceased to be a member within a year of the commencement of the winding up, but only for the debts and liabilities contracted by the company before he ceased to be a member.

The amount of the guarantee must be stated in the memorandum and is frequently as little as £1, although it may be greater.

A guarantee company does not usually have a share capital. Its memorandum and articles must correspond with the form set out in Table C of the Act and it must register its articles of association. A guarantee company having a share capital usually requires this initial capital to purchase business premises. Its memorandum and articles must correspond with Table D of the Act. Shareholders of such a guarantee company will have a twofold liability, to pay for their shares and to honour their guarantee in the event of the company being wound up.

Guarantee companies formed prior to the 1980 Companies Act may be either private or public companies. This Act introduced changes affecting guarantee companies. It provides that no company may be formed as, or become, a guarantee company with share capital on or after the appointed day. It also provides that the present guarantee company having a share capital may become a 'new public company' by re-registration as long as it satisfies the requirements of the 1980 Companies Act. Schedule 1 of the Companies Act 1980 includes an example of a memorandum of association of a public company limited by guarantee, and having a share capital. A guarantee company without a share capital cannot be registered as a new public company as it cannot satisfy the requirements relating to capital, and is therefore a private company.

(b)   Unlimited companies

This type of company is defined as 'a company not having any limit on the liability of its members'. Every member is liable for the debts contracted by the company while a member but the liability will only arise if the company is wound up and is unable to meet its debts. It is possible for the members to restrict or even avoid liability, by the device of the company issuing a policy, or entering into a contract, whereby the member's liability is restricted, or the company's funds alone are liable in respect of the policy or contract. All unlimited companies are private companies (1980 Companies Act, section 1).

Unlimited companies are comparatively rare but the changes introduced by the Companies Act 1967 has increased their number. The 1967 Act provides that if certain requirements are fulfilled an unlimited company is exempt from filing its accounts and directors' and auditors' reports with the Registrar, thus keeping its financial affairs private (i.e. it does not have to comply with section 1 of the Companies Act 1976).

Unlimited companies may be formed with or without a share capital. If a company has a share capital it must submit an annual return. Its articles must correspond with Table E of the Act.

An unlimited company is not governed by the rules relating to the alteration of capital as are the other types of companies, so that it may reduce its capital (if it has a share capital) and pay back share capital to its members, without restriction. It is also allowed to purchase its own shares and use its own assets for this purpose.

The Companies Act 1967 allows a share company or a guarantee company to be re-registered as an unlimited company. All the members must consent and the memorandum and articles must be altered. After all the formalities have been completed, a new certificate of incorporation will be issued by the Registrar, and a notice published in the *London Gazette*.

The converse is allowed, and an unlimited company may re-register as either a company limited by guarantee, or limited by shares (see below). The steps to be taken are as for re-registration of limited to unlimited, except that the consent of all the members is not required, only that of 75 per cent of the membership (i.e. sufficient to pass a special resolution). If an unlimited company seeks to re-register as a public company it must also satisfy the new requirements of the Companies Act 1980 relating to public companies.

(c)   Companies limited by shares

A company limited by shares has 'the liability of its members limited by the memorandum to the amount, if any, unpaid on the shares held by them'. No further liability attaches to the holder of a fully paid share. Should the company become insolvent, he will not be required to contribute to the payment of its debts.

Public and private companies

The promoters of a company will have to decide whether a company should be formed as a private or a public company. A private company does not require a large amount of capital and is therefore suitable for small businesses and family concerns. It cannot seek public investment for its shares, but is not subject to the capital requirements of a public company. It is estimated that the 14661 public companies registered in England and Wales (as at 31 December 1979) account for 70 per cent of the total capital invested in companies. The remaining 677376 private companies account for a mere 30 per cent of this capital.

Definitions

The 1980 Companies Act has introduced a new criterion for establishing whether a company is a public or a private company. A public company must:

(i) State in its memorandum that it is a public company;
(ii) End its name with the designations 'public limited company' or 'p.l.c.', or their Welsh equivalents;
(iii) Have a minimum share capital of £50000.

A private company is any company that is not a public company (1980 Companies Act, section 1).

Prior to the 1980 Companies Act a company was a public company unless it could satisfy the requirements relating to private companies. A private company, by its articles:

(i) Restricted the right of its members to transfer its shares;
(ii) Limited the number of its members to fifty, excluding past and present employees;
(iii) Prohibited any invitation to the public to subscribe for its shares or debentures.

The 1980 Companies Act provides that, after 22 December 1980, known as the appointed day, no company may be formed as a guarantee company with a share capital (section 1). Therefore all public companies formed in the future will be companies limited by shares. This Act also makes provisions for existing companies. The present public and private companies must decide, within fifteen months of the appointed day, whether they wish to re-register, or register as public companies.

Registration and re-registration

If a public company decides to re-register as a new public company it must satisfy the Registrar that its memorandum has been changed by a resolution of the directors, and that it has fulfilled the share capital requirements. The Registrar will then issue a certificate of incorporation stating that the company is a public company, and the company becomes a new public company.

If an old public company does not have sufficient capital 'to re-register' as a new public company, it may deliver a declaration to the Registrar that it does not satisfy the share capital requirements of a new public company, and will then be issued with a certificate stating that it is a private company. An old public company which can satisfy the capital requirements may pass a special resolution not to re-register. Such a resolution may be challenged by a minority of members within twenty-eight days. If their objection is not upheld by the Court, the Registrar will issue a certificate stating that the company is a private company.

An old public company must make a positive decision as to its future within the allotted time, for if it fails to obtain a new classification (i.e. to re-register as a new public company or as a private company), both the company and its officers are subject to a fine, and the Secretary of State may apply to the Court for the company to be wound up. The Court may wind up such a company if, in its opinion, it would be just and equitable to do so.

A private company may re-register as a public company, as may an unlimited company. It may do so by passing a special resolution to alter its memorandum and articles to conform with the requirements of a public company; complying with the share capital requirements; and submitting specified documents to the Registrar. The Registrar will then issue a certificate of incorporation and the company becomes a public company.

Many of the traditional advantages associated with private companies have been abolished by the Companies Act 1980. In the past most private companies were able to convert to public companies by passing a special resolution altering its articles and, if necessary, increasing the number of its members. This avoided the formalities associated with public company formation. The old public company had to have a minimum of seven members, but the new public company needs only two.

A private limited company with a share capital will, as before, be prohibited from offering its shares and debentures to the public (1980 Companies Act, section 15).

The previous restriction on the rights of members of private companies to transfer their shares has been repealed. However most private companies will continue to insert such a clause in their articles to ensure that control is retained within the company.

The differences between private and public companies are likely to become even more pronounced in the future, as the E E C directives relating to the raising and maintenance of capital and the payment of dividends need only be implemented by public companies.

Characteristics of public and private companies

Some of the characteristics of a public company are as follows:

(a) A public company may be registered with only two members.
(b) It must have a minimum capital of £50 000.
(c) It cannot commence business or borrow until section 4 of the 1980 Companies Act is complied with, and the Registrar has issued a certificate.
(d) It must have a minimum of two directors, unless it was registered before 1 November 1929, in which case one director is sufficient.
(e) Directors, other than the first directors, have to be voted into office individually at a general meeting.
(f) Directors must, unless otherwise resolved, retire at the age of seventy.
(g) At a general meeting proxies are allowed to vote but, unless the articles provide otherwise, are not allowed to address the meeting.
(h) No distribution of the company assets may be made if it results in the value of the assets being below that of its liabilities and capital.
(i) Its secretary must have the requisite knowledge, experience and an appropriate qualification.
(j) If the net assets of the company falls to half of its called up share capital, an extraordinary general meeting must be summoned.

A private company must have a minimum of two members. There is no upper limit on the number of members it may have.

(a) It needs only one director, and a director need not retire at the age of seventy unless the company is a subsidiary of a public company.
(b) At a general meeting, proxies may not only attend and vote but may also address the meeting.
(c) It cannot, however, offer its shares or debentures to the public.

Oversea companies

These are companies incorporated outside Great Britain who establish a place of business within Great Britain (section 406). For the purpose of this section Great Britain is defined as England, Wales and Scotland, but not the Channel Islands or the Isle of Man. Certain provisions of the Act apply to these companies. An oversea company incorporated in the Channel Islands or Isle of Man is known as an island company.

Within one month of establishing a place of business within Great Britain, such a company must file with the Registrar:

(i)   A certified copy of its charter or memorandum and articles;

(ii) A list of directors and secretary;

(iii) The name and address of at least one person resident in Great Britain authorised to accept service of process on behalf of the company.

If any alteration is made in any of the above particulars, the company must notify the registrar. An oversea company must exhibit in every place where it carries on business its name and the name of the country in which it is incorporated. If it is a limited company, it must also state this outside every place of business. This information must also appear on all the company's letters, notices and official publications.

The content of a prospectus issued by an oversea company is very similar to a prospectus issued by an English company. In addition, an oversea company must state the country of its incorporation, and the prospectus must also contain particulars of the company's constitution and of the enactment under which it is incorporated.

An oversea company must prepare accounts. If the company is a holding company it must also prepare group accounts in such a form as if it were incorporated in Great Britain. Copies of these accounts must be delivered to the Registrar. This does not apply if the form of the company is such that it would be regarded as an unlimited company if it were incorporated in Great Britain.

Accounting classification

The Companies Act 1981 creates, for accounting purposes, a new classification of companies:

(a)   A small company is a company which satisfies two of the following conditions:

 (i)   Its turnover must not exceed £1 400 000;
 (ii) Its balance sheet total must not exceed £700 000;
(iii) The average number of employees, in a financial year, does not
       exceed 50.

It is not required to file a profit and loss account or directors' report,
and only has to file an abbreviated version of its balance sheet.

(b)   A medium-sized company is one which satisfies two of the
following conditions:

 (i)   Its turnover must not exceed £5 750 000;
 (ii) Its balance sheet total must not exceed £2 800 000;
(iii) The average number of employees, in a financial year, does not
       exceed 250.

It has to file a full balance sheet and directors' report, but is only
required to file a modified profit and loss account, which does not
disclose turnover and gross profit margin.

   Group accounts may also be prepared in a modified form when a
group of companies fulfils the small- or medium-sized company
criteria. Dispensation will not be given if one of the companies in the
group is a public, banking, insurance or shipping company.

(c)   Companies which do not satisfy the small or medium-sized
criteria, public companies, and insurance, banking and shipping companies must prepare their accounts fully in accordance with the Act.

4

The Memorandum of Association

A company's memorandum is a document which outlines a company's constitution and defines the scope of a company's powers. It is in effect a company's charter and regulates a company's relationship with the outside world. It is filed with the Registrar on a company's incorporation and may be inspected by any member of the public.

The form of the memorandum

The form and requirements of the memorandum are set out in the Act (section 2) and consists of six basic clauses:

(i) The company's name with 'limited' as the last word, if it is a private limited company or a company limited by guarantee. If it is a public limited company, the name must end with the words 'public limited company'. A company whose registered office is to be found in Wales may use the words 'cyfyngedig' for limited and 'cwmni cyfyngedig cyhoeddus' for public limited company. The permitted abbreviations are ltd, p.l.c., cyf. and c.c.c.

(ii) The country in which the registered office will be situated. This establishes a company's domicile.

(iii) The objects of the company.

(iv) In the case of a limited company, a declaration that the members' liability is limited.

(v) The amount of the share capital and its division into shares of a fixed sum. This does not apply to unlimited companies and to companies not having a share capital.

(vi) The memorandum concludes with an association clause and must be signed by a minimum of two subscribers. Each states against his name the number of shares he takes.

Specimen memorandum

Schedule 1 of the 1980 Companies Act illustrates the form of memorandum of association of a public company limited by shares.

1   The name of the company is 'The Western Steam Packet, public limited company'.
2   The company is to be a public company.
3   The registered office of the company will be situated in England and Wales.
4   The objects for which the company is established are, 'the conveyance of passengers and goods in ships or boats between such places as the company may from time to time determine, and the doing of all such things as are incidental or conducive to the attainment of the above object'.
5   The liability of the members is limited.
6   The share capital of the company is £50000 divided into 50000 shares of £1 each.

We, the several persons whose names and addresses are subscribed are desirous of being formed into a company, in pursuance of this memorandum of association, and we respectively agree to take the number of shares in the capital of the company set opposite our respective names.

Names, Addresses and Descriptions of Subscribers	Number of shares taken by each Subscriber
'1 Thomas Jones in the county of merchant	1
2 Andrew Smith in the county of merchant	1
Total shares taken	2'

Dated   day of   19 .

Witness to the above signatures

A. B., 13 Hute Street, Clerkenwell, London.

The contents of the memorandum

The name of the company

The Companies Act 1981 simplifies the arrangements of the approval of company names. The Registrar keeps an index of the names of existing companies, and the promoters of a company will be able to select its name, by a simple comparison with the list in the index. (The Registrar's prior approval of a company's name before registration is no longer required.)

Certain restrictions are, however, imposed. The Registrar may not register a company by a name:

(i)   which includes ltd, plc or unlimited other than at the end of the name;
(ii) which is the same as a name already on the index;
(iii) which is offensive;
(iv) which would, by its use by a company, constitute a criminal offence.

Except with the approval of the Secretary of State, a company may not register a name which suggests a connection with the government or with a local authority. The Secretary of State may also specify that the use of certain words or expressions, as part of a company's name, requires his prior approval.

If the Secretary of State is of the opinion that a company has registered a name which is too like an existing name in the index, he may within twelve months direct the company to change its name. If a company has provided misleading information in order to register a particular name, the Secretary of State may, within five years of registration, direct the company to change its name. A company may also be directed to change its name when a name has been registered which gives so misleading an indication of the company's activities as to be likely to cause harm to the public.

An action is also available at common law to an 'existing' company to seek an injunction to restrain another company from carrying on a business, or proposing to carry on a business, under a name which is likely to cause the public to believe that the business of the company is that of the 'existing' company.

In *Ewing v. Buttercup Margarine Co. Ltd*, a company was registered as the Buttercup Margarine Co. Ltd. to manufacture and deal in margarine. Unknown to the directors, another company had been registered as the Buttercup Dairy Co. Ltd. This company owned a chain of shops retailing dairy products in Scotland and Northern England. It was held that the names were so alike as to cause confusion, and the Buttercup Margarine Co. was restrained by injunction from carrying on its business under that name.

A private guarantee company formed to promote commerce, art, science, education, religion, charity or any profession need not use the word 'limited' as long as it submits a statutory declaration that it fulfils the following conditions: The memorandum or the articles of association must state that the company intends to apply its income or profits solely for promoting its objects. It must also prohibit the payment of any dividend to its members and must provide that on its winding up it will transfer all its assets, otherwise available for distribution to its members, to similar companies.

A company may change its name at any time by special resolution. Its new name is subject to the same scrutiny as a first registration. The Registrar then issues a certificate of incorporation in the company's new name. However, a company changing its name from ltd to plc or *vice versa* does not require the approval of a special resolution.

Every company is required to publish its full name outside its registered office and all places where it carries on business. The name must also be engraved on its common seal and be mentioned on its bills of exchange, cheques, promissory notes, invoices, receipts and business letters. The company and its officers may be fined for not complying with these provisions.

An officer of the company may incur personal liability if the company's name is incorrectly mentioned on a bill, cheque, or order for goods, unless the debt is paid by the company. In *Atkins & Co. Ltd v. Wardle* it was held that the directors of the South Shields Salt Water Baths Co. Ltd, were personally liable when they accepted a bill of exchange on the company's behalf with the word 'Ltd' having been omitted.

The 1980 Companies Act creates the offence of trading under a misleading name. It provides that a person who is not a public company, or an old public company (after the end of the transitional period), is guilty of an offence if he carries on trade or business under a name which includes the words 'public limited company'. It also provides that a public company shall be guilty of an offence if it uses a name to create the impression that it is a private company in circumstances which are likely to be material (section 76).

The registered office

The memorandum must state whether the registered office is to be situated in England, Wales or Scotland. This will determine a company's nationality and domicile. A company registered in England has British nationality, an English domicile and is subject to English law, whereas a company registered in Scotland has British nationality, a Scottish domicile and is governed by the laws of Scotland.

A company must have a registered office at all times, to which all communications and notices may be addressed. The location of the registered office can be altered at any time, on giving notice to the Registrar, but only within the country of its domicile. The location of a registered office cannot be changed from England to Scotland or *vice versa*.

Documents, including notices and writs, are served on a company at its registered office.

A company must also keep certain registers and documents at its registered office. These include a register of members, a register of directors and secretaries, a register of mortgages and charges, a register of debenture holders, a register of directors' interests in shares or debentures and a register of interests in shares, along with copies of directors' service contracts and the minute books of general meetings.

The objects clause
This clause sets out the objects for which the company is formed, which must be lawful. A company cannot enter into activities and contracts which are outside its objects clause as it would then be acting *ultra vires*, or beyond its powers. In *Ashbury Railway Carriage Co. Ltd v. Riche*, a company was formed to manufacture and repair railway carriages, and purchase, lease and work mines, minerals and land. The directors purchased a concession for building a railway in Belgium. It was held that the contract was *ultra vires* and void as it was beyond the objects of the company.

This clause offers protection to both shareholders and creditors. A company's shareholders are made aware of the purposes for which their investment can be applied, while any person contemplating dealing with the company is made aware of the limits of the company's contractual powers.

A company's objects should be reasonably interpreted. Whatever is incidental to the objects set out in the memorandum should be regarded as *intra vires* (i.e. within the company powers), unless expressly forbidden. If a company's objects are as stated in the specimen memorandum – 'the conveyance of passengers and goods in ships or boats between such places as the company may determine' – a company would be given certain ancillary powers to achieve these objects. It could borrow money, have a bank account, contract for supplies, employ labour, bring and defend actions, pay pensions to its employees and lease premises. It must be shown that there is a connection between the power and the company's objects, and that the company will benefit from the exercise of the power.

Borrowing cannot exist as an independent activity, even though a company has been given borrowing powers in its object clause. It must be used to further an activity which is *intra vires* the company. In *Re Introductions Ltd*, a company was formed to provide entertainment and accommodation for overseas visitors. It had a power 'to borrow and raise money in such manner as the company' should think fit, and borrowed money from the bank to start a pig breeding business. It was held that such borrowing was *ultra vires*.

The objects clause quoted above consists of one short paragraph. Modern object clauses have a large number of paragraphs which confer on a company a wide range of powers. Companies often need powers, which the courts will not readily imply, in order to achieve their objects – for example, if a company is not expressly given power in its objects clause to acquire shares in another company, it cannot be a holding company.

The Courts have evolved certain rules in interpreting the object clause, the most important of which is the main object rule.

According to the Courts, the first paragraph sets out the company's main object. Such a paragraph controls and limits the operation of the succeeding paragraphs. Should the main object fail, then the substratum of the company is destroyed and the company may be wound up. In *Re German Date Coffee Co.* a company was formed to extract coffee from dates by the use of a German patent. The patent was not obtained, but the company successfully used a Swedish patent. It was held that the company should be wound up. Its main object had failed as it envisaged the use of a German patent.

Companies have sought to exclude this rule by various means.

In *Cotman v. Brougham*, a rubber company's objects clause concluded with a statement that each of its thirty sub-clauses should be considered as a separate and independent main object. One clause authorised the company to deal in shares in other companies, and it underwrote shares in an oil company. It was held that the underwriting was valid.

In *Bell Houses v. City Wall Properties* the memorandum of a property company contained a clause which authorised the company, 'to carry on any trade or business whatsoever, which can in the opinion of the board of directors be advantageously carried on by the company in connection . . . with the general business of the company'. The directors entered into a contract to introduce another company to a financier in return for a commission. It was held that such a contract was valid.

In *Re New Finance and Mortgage Company Ltd*, a clause in the objects clause allowed the company to act as 'financiers, capitalists, concessionaires, bankers, commercial agents, mortgage brokers, financial agents and advisers, exporters and importers of goods and merchandise of all kinds and merchants generally'. It was held that the phrase 'merchants generally' gave the company authority to operate garages, selling petrol, cars and car accessories.

The ultra vires doctrine

The effect of the *ultra vires* doctrine has been modified by section 9(1) of the European Communities Act 1972. This provides that where a person deals with a company in good faith, he will be able to rely upon the transaction being within the capacity of the company, as long as the transaction has been decided upon by the directors.

If a company enters into a contract which is *ultra vires*, but the other contracting party is unaware of this, he can enforce the contract as long as he has acted in good faith (i.e. was unaware of the nature of the transaction, or was not put on inquiry by unusual or suspicious circumstances). The company cannot sue him, as an *ultra vires* transaction is regarded as void and having no rights or obligations.

If he is aware of the *ultra vires* nature of the contract he is not protected by section 9(1) of the European Communities Act. If he has read the memorandum he is deemed to be aware of its *ultra vires* nature. He also loses the protection of section 9(1) if the directors have not approved the transaction. (A transaction can be entered into by a single director if he has been delegated such power by the board, or the board consists of one member.) He may, however, be able to trace money paid or any property delivered to the company.

A company can sue a director who has spent the company's money or disposed of property for an *ultra vires* purpose, even though he may have acted in good faith.

Alterations of objects

A company may change its objects, by special resolution, in order to enable it to meet changed circumstances. It can only do so within certain limits.

Section 5 allows a change of objects so that a company may:

Carry on its business more economically or efficiently;
Attain its main purpose by new or improved means;
Carry on some business which under existing circumstances may conveniently or advantageously be combined with the existing business;

Change or enlarge the local area of operations;
Sell or dispose of the whole or part of its undertakings;
Restrict or abandon any of the existing objects;
Amalgamate with any other company or body of persons.

Minority dissenting shareholders may petition the court to cancel the alteration. If this is done within twenty-one days of passing the resolution the Court will suspend the alterations. The dissenting shareholders must hold at least 15 per cent of the issued capital of the company, or 15 per cent of the issued shares of any class (if the company has two or more classes of shares). An application may also be made by the holders of 15 per cent of any debentures issued before 1 December 1947 and secured by a floating charge. Accordingly notice of a special resolution to alter the objects clause must also be given to such debenture holders.

Only those individuals who voted against the resolution, or abstained, or who were not at the meeting, can object.

The Court may confirm the alteration, or cancel the alteration, or confirm the alteration subject to conditions, or it may adjourn the proceedings so that agreement may be reached for the purchase of the shares of the dissenting shareholders.

If no application opposing the alteration is made within the twenty-one days, the company must, within a further fifteen days, deliver to the Registrar a printed copy of its memorandum as altered.

If an application is made, the company must notify the Registrar immediately, and when the Court order is made the company must within fifteen days file a copy of the order together with a printed copy of the memorandum, if it has been altered.

The limited liability clause
This clause provides that 'the liability of the members is limited'. Similar words are used in a memorandum of a company limited by shares, as in a company limited by guarantee.

In the case of a company limited by shares, its effect is that a member shall only be liable to contribute the amount unpaid on his shares. In the case of a company limited by guarantee, a member's liability must not exceed the amount of his guarantee. If the guarantee company has a share capital a member's liability must not exceed the amount of his guarantee, plus any amount which remains unpaid on his shares. A typical guarantee clause is found in the first schedule of the 1980 Companies Act:

Every member of the company undertakes to contribute to the assets of the company in the event of its being wound up while he is a member, or within one year afterwards, for payment of the debts and liabilities of the company, contracted before he ceases to be a member, and the costs, charges and expenses of winding up the same and for the adjustment of the rights of the contributories amongst themselves, such amount as may be required, not exceeding £20.

The effect of the limited liability clause is that the liability of a member cannot be altered without his consent. He cannot be compelled to take more shares, or to increase his liability to contribute more money, unless he agrees to this in writing.

If a limited company wishes to re-register as an unlimited company, it may only do so with the written consent of all its members, as their liability will be dramatically altered. A member's liability will also be altered if a company carries on business without having at least two members for more than six months. The surviving member who is aware of the fact is liable (jointly and severally with the company) for the debts of the company contracted after the six month period.

A company's memorandum may state that the liability of its directors is unlimited. Any person who is invited to join the board of directors of such a company must be informed in writing of the existence of this clause (section 202).

The capital clause
The capital clause sets out the amount of the nominal capital and its division into shares of fixed amounts (e.g. the share capital of the company is £40000 divided into 40000 shares of £1 each).

If the shares are divided into various classes (e.g. 20000 £1 ordinary shares, 20000 £1 preference shares) it is unnecessary to specify this in the memorandum as reference to the types of shares and their respective rights is found in the articles.

It is comparatively easy for the company to increase its authorised capital at a later date. All that is required is an ordinary resolution (section 61), but if a company wishes to reduce its capital it requires a special resolution and the Court's approval (section 66).

The association clause
The memorandum concludes with an association clause by which the subscribers declare that they desire to be formed into a company. There must be at least two subscribers. Each signs in the presence of a witness for a minimum of one share. The witness attests each signature, and one person may witness all the signatures.

Other clauses

Clauses are sometimes inserted in the memorandum which are normally found in the articles. Such clauses may define the rights which attach to different classes of shares with regard to dividend, voting, and participation in the company's assets on a winding up. These can be altered in the same manner as the objects clause (i.e. a special resolution, and a provision allowing for minority dissent).

If the memorandum provides a procedure for the alteration of these clauses, this must be followed, rather than the procedure mentioned above. A company may render these clauses unalterable by inserting a provision in the memorandum prohibiting their alteration.

5

The Articles of Association

The articles contain the internal regulations for the management of the company's affairs. They govern the rights of the members among themselves and set out the manner in which a company must conduct its affairs. As the articles are subsidiary to the memorandum, any article which is inconsistent with the provisions in the memorandum is invalid. An article may not contain anything illegal or authorise anything impliedly or expressly forbidden by the Act, for example, the payment of a dividend out of capital, or the issue of shares at a discount.

The Act sets out a specimen set of articles in the First Schedule, namely Table A. (The articles mentioned in the text are the articles found in Table A.) A share company may adopt Table A instead of registering its own articles, or it may specifically exclude Table A and set out its own articles. The third alternative is for a company to set out its own articles and adopt part of Table A.

If a company's own articles are silent on a particular point the appropriate provisions of Table A will apply, unless it is stated that Table A has been specifically excluded. In practice some modification of Table A is invariably found to be necessary. Companies often modify provisions as to class rights, directors' rights and quorums to suit their own circumstances.

All the major Companies Acts since 1862 have contained a model set of articles in the form of Table A and each has differed in some respects from the previous model. The Table A which applies to a company is the Table A in force at the date of a company's incorporation; for example, a company formed in 1906 is subject to Table A of the Companies Act 1862, a company formed in 1945 is subject to Table

A of the Companies Act 1929, a company formed in 1979 is subject to Table A of the 1948 Companies Act.

Model forms of memoranda and articles for guarantee companies are set out in Tables C and D, and for an unlimited company having share capital in Table E of the Act.

If articles are registered they must be printed, divided into separate consecutive paragraphs, and signed by the subscribers to the memorandum.

The contents of the articles

The articles usually include provisions dealing with the following:

The allotment of shares;
Share capital and variation of class rights;
Lien and calls on shares;
Forfeiture, transfer and transmission of shares;
Conversion of shares into stock;
Increase and reduction of capital;
Borrowing powers;
General meetings;
Voting at meetings;
Appointment, duties and powers of directors and managing directors;
Appointment and remuneration of the secretary;
The company seal;
Accounts and audit;
Dividends, reserves and capitalisation of profits;
Serving of notices;
Special provisions relating to winding up.

Alteration of the articles

A company is given power to alter or to add to its articles by special resolution (section 10). A company cannot deprive itself of this power, and any article may be altered as long as the alteration is not inconsistent with the Act and the company's memorandum.

The alteration is invalid if it amounts to an oppression of, or fraud upon, a minority. If an alteration of an article is beneficial to a company, but prejudices a minority, the alteration will be upheld. In *Allen v. Gold Reefs of West Africa*, the company had a lien on partly paid shares only. A shareholder, the only holder of fully paid shares, died indebted to the company. The company altered its articles to impose a lien on all shares, thus giving it a lien over the deceased shareholder's shares. It was held that such an alteration was valid. In *Sidebottom v. Kershaw Leese and Co. Ltd* the company's articles were altered to allow the company to require any member who carried on a business competing with the company to sell his shares at a fair price to nominees of the directors. Sidebottom, a shareholder, operated mills in competition with the company. It was held that the alteration was valid as a shareholder who was also a business competitor might cause loss to the company.

In *Greenhalgh v. Arderne Cinemas* the majority shareholders wished to sell their shares to a third party. The articles contained a clause which stipulated that any member who wished to sell his shares to a non-member must first offer his shares, at a fair price, to his fellow members. The company altered its articles so that any shareholder could sell his shares to a third party, if permitted to do so by an ordinary resolution. This was held valid and for the benefit of the company as a whole, despite the fact that a minority shareholder would have to firstly offer his shares to the majority under the existing clause.

In *Brown v. British Abrasive Wheel Co.*, the company required further capital. The holders of 98 per cent of the company's share capital were prepared to advance additional capital if they could acquire the remaining 2 per cent shareholding. The minority share-holders refused to sell and the company passed a resolution enabling a 90 per cent majority to acquire the shares of any dissenting minority. This was held to be invalid as it was solely for the benefit of the major-ity shareholders and not for the company's benefit.

If a company is in breach of contract as a result of altering its articles such an alteration is nevertheless valid, the other party cannot obtain an injunction to prevent the alteration; the remedy lies in damages. In *Southern Foundries v. Shirlaw*, Shirlaw was appointed by contract to be managing director for ten years. As a result of a merger, the articles were altered so that Shirlaw could be removed from office before the end of the ten-year period. It was held that he was entitled to damages for wrongful dismissal.

An alteration that increases the liability of a member to contribute to the company, for example by increasing his shareholding, or his liability to pay money to the company, is not binding unless he agrees to this in writing.

The memorandum and articles filed with the Registrar may be inspected by any person and the company must supply a copy of the memorandum and articles on payment of not more than five pence per copy.

The effect of the memorandum and articles

The Act provides that the memorandum and articles shall, when registered, bind the company and its members as if they had been signed and sealed by each member and contained agreements on the part of each member to observe all their provisions (section 20).

The result is that the articles and memorandum form a contract between the company and each member, and each member in his capacity as member is bound to the company by the provisions found in the articles. A member is bound by contract to pay the amounts outstanding on his share and a member of a guarantee company is similarly bound to contribute the amount of his guarantee on the winding up of the company. The Act provides that these are specialty debts which may be recovered by the company within twelve years. In *Hickman v. Kent or Romney Sheep Breeders Association*, a dispute arose between Hickman, a member, and the company, relating to the company's refusal to register certain of his flock in the Association's stud book. One of the company's articles specified that any dispute between the company and its members should be submitted to arbitration. Hickman nevertheless brought an action in the High Court against the company. It was held that the company was entitled to have the court action stayed and the dispute referred to arbitration.

A member may sue a company if it denies him those rights accorded to him in the articles or the memorandum. A member has compelled a company to restore his name to the register when it was wrongfully removed; to pay dividends; return his capital on a winding up. In *Pender v. Lushington*, the articles of a company provided that a member should not be entitled to more than 100 votes. Certain shareholders who held more than 100 shares transferred certain shares to nominees in order to exercise greater voting power. The company refused to recognise the votes of the nominees. It was held that the company was contractually bound by the articles to allow those votes to be recorded.

The memorandum and articles also have effect as a contract between the members themselves, which may be enforced directly by one member against another without the aid of the company. In *Rayfield v. Hands*, the articles of a private company provided that if a member intended to transfer shares he should inform the directors 'who will take the said shares equally between them at a fair value'. The directors refused to buy Rayfield's shares. It was held that the articles bound the directors, as members, to purchase the shares.

In *Borland's Trustee v. Steel Brothers and Co. Ltd*, the articles provided that the shares of any member who was adjudged bankrupt should be sold to certain persons at a fair price, not exceeding par. Borland became bankrupt and it was held that his trustee must sell his shares in accordance with the articles.

The memorandum and the articles do not bind the company to an outsider, nor do they form a contract with a member other than in his capacity as a member. In *Eley v. Positive Government Security Life Assurance Co.*, the articles provided that Eley should be employed for life as a solicitor to the company and should not be removed except for misconduct. He became the company's solicitor and later became a shareholder. The company ceased to employ him as its solicitor and he sued for breach of contract. It was held that he could not succeed, as the contract which be sought to enforce was not conferred upon him in his capacity as a shareholder.

However a provision in the memorandum or articles can be evidence of the existence of a contract. In *Re New British Iron, Ex Parte Beckwith*, the articles of a company provided that the directors should have a share qualification and should be paid fees of £1000 a year. The company was wound up and a director claimed for his fees. It was held that although the articles did not constitute a contract, yet they were evidence that the director had accepted office on the basis of the articles, and the company was liable to pay his fees.

6

The Promoter

Definition

A promoter has been defined as 'one who undertakes to form a company . . . and to set it going, and who takes the necessary steps to accomplish that purpose' (*Twycross v. Grant*). Any person who takes part in forming a company or in raising capital for a proposed or newly formed company is *prima facie* a promoter. A person may take a relatively minor part in promoting a company and yet find himself a promoter of that company. Individuals who have issued a prospectus, negotiated contracts for the purchase of property, obtained directors, and placed shares have been held to be promoters of companies.

A person who acts in a professional or technical capacity for a promoter – a solicitor who undertakes legal work for a company's formation, or an accountant or valuer who prepares accounts or valuations for a promoter – will not be regarded as a promoter.

Duties of a promoter

Theoretically a promoter is allowed to make a profit from promoting the company, as he is not a trustee or an agent for the company, as it is not yet in existence. In practice, the courts have ruled that as the promoter stands in a fiduciary relationship to the company he must not make, either directly or indirectly, any profit from the promotion unless the company assents.

A promoter must disclose any profit which he is making by promoting the company, either to an independent board of directors or to the existing and intended shareholders, for example by means of a prospectus. Disclosure to an independent board is rarely possible as the promoters are usually the first directors of the company.

In *Erlanger v. New Sombrero Phosphate Co.*, a syndicate managed by Erlanger purchased for £55000 an island reputed to contain large quantities of phosphate. Erlanger formed a company to purchase the island from the syndicate for £110000. The company's directors were nominated by him. The profit made by the promoters was not disclosed to the shareholders or to an independent board. The original directors were later removed from office, and the company successfully sued for rescission of the contract and for the recovery of the purchase money from the syndicate.

Remedies against a promoter

The following remedies may be available to a company if a promoter has failed to make full disclosure of any profit made by him.

Firstly, rescission of any contract made with the promoter. This was possible in the case of *Erlanger v. New Sombrero Phosphate Co.* This remedy is not available if it is not possible to restore the promoter and the company to their former positions, for example where the company has resold the property to a third party.

Secondly, the company may compel the promoter to account for any secret profit made by him. If a company succeeds in an action for rescission any secret profit is normally recovered as a result of the action, but such a profit may be recovered even though the company does not sue for rescission of the contract. In *Gluckstein v. Barnes*, a syndicate purchased Olympia for £140000, and formed a company which purchased the property from the syndicate for £180000. The directors, who were members of the syndicate, disclosed this profit. The syndicate had also purchased debentures in Olympia at a very low price. As a result of the sale to the company, the debentures were repaid in full and the syndicate made an additional profit of £20000, which they did not disclose. It was held that the directors must account for this sum to the company.

Thirdly, the company can sue for damages for breach of a fiduciary duty on the basis that the promoter is negligent in not disclosing his interest. In *Re Leeds and Hanley Theatre of Varieties Ltd*, a company purchased two music halls for £24000 and conveyed these properties to its nominee. The company promoted another company and instructed their nominee to sell the properties to the second company for £75000. No mention was made of the first company's interest in the transaction in the prospectus or elsewhere. The promoters were held liable in damages.

A dishonest promoter may find himself liable at a later date. If the company is wound up, a promoter may be sued for misfeasance and he may be ordered by the Court to make restitution to the company (section 333).

Payment of a promoter

As a company does not have legal capacity before its formation, a promoter is not able to make a contract with the company to be paid for promotion services, or to be indemnified for any expenses incurred by him. The articles usually give authority to the directors to pay the promoters for their services. Article 80 provides that 'the directors . . . may pay all the expenses incurred in promoting and registering the company'. There is usually no problem in practice as the promoters or their nominees are usually the first directors of a company.

Payment can be made to a promoter in various ways. He may be paid a commission for promoting a company. Alternatively, he may be allotted shares as payment for his services. These are usually ordinary shares, but sometimes promoters are given deferred or founders' shares. In other cases promoters are given the option to subscribe for shares at par. This can be a valuable form of payment if the shares are likely to go to a premium. Promoters can also be given debentures as payment.

Any amount paid or benefit given must be disclosed by the promoter to the company, and also by the company in any prospectus issued within two years.

Pre-incorporation contracts

A promoter who enters into a contract on behalf of a company before its incorporation (i.e. a pre-incorporation contract) may face certain problems. As the company was not in existence at the time of making the contract it cannot ratify such a contract after its formation. Any person who acts as an agent for such a company is personally liable on the contract. Section 9(2) European Communities Act states that 'where a contract purports to be made by a company, or by a person as agent for a company, at a time when the company has not been formed, then subject to any agreement to the contrary the contract shall have effect as a contract entered into by the person purporting to act for the company or as agent for it, and he shall be personally liable on the contract accordingly'.

In *Kelner v. Baxter*, three individuals entered into a contract for the supply of wines and spirits on behalf of the Gravesend Royal Alexandria Hotel Company, which had not at that time been incorporated.

The company was incorporated, experienced financial difficulties and was wound up. It was held that the promoters were liable for its pre-incorporation contracts.

A recent decision (*Phonogram Ltd v. Lane*) illustrates the operation of section 9(2) of the European Communities Act. A contract was made by Lane 'for and on behalf of' an unformed company, with Phonogram Ltd. The company was never incorporated, although incorporation was originally intended. Phonogram Ltd sued Lane for the sum advanced under the contract, which was returnable under the terms of the contract. It was held that Lane was personally liable for repayment of this sum.

A promoter may avoid this liability by providing in the contract that his liability shall cease if the company enters into a new contract on similar terms, or by inserting a clause that either party may rescind the contract if it is not adopted by the company within a specified time (e.g. three months). Alternatively, a contract may be prepared in draft form to be entered into by the company and the other party, after incorporation.

A company is not bound by a pre-incorporation contract. In *Re English and Colonial Produce Company Ltd*, it was held that a solicitor, who had drafted documents for a company before it was incorporated, was unable to recover his fees from the company.

A company cannot enforce a pre-incorporation contract against the other party. In *Natal Lane & Colonisation Co. v. Pauline Colliery & Development Syndicate*, the Pauline Colliery Syndicate had, before its incorporation, taken an option on some lands. When the syndicate sought to exercise the option, the other party refused to grant a lease. It was held that the contract could not be enforced.

If a public company enters into a contract before it receives its section 4 certificate from the Registrar, the contract will be binding. Should the company fail to meet its obligations under the contract, its directors will be jointly and severally (individually and collectively) liable to indemnify the other party to the contract.

7

Raising Capital

Companies raise money and finance their activities in various ways. The method chosen will depend on a number of factors, including the cost of raising the required capital and the amount of interest or dividend to be paid to investors or shareholders. A public issue of shares is unsuitable for a small company, as this is a costly exercise which could not be justified in terms of the amount that could be raised.

Small companies generally finance their activities in other ways. It may be cheaper to lease machinery and equipment, rather than purchase these items. Alternatively, a company may acquire such items on hire purchase or under a credit sale agreement, thus spreading the cost over a longer period of time.

It may be possible for a company to negotiate a private loan from a bank, or a merchant bank, or an insurance company.

A company may also negotiate privately with individuals to invest in its shares or debentures. In the case of a small company the negotiations are usually conducted by its directors, but a large company seeking to obtain a substantial investment will usually employ an intermediary, such as a bank or an issuing house, to act on its behalf. This is known as a private placing.

A company is under no obligation to distribute the whole of its profits as a dividend. A prudent company makes provision for the depreciation of its fixed assets, such as plant and machinery, by allocating a fraction of its profits to a fund to finance purchases of equipment.

It may also allocate part of its profits to finance the future expansion of its business. The articles usually give the directors authority to create a reserve out of the company's profits, which may be used 'for any purpose to which the profits of the company may be properly applied' (Article 117).

As shareholders expect to be paid a dividend, a company may have to find a method of satisfying members whilst retaining profits. This can be achieved by capitalising profits and issuing fully paid bonus shares or debentures to its shareholders. The shareholders may then, if they so wish, sell their bonus shares and debentures to compensate them for their loss of dividend.

A company may raise additional capital by a rights issue. It sends to each existing shareholder or debenture holder a circular, known as a letter of rights, inviting him to subscribe for additional shares or debentures in proportion to his original holding. The letter of rights is usually renounceable, so that the recipient can sign the renunciation and sell his right to subscribe to some other person. The modern practice is to send the shareholder or debenture holder a provisional letter of allotment by which these new shares or debentures are actually allotted, subject to his right to reject them if he does not wish to subscribe.

A public company may 'place' its shares or debentures with an issuing house, or a firm of stockbrokers at an agreed price. The issuing house will place the securities with its clients or associates, at a price above that paid to the company. In most cases a prospectus will not be necessary, as an issuing house usually restricts its offer to a few selected clients. Should the offer to purchase these securities be made to a wider clientele, the placings would in all probability have to satisfy the requirements of a prospectus.

A public company may invite the public to subscribe for its shares or debentures, by issuing a prospectus. A company will make a direct public issue only if it is confident that due to its reputation, or the price of its shares, all the issue will be taken up. A prudent company will, nevertheless, arrange for such an issue to be underwritten.

8

The Prospectus

Definition of prospectus

If a company wishes the public to subscribe for its shares or debentures it must issue a prospectus. It usually takes the form of a circular or newspaper advertisement, and may be published by the promoters, by the company, by an issuing house, or by a share broker.

It is defined by the Act as 'any prospectus, notice, circular, advertisement or other invitation offering to the public for subscription or purchase any shares or debentures of a company' (section 455). The object is to ensure that whenever the shares or debentures of a public company are offered to the public, any prospective investor is given the necessary basic information to enable him to assess the advisability or otherwise of investment in the company.

It would appear from the definition that a prospectus must be in writing, so that an oral invitation is not a prospectus. The definition covers payment in cash, as an invitation to invest in securities other than in cash is not a prospectus governed by the Act, but is dealt with under the Prevention of Fraud (Investments) Act 1958.

What constitutes an offer to the public is a matter of fact and will depend on various circumstances. 'Public' has been defined in the Act as any section of the public, whether selected as members, or debenture holders of the company, or as clients of the person issuing the prospectus (section 55).

In *Re South of England Natural Gas Co. Ltd*, a gas company distributed a circular to 3000 members of other gas companies offering its shares for subscription. Although the circular was headed 'for private circulation only', it was held that there was an offer to the public and that the circular was a prospectus.

An offer is not to be regarded as made to the public if it is not calculated to result in the shares or debentures becoming available to persons other than those receiving the offer, or it can be regarded as a matter of domestic concern to those making and receiving it (section 44).

In *Nash v. Lynde* a director sent a circular to a solicitor suggesting that he might care to bring it to the notice of his clients. The solicitor sent it to a friend who handed the circular to a relative. It was held that there had been no publication so as to bring the circular within the Act.

In *Government Stock and Other Securities Investment Co. Ltd v. Christopher*, a shipping company offered to acquire all the shares in two other companies in exchange for its own shares. The circular containing the offer was sent to the shareholders of the two companies with a form of acceptance and transfer. It was held that as there was no offer to the public, the circular was not a prospectus.

The contents of the prospectus (section 38, 4th schedule)

1 The company's share and loan capital

(a) The number of founders', or management, or deferred shares and the extent of their interest in the company's property and profits. (Not common today, but if issued have a small value in relation to the capital of the company. Such shares may be entitled to a large proportion of the profits above a stated figure.)

(b) The voting, capital and dividend rights of each class of share.

(c) Particulars of any option to take shares or debentures, together with the name of the person entitled to the option, the price to be paid, the consideration to be given and the time for its exercise. (If the option price is below the market price, and is given for an inadequate consideration, the option holder has a distinct advantage over the other subscribers.)

(d) Details of any shares offered and allotted for cash within the previous two years, together with the number of shares or debentures issued as fully or partly paid up within that time, for a consideration other than cash.

2 The company's capital requirements

(a) The amount payable on application and allotment on each share including the amount, if any, payable as a share premium.

(b) The minimum subscription, that is the minimum amount which in the directors' opinion must be raised in cash by the issue of the shares to provide for:

(i)   The purchase price of any property to be acquired;

(ii)   The preliminary expenses incurred in forming the company including underwriting commission;

(iii)   The repayment of money borrowed for those purposes and working capital.

(iv)   An estimate of preliminary expenses and of the expenses of the issue. If these expenses have been paid for by persons other than the company (e.g. promoters) these persons must be named.

(c)   The amount or rate of underwriting commission (if applicable).

3   The company's financial record

(a)   If the company has been carrying on business for less than three years, or if the business to be acquired out of the proceeds of the issue has been carried on for less than three years, the length of time it has been in business.

(b)   The auditors must also submit a report on its profits and losses in each of the last five financial years; its assets and liabilities at the date of the last accounts; the rates of dividends paid in respect of each class of share in the last five financial years; the cases where no dividend has been paid.

(c)   If the company has subsidiaries the report must deal with the profits or losses and assets and liabilities of its subsidiaries, and if the proceeds of the issue are to be used to purchase a business a similar report must be submitted by a named accountant in respect of that business.

4   Details of any property to be acquired with proceeds of issue

(a)   The names and addresses of the vendors with the amount payable in cash, shares and debentures to each. The goodwill must be specified separately.

(b)   Any transaction relating to the property in the previous two years in which any vendor, promoter, director or proposed director had an interest, apart from the contracts entered into in the ordinary course of business, or where the amount of purchase money is not material.

A person is a vendor if he has entered into any contract for the sale or purchase, or for an option to purchase, any property to be acquired by the company and:

(i)   The purchase money is not fully paid when the prospectus is issued; or

(ii)   The purchase money is to be paid wholly or partly out of

the proceeds of the issue of securities offered by the prospectus; or
(iii)   The contract depends upon the result of the issue.

5   Directors, promoters and auditors

(a)   The names, addresses and descriptions of the directors, or proposed directors, and the number of qualification shares fixed by the articles (if any), and any provision in the articles as to directors' remuneration.
(b)   The interest of every director in the promotion, or property to be acquired by the company and any sum paid to induce him to become a director, or as a share qualification, or for services in promoting the company.
(c)   Any amount or benefit given to promoters within the preceding two years, or intended to be given, and the consideration.
(d)   The names and addresses of the auditors (if any).

Every prospectus issued by or on behalf of a company must be dated, signed by every person named in the prospectus as a director or proposed director, and must be filed with the Registrar on or before the date of publication.

There must also be endorsed on or attached to the prospectus any of the following documents which are applicable:

(i)   An expert's consent to the inclusion of any report or statement made by him.
(ii)   A copy of any material contract referred to in the prospectus.
(iii)   The auditor's statement of any adjustment made in his report in the prospectus and the reasons for it.

Offer for sale

An offer for sale by an issuing house is not a prospectus issued by or on behalf of a company, but is nevertheless within the scope of the prospectus provisions of the Act, which provides that any document containing an offer of shares or debentures for sale to the public is to be deemed a prospectus issued by the company.

In addition to the matters required to be contained in a prospectus, the offer must also contain the net amount to be received by the company and the place and time at which the contract with the issuing house may be inspected.

The Act also provides that the persons making the offer are liable as if they were the directors of the company.

Unless the contrary is proved it will be evidence that an allotment was made with a view to an offer to the public if:

(i) The offer is made within six months of the allotment or agreement to allot;

(ii) At the date of the offer the whole consideration to be received by the company in respect of the shares or debentures had not been so received.

Abridged prospectus

The detailed and strict requirements of the 4th schedule are relaxed in certain circumstances:

(i) If a prospectus is issued more than two years after the company is entitled to commence business, the information in respect of directors and preliminary expenses is not required to be disclosed.

(ii) If a company proposes to issue a prospectus to the public and to apply for a stock exchange listing, it may apply to the Stock Exchange for a certificate of exemption if it finds that it would be unduly burdensome to comply with 4th schedule requirements (e.g. because of the size of the issue). As long as the particulars required by the Stock Exchange are then published, the company is deemed to have complied with the requirements of the 4th schedule (section 39).

When a prospectus is not required

An application for shares or debentures does not require a prospectus when:

(i) Shares or debentures are offered to existing shareholders or debenture holders;

(ii) The issue relates to shares or debentures which are identical to ones already issued and being listed on a prescribed stock exchange;

(iii) A person is invited to underwrite an issue;

(iv) The issue is not offered to the public.

Underwriting

Before a company offers shares or debentures to the public it will usually enter into a contract to have the issue underwritten. This is an agreement with an underwriter, that in the event of the public not taking up the whole of the issue or the number specified in the agreement he will, for a commission, take an allotment of those shares that are not taken up by the public. The underwriting agreement may be made with a broker, an issuing house, an insurance company, a syndicate or a bank.

The underwriting commission is calculated on the number of shares underwritten, and is payable whether or not the underwriter is called upon to take up any shares. The commission may be a payment of newly issued shares, or money received for them, but it is also permissible to give underwriters an option to subscribe for shares at a specified price, within a specified time.

The terms of the agreement may be contained in an underwriting letter, but are usually found in an underwriting agreement concluded between the company and the underwriters.

The underwriters will usually enter into a subsidiary contract with sub-underwriters to relieve them of some of their liability. A commission will be paid by the underwriters to the sub-underwriters, and this is known as an over-riding commission.

The Act allows payment of underwriting commission as long as certain requirements are fulfilled. Section 53 states that a company may pay a commission to any person in consideration of his subscribing or agreeing to subscribe for, or procure subscriptions for any shares in a company if:

(i)   Payment of the commission is authorised by the articles;
(ii)   The commission does not exceed 10 per cent of the issue price of the shares, or the amount, or rate authorised by the articles, whichever is the less;
(iii) The amount, or rate agreed is disclosed in the prospectus, or in the case of shares not offered to the public, is disclosed in a statement filed for that purpose;
(iv)   The number of shares which the underwriters have agreed to subscribe for absolutely is disclosed.

Section 53 does not apply to the underwriting of debentures, which may be issued at a discount. If commission is paid for such underwriting, the details of the amount or rate must be filed with the Registrar and must be disclosed in any prospectus issued within two years of the issue of the debentures.

Brokerage

This is a payment made to an issuing house or brokers in return for their placing the company's shares or debentures. The distinction between brokerage and underwriting is that brokerage does not involve the brokers in any risk of having to take up the shares and they are not personally involved in the issue.

Payment of brokerage is allowed if it is authorised by the articles (Article 6). The amount or rate must be reasonable in the ordinary course of business (¼ per cent is regarded as reasonable) and must be disclosed in any prospectus within two years of the issue of the shares or debentures.

9

Liability for False Statements in a Prospectus

A company, an issuing house, or any other person making a false or misleading statement in a prospectus, or omitting essential details from a prospectus, may face civil or criminal liability.

Civil liability

It is essential for a person seeking redress to show that he has been induced to subscribe on the strength of a false or misleading statement in a prospectus.

He may have claims:

1 Against the company;
2 Against the directors, promoters or persons who have authorised the issue of the prospectus;
3 Against the experts.

1 Rights against the company

The main remedy against the company is for rescission of the contract, that is the cancellation of the contract, removal of the plaintiff's name from the register, and repayment of any money paid to the company.

The plaintiff must prove that the statement complained of was a statement of fact, not of opinion. If a prospectus gives an opinion regarding the company's prospectus and future profits and these are not fulfilled, a subscriber will have no remedy. In *Aaron's Reef v. Twiss* a statement in a prospectus that a gold mine had been proved rich, when in fact three companies had unsuccessfully attempted to work the mine, was held to be a misrepresentation, and entitled Twiss to a rescission of his contract to purchase 100 shares.

A statement is deemed to be untrue if it is misleading in its context, even though the statement is literally true. In *R v. Kylsant*, a prospectus issued by the Royal Mail Company stated that 'the dividends on the ordinary stock during the last seventeen years have been as follows', and set out the dividends from 1911 to 1927. The company had suffered trading losses from 1921 to 1927, and was only able to declare a dividend by using accumulated reserves and tax rebates from excess profits paid by the company during the 1914–18 war. It was held that the prospectus was 'false in a material particular'.

An omission can be a material misrepresentation of fact, if the omission makes that which is stated misleading. In *Coles v. White City (Manchester) Greyhound Association Ltd*, a piece of land was described in the prospectus as 'eminently suitable', although the land was subject to a planning resolution by the local authority. No compensation would be paid for any buildings that had to be demolished, unless the local authority had given permission for their erection. Consent to build a greyhound stadium was refused. It was held that the description of 'eminently suitable' was misleading in view of the omission of these facts, and the shareholders who applied for shares on the basis of the prospectus were entitled to rescind their contracts.

Rescission is only available to the allottee, so that a person who buys shares on the market on the basis of statements in the prospectus has no remedy against the company. In *Peek v. Gurney*, Colonel Peek purchased 2000 shares from the original purchaser after reading the company's prospectus. The statements were false, the company went into liquidation, and Colonel Peek had to pay as a contributor £100000 in respect of the shares. It was held that he had no rights against the company as the prospectus was directed at the original allottee only.

Any such contract is valid, though voidable, until rescinded. Even a short delay after the discovery of the mis-statement may be disastrous and deprive the individual of his right to set aside the contract. This right will be lost if there is an implied ratification, for example where individuals, being aware of the mis-statement, have endeavoured to sell their shares, have attended and voted at meetings, executed transfers of shares or have simply treated the contract as subsisting by accepting dividends. The right to rescind will also be lost if the company goes into liquidation, or where it is impossible to restore the parties to their former position, as when the shares are sold.

The deceived shareholder may sue the company for damages if the company has fraudulently misrepresented material facts. The action is for the tort of deceit. The shareholder must prove that the misrepresentation was one of fact, that it was material and that as a result of acting upon it he has suffered loss or damage. He must also prove that those acting on the company's behalf were so authorised and had acted fraudulently, so that a company is vicariously liable for the torts of its employees if they act within the scope of their employment.

If the misrepresentation was made innocently (i.e. the company was unaware that it was untrue) the company may be liable in damages. The company may be able to avoid liability if it can prove that it had reasonable grounds to believe, and did believe up to the time the shares were issued, that the facts represented were true.

2   Rights against directors or promoters

If the directors have been fraudulent in misrepresenting facts stated in the prospectus, they will be liable in damages for the tort of deceit. In order to prove fraud, the plaintiff must show that the defendant 'makes a statement to be acted upon by others, which is false and which is known by him to be false, or is made recklessly or without care whether it is true or false'.

A director will not be liable for deceit for a false statement made in a prospectus if he honestly believes the statement to be true, even if there are no reasonable grounds for his belief. In *Derry v. Peek*, a prospectus stated that the Plymouth and District Tramways Co. had the right to work its trams by steam instead of horses, by virtue of a special Act of Parliament. The consent of the Board of Trade had to be obtained for such a change. It refused to give its consent and the company had to be wound up. Peek, who had taken shares on the strength of the prospectus, sued the directors for fraud. It was held that they were not liable as they honestly believed the statement as to steam power to be true.

An individual who buys shares in the market on the strength of a prospectus has no right against the directors if the prospectus contained a misrepresentation (as in *Peek v. Gurney*), unless the directors intended by issuing the prospectus to encourage and induce purchases in the market. In *Andrews v. Mockford*, a father and son concocted a prospectus for the Sutherland Reef Company, a gold mining company which never existed. A copy of the prospectus was sent to Andrews, amongst others. He decided not to purchase any shares but kept the prospectus. A few months later he read that the company had made a rich discovery on its property and that the main shaft was down fifty feet. The newspaper report was based on a bogus telegram and Andrews bought shares on the stock market. The company was wound up, and Andrews sued Mockford for damages on the basis that there was one continuous fraud which had induced him to purchase the shares. It was held that the action succeeded.

Compensation under section 43

A director, promoter and every person who authorises the issue of a prospectus is liable to compensate any person who subscribes for shares on the faith of a prospectus – for damages sustained by any untrue statement contained in it.

The statement is untrue if it is misleading in the form and context in which it is issued.

The defences

There are certain defences that are available under section 43:

(i)   He had withdrawn his consent to become a director before the prospectus was issued and it was issued without his consent; or

(ii)   It was issued without his knowledge or consent and on becoming aware of the issue, he gave reasonable public notice of this fact; or

(iii)   After issue, but before allotment, and on becoming aware of the untrue statement he withdrew his consent and gave public notice of its withdrawal and the reason for it; or

(iv)   He had reasonable grounds to believe and did up to the time of allotment believe the statement to be true; or

(v)   The statement was fairly represented and made by an expert. He believed the expert competent and the expert had given his consent; or

(vi)   It was a correct and fair representation of a statement made by an official, or correct and fair copy of an extract from a public official document.

A director cannot escape liability for non-disclosure of a material contract of the existence of which he was aware, by professing ignorance of the contents, or materiality of the contract, or by alleging that he left the matter to his legal advisers.

Damages for non-compliance with section 38

An omission from a prospectus of a matter to be included may give rise to an action for damages, at the instance of a subscriber who has suffered loss (even if the omission does not make a prospectus false or misleading).

A director is not liable:

(i)   If he did not know of the matter not disclosed; or

(ii)   If non-compliance arose from an honest mistake of fact on his part; or

(iii)   If non-compliance was not material or the court thinks he ought to be excused.

3 Remedies against experts

An expert who has given his consent to a statement in a prospectus may be liable, if the statement is untrue, under section 43, as a person who has authorised the prospectus.

The expression 'expert' includes an engineer, valuer, accountant and any other person whose profession gives authority to a statement made by him (section 40).

He may be sued for damages, or for compensation under section 43 and the defences that are open to him are:

(i)   He withdrew his consent in writing before the registration of the prospectus; or

(i)   After registration but before allotment, on becoming aware of the untrue statement, he withdrew his consent in writing and gave reasonable public notice of the withdrawal and the reason for it; or

(iii) He was competent to make the statement and up to the time of the allotment believed on reasonable grounds that the statement was true.

Negligence

It may be possible to claim damages for negligent misrepresentation under the principle in *Hedley Byrne v. Heller & Partners*. This provides that if a person negligently makes a false statement in circumstances where he should have foreseen that another party would act upon that statement to his detriment he is liable for any financial loss suffered by that other party. It was held in *Dimant Manufacturing Co. Ltd v. Hamilton* that a company's auditors were liable to a purchaser of shares to whom they had handed an audited copy of the company's balance sheet, which was later found to be incorrect. The purchaser had entered into the contract on the basis of a representation as to the accuracy of the balance sheet.

Few cases are likely to arise under this principle, as it is far easier to satisfy the requirements of proof of section 43 than to establish negligence.

Criminal liability

Any person who authorises the issue of a prospectus containing a false statement is guilty of an offence, and may on conviction on indictment be subject to two years' imprisonment or a fine or both. If it is treated as a summary offence he may on conviction be sentenced to a term of imprisonment not exceeding six months or to a fine not exceeding the statutory maximum, or both (section 44 as amended by the 1980 Companies Act). Examples of individuals found guilty under this section have been directors and auditors of a company, a managerial official of an issuing house and an expert whose report was referred to in a prospectus.

There are two possible defences to an accused under this section, laying the onus of proof of innocence on the accused. The defences are that:

(i)   The statement was not material; or
(ii) That he had reason to believe and, up to the time of the issue of the prospectus, did believe the statement to be true.

Section 19 of the Theft Act 1968 provides that where an officer of a company, with intent to deceive its members or creditors about its affairs, publishes or concurs in publishing a written statement or account which to his knowledge is or may be misleading, false or deceptive in a material particular, is liable to imprisonment for a term not exceeding seven years. It was under a forerunner of this section in the Larceny Act that Lord Kylsant was convicted (*R v. Kylsant*).

10

Membership of a Company

How persons become members

A person becomes a member of a company when he agrees to become
a member and his name is entered in the register of members (section
26). In the case of a share company its shareholders are its members.

A person becomes a member in one of the following ways:

(a) By purchasing shares from a previous member, e.g. on a stock
    exchange. The company registers the transfer and enters his
    name on the register of members.
(b) By applying to the company for an allotment of shares. When
    shares are allotted to him, the company will enter his name on the
    register.
(c) By subscribing to the company's memorandum. As soon as the
    company is registered, the subscriber's name is entered on the
    register.
(d) By signing and filing an undertaking, as a director, to take and
    pay for qualification shares.
(e) By succeeding to shares on the death or bankruptcy of a member.

Any person not under a disability may become a member, unless the
company's articles impose a restriction as they often do, in the case of
minors and aliens. Articles often give a power to the directors to refuse
a transfer to persons of whom they do not approve.

Who may become members?

Companies

A company may become a member of another company if its memorandum contains a power to hold shares, or if it takes shares in pay-

ment of a debt by way of compromise. It attends meetings by appointing a duly authorised representative to attend and vote on its behalf. A company may only acquire its shares in one of the following ways:

(i)   The acquisition by a company of any of its fully paid shares, other than for a valuable consideration (e.g. a gift of its own shares to a company in a bequest).
(ii) The acquisition of its shares in a reduction of capital.
(iii) The redemption or purchase of any shares in accordance with the Companies Act 1981.
(iv) The purchase of its shares as a result of a Court Order under section 75 of the 1980 Companies Act when the minority complain of unfair prejudice, or as a result of an alteration of the company's objects.
(v)   The forfeiture or surrender of shares.

   In situations (ii) and (iii) and (iv) the company must immediately cancel the shares; in situations (i) and (v) the shares must either be disposed of or cancelled within three years (1980 Companies Act, section 35).
   If a person acquires shares in a limited company as a nominee of that company he is deemed to hold the shares on his own account with the company having no interest in the shares. If the nominee does not pay the company the sums due on the shares, the directors shall be jointly and severally liable with the nominee for payment of any outstanding sums.
   The general prohibition on a company and its subsidiaries giving financial assistance (by means of a gift, loan, guarantee or otherwise) for the purchase of its own shares was modified by the Companies Act 1981, sections 42–44. The prohibition does not apply if the company's principal purpose in giving financial assistance is incidental to some larger purpose, and the assistance was given in good faith in the interests of the company.
   A company may provide financial assistance in the following circumstances:

(i)   The loan is made in the ordinary course of business by a company whose ordinary business is lending money.
(ii) Money is provided for the purchase of shares in the company or its holding company, for an employee share scheme.

An employee share scheme is a scheme for encouraging or facilitating the holding of shares or debentures in a company (or its holding company) for the benefit of its employees or former employees, or the wives, husbands, widows, widowers and infant children of such employees.

(iii)　Loans to employees, other than directors, to purchase fully paid shares in the company.

A public company may only provide financial assistance in these circumstances, from its distributable profits. The penalty for contravention by the company and every officer of the company in default, is a maximum fine of £1000 and a maximum term of two years' imprisonment (section 42).

The prohibitions imposed in section 42 are relaxed in the case of private companies. In general a private company may provide financial assistance to any person, including a director, for the acquisition of its own shares. Such financial assistance may only be provided from the company's distributable profits. A subsidiary may not provide financial assistance for the acquisition of shares in its holding company, if it is also a subsidiary of a public company, which is itself a subsidiary of that holding company.

A special resolution must sanction the financial assistance to be given, unless the company proposing to give the financial assistance is a wholly owned subsidiary.

The directors of the company proposing to give the financial assistance must make a statutory declaration that they have formed the opinion that after giving this financial assistance the company will be able to pay its debts in full over the following year. The auditors must also append a report to the effect that they are not aware of anything to indicate that the directors' declaration is unreasonable in the circumstances (Companies Act 1981, section 43).

The holders of 10 per cent of the issued shares or capital of the company or 10 per cent of the membership (if the company is limited by shares) who did not vote in favour of the resolution may apply to the Court for the resolution to be cancelled. The Court may confirm the resolution, cancel the resolution or make an order for the purchase of the interests of dissentient members and may make these orders on such terms and conditions as it thinks fit.

The relaxation of this prohibition will make it easier to carry out a 'management buy-out'. Managers of private companies who wish to buy up the shares of their company from the existing owners will be allowed to secure loans on the company's assets.

Subsidiary companies

As a general rule a subsidiary company may not hold shares in its holding company (section 27) unless:

(a)   The subsidiary was a member of its holding company before 1 July 1948. It may continue to be a member, but it cannot vote at the meetings of its holding company.

(b)   The subsidiary holds the shares as a personal representative or trustee and neither company has any beneficial interest under the trust, other than in the ordinary course of business (e.g. a bank's subsidiary company, dealing with executorship and trustee matters may hold the bank's shares as a result of being appointed an executor or trustee).

Joint holders

Shares may be allotted to two or more persons jointly, and will be registered in their names. The articles usually state that the company shall not be bound to issue more than one share certificate, and that only the first named in the register is entitled to a share certificate, to a dividend, to notice of meetings, and to a vote. When such a share is transferred, the joint holders must join in the transfer, and on the death of one joint holder the shares are vested in the survivor.

Minors

A minor (i.e. a person under the age of eighteen) may become a member unless forbidden in the articles. A minor may repudiate a contract to take shares before or within a reasonable time of becoming eighteen (i.e. the contract is voidable). If he does repudiate, he cannot recover any money paid for the shares unless there has been a total failure of consideration. In *Steinberg v. Scala (Leeds) Ltd*, an infant agreed to take 500 £1 shares in a company and paid 10s (50p) on each share. She did not receive a dividend on the shares and whilst an infant sued to recover the money she had paid, and sought a declaration that she was not liable for future calls. It was held that she was not liable for future calls, but as the shares had at one time had a market value she could not recover the money she had already paid.

Bankrupts

A bankrupt may be a member of a company and, unless the articles provide otherwise, a shareholder does not cease to be a member if he becomes bankrupt. As a member he is entitled to vote at meetings, but the articles usually provide that notice of meetings is to be sent to the trustee in bankruptcy (Article 134), and so the bankrupt will vote in accordance with the dictates of the trustee. However, an undischarged bankrupt may not become a director without the leave of the Court by which he was adjudged bankrupt.

Personal representatives

A member's personal representatives, i.e. his executor (if a will has been made) or an administrator (if no will was made), will succeed to his shares on a member's death. A deceased member's estate remains liable for calls if the shares are not fully paid.

A personal representative is entitled to transfer the shares and receives all dividends, bonuses or other benefits from the shares without being registered as a member, but the articles usually preclude him from voting.

The articles usually provide that a personal representative may choose to be registered as a member (Article 30), or he may be required by the directors to either register as a member or transfer the shares. If he does not elect within ninety days, the directors are empowered to withhold payment of all dividends, bonuses or other monies payable until he does elect (Article 32).

If he chooses to be registered as a member he becomes personally liable for calls, although he is entitled to an indemnity from the estate of the deceased member.

Firms

As a firm is not a legal entity it should be registered as a member and the partners should be asked for their consent to registration as joint holders.

Lenders

A person who lends money to the company on a mortgage of its shares may become liable as a member if the shares are registered in his name. In *Re Patent Manufacturing Co. Addison's Case*, Addison lent the company £500 and took 100 £5 shares as security for the loan, with a proviso that the money was to be repaid on a month's notice and that the shares should then be cancelled. Notice was given and the money was repaid, but it was later held that Addison was liable to pay £500 for the shares.

Rights and liabilities of members

In a share company, the member's liability is to pay for his shares in full, that is for the whole nominal amount of his shares. If he was allotted shares as a result of a prospectus application, he is liable for the amounts due on application and allotment, and for any instalments specified in the terms of issue. Any further amounts outstanding on the shares may be called up by the directors at some future date. Should any amount remain unpaid and the company is wound up, the liquidator will call upon the shareholder to pay the outstanding amount.

If a shareholder transfers partly paid shares he may incur liability in the event of the company being wound up within one year. Should the existing shareholders be unable to pay their contributions, previous shareholders may be placed on the 'B' list of contributories.

If the company carries on business for more than six months with less than two members, the remaining member may become liable for the company's debts contracted after the six month period, without limit of liability.

A member has major rights in that he is entitled to a dividend, when a dividend has been duly declared. He has a right to vote at meetings and can appoint anyone as his proxy to attend and vote in his place. He has a right in the winding up of the company to receive a proportionate part of the capital (after the payment of the company's debts), or to participate in the distribution of the company's assets.

He has the right to transfer his shares to whomsoever he wishes, unless he is forbidden to do so or is restricted by the articles.

A member is entitled to a share certificate, to a copy of the memorandum and articles and, unless provided otherwise by the articles, to receive a notice of general meetings. He is entitled to receive a copy of every balance sheet laid before a general meeting, and has the right to inspect copies of directors' service contracts, various registers, and the minutes of general meetings.

He may, on his own or with other members, requisition a general meeting, circulate resolutions and petition the Court for the winding up of the company, or for relief where the members are unfairly prejudiced.

Termination of membership

A person ceases to be a member when his name is removed from the register on the occurrence of any of these events:

1 A transfer of all his shares.
2 The forfeiture or surrender of all his shares.
3 The sale of all his shares by a company to enforce a lien.
4 The death of the member and the transfer of his shares to his personal representative.
5 The expulsion of the member from a company.
6 The bankruptcy of the member and the registration of the shares in the name of his trustee in bankruptcy, or their disclaimer by the trustee.
7 The issue of share warrants.

8   The redemption of redeemable shares.
9   The winding up of a company.

Register of members

A company must keep a register of its members containing:

(a)   The name and address of each member.
(b)   A statement of the shares held by each member. If the shares are of different classes, each class must be distinguished.
(c)   The amount paid or agreed to be considered as paid upon the shares.
(d)   The date on which each person became a member.
(e)   The date on which each person ceased to be a member (section 110).

A company with more than fifty members must keep an index of its members, and the register and index must be open to inspection during business hours, free of charge, to members. Non-members may be charged 5 pence (or less), if the company so prescribes, for inspecting the register. Any member or any other person may require the company to provide a copy of the register on payment of 10 pence per 100 words. The company must provide this copy within ten days of its being requested.

The Court has power to rectify the register if a person's name is entered or omitted from the register, without sufficient cause; or default is made; or unnecessary delay takes place in entering the fact that a person has ceased to be a member.

As well as rectification, the Court may order the payment by the company of any damages sustained by the aggrieved party (section 116).

Notice of trusts

Notice of a trust cannot be entered on the register, even if the company has constructive notice of the existence of a trust. In *Simpson v. Molsen's Bank*, the executors of a will transferred shares to a third party in breach of the terms of the will, and he was registered by the company as the holder of the shares. Not only did the company have a copy of the will, but one of its directors was an executor of the will. It was held that the company's sole responsibility was to satisfy itself that the executors were properly appointed and had authority; it was not concerned with the contents of the will.

As far as a company is concerned the person whose name is entered on the register is the beneficial owner of the shares. If the shares are held by a trustee the company is not liable to any beneficiary for any breach of trust, or for any fraudulent transfer of the shares by the trustee. The trustee is liable for any calls on the shares, even though the calls exceed the value of the trust property in his hands.

A beneficiary can protect his interest by serving a 'Stop Notice' on a company. He makes an application to the Court, with a supporting affidavit, giving particulars of his interest and this is served on the company. If a company receives any request to transfer the shares or pay a dividend on them, it must inform the person who lodged the notice, and must not accept the transfer, or pay a dividend until eight days have expired after giving such notice. This enables the person lodging the notice to obtain an injunction within the eight days and so prevent the company from transferring the shares or paying a dividend.

Register of interests in shares

If a company's shares are listed on a stock exchange it must also keep a register of any person who becomes interested in 5 per cent or more of its issued shares which carry an unrestricted right to vote at general meetings. (This percentage may be amended by the Secretary of State by means of a statutory instrument.)

A person is 'interested' if he is the registered holder of the shares or if his interests include those listed in section 28 of the 1967 Companies Act (as amended by the Companies Act 1981) relating to directors' interests.

If a person already has a 5 per cent holding and either increases or diminishes his holding by 1 per cent without reducing his holding to below 5 per cent, he must also inform the company, as must a person whose holding falls below 5 per cent.

The Companies Act 1981 imposes obligations on members of a 'concert party' to notify a public company (the target company) of interests in voting shares. A concert party agreement is any agreement to acquire an interest in the shares of a public company. Each party to the agreement relies on the other party to retain the shares acquired, as a result of obtaining this interest. They must inform the target company of their collective holding. They may appoint an agent for this purpose, but if they do not, they must notify the company individually. Each party is under a duty to inform the other parties of their holding, so that they may comply with their obligation to notify the company when (or if) it arises.

A public company may require any person who during the last three years has been interested (or who it believes has been interested) in its voting shares to provide information to the company as to the extent of his interest. In the event of obtaining unsatisfactory replies, or no replies, the company may apply to the Court for restrictions (e.g. non-payment of dividends, no votes to be exercised) to apply to its shares. Members holding 10 per cent or more of the company's shares may require the company to use this power to investigate the owner-ship of shares.

A register of the results of the enquiries undertaken in connection with such interests, must be kept and made available for inspection by the members and the public.

The annual return

Every company having a share capital is required to make an annual return to the Registrar stating:

1   The address of its registered office.
2   The address where the registers of members and debenture holders are kept (if not kept at the registered office).
3   A summary (called the annual summary) between shares issued for cash and shares issued for a consideration other than cash and stating:

    (a)   The amount of share capital and the number of shares author-ised and issued;
    (b)   The amounts called up, paid and unpaid on each share;
    (c)   The amounts paid by way of commission, and the discounts allowed on the issue of shares and debentures;
    (d)   The number of shares forfeited;
    (e)   The number of share warrants and the number of shares comprised in them.

4   The total amount of debts secured by mortgages and charges.
5   A list of names and addresses of members and of those ceasing to be members since the last return, stating the number of shares held and the number transferred.
6   Particulars of the directors and secretary.

11

Share Capital

Various terms are used in respect of share capital:

(a) Nominal or authorised capital is the nominal value of shares which a company may issue. This amount is stated in the memorandum of association and may be increased or reduced.

(b) Issued capital is the nominal value of the shares which have actually been allotted by the company, whether for cash or some other consideration.

(c) Paid up capital is the total amount paid up or credited as paid up on the shares issued.

(d) Uncalled capital is the total amount not called up on the shares issued.

(e) Reserve capital is that part of the uncalled capital which may only be called up in the event of the company being wound up.

(f) Equity share capital is that part of the issued capital which gives its holders an unrestricted right to participate in dividends and distribution of capital. It normally consists of the ordinary shares or the ordinary and deferred shares.

Classes of share capital

A company may confer different rights on different classes of shares. Article 2 provides that 'any share in the company may be issued with such preferred, deferred or other special rights or such restrictions, whether in regard to dividend, voting, return of capital . . . as the company may . . . determine'. The various rights attaching to the various classes of shares are usually set out in the company's articles, or in the terms of issue of the shares. Different classes of shares attract different types of investors. While the ordinary shares offer the promise of greater financial rewards, the preference shares promise a more secure if less spectacular return on investment. If additional capital is only required for a limited time, a company may issue redeemable shares.

The main classes of shares are:

(a)   Ordinary shares.
(b)   Founders' or deferred shares.
(c)   Preference shares.

(a)   Ordinary shares

Ordinary shares are often referred to as the equity capital of the company. The holders of these shares are entitled, in the absence of any deferred shares, to the balance of the distributed profit and in a winding up to the balance of the assets.

Companies are allowed to issue non-voting shares, but such shares are frowned upon by the Stock Exchange. Non-voting ordinary shares are a separate class of shares from the ordinary voting shares.

(b)   Founders' or deferred shares

The holders of these shares are only entitled to a dividend if the dividend on the ordinary shares reaches a fixed amount, for example the deferred shareholders may be entitled to 25 per cent of the profits, after a dividend of 10 per cent has been paid on the ordinary shares.

These shares are rarely issued today, but at one time they were fairly common. They are sometimes referred to as founders or management shares as they were often issued to the promoters who were prepared to wait until the very last for their share of the profits, thus showing their confidence in the company. Unfortunately, many of these shares were issued by unscrupulous promoters who perpetrated frauds on the public and this type of share became very unpopular with investors.

The Act does recognise the existence of such shares and a prospectus issued by a company must state the number of founders or management or deferred shares (if any), their voting rights, and their interests in the company's property and profits (section 38). Most deferred shares have now been converted into ordinary shares.

(c)   Preference shares

These are shares which are given certain preferential rights over the other shares in a company. There are different types of preference shares and their rights vary accordingly, but the two principal rights usually enjoyed by those shares are:

(i)   a right to preference in the payment of a dividend; and

(ii)   a right to preference in the repayment of capital in a winding up.

Preference shareholders are entitled to receive a dividend which is expressed as a percentage of the nominal amount of the share (e.g. 6 per cent preference share) when a dividend is declared. A preference shareholder is not entitled to 6 per cent per annum but to preferential treatment on the declaration of a dividend.

Unless stated otherwise a preference share is cumulative, that is, if no dividend is declared on the preference share in any year, the arrears of dividend are carried forward and must be paid before any dividend is paid on the ordinary shares. For example, if no dividend is declared on 6 per cent preference shares in 1980, 1981 and 1982 they would be entitled in 1983 to arrears of 24 per cent before the ordinary shareholders were paid any dividend.

The articles may provide that the shares are participating in that after the preference and ordinary shares have received specified dividends, the preference shareholders will be entitled to participate in the surplus profits of the company.

The general rule in a winding up is that all shareholders should be treated equally, so that if any group of shareholders is to receive preferential treatment this must be expressly stated in the articles or the terms of issue of the shares. Most articles give preference shareholders priority to repayment of capital in a winding up, and if no other rights are given it is assumed that they are not entitled to share in any assets which remain after the repayment of the capital.

If the articles or terms of issue of the shares do not grant preference shareholders any priority in winding up, they will be entitled to share equally with the ordinary shareholders in the repayment of capital and in the division of any surplus assets.

Preference shareholders have no rights in a winding up to any outstanding arrears of dividend unless the articles specifically give that right.

Redeemable shares
A company limited by shares may, if authorised by its articles, issue redeemable shares which may be redeemed at the option of the company or the shareholder. These shares are issued when the company requires additional capital for a limited time only.

Under section 45 of the Companies Act 1981:

(i)   The shares may only be redeemed if they are fully paid.
(ii)   The shares may only be redeemed out of the distributable profits available for dividend, or out of the proceeds of a fresh issue of shares made for the purpose.

(iii) If the shares are redeemed from profits, profits equal to the nominal amount of the shares redeemed must be transferred to a capital redemption reserve fund.

(iv) The capital redemption reserve fund may be used to pay up unissued bonus shares to be issued as fully paid to members.

 (v) Any premium payable on redemption must be provided out of distributable profits or out of a fresh issue of shares made for the purposes of redemption.

(vi) When a company is redeeming shares, it may issue shares to an equivalent nominal amount of the redeemed shares, without being regarded as having increased its share capital, as long as the old shares are redeemed within one month of the issue of the new shares.

Notice of the redemption must be given to the Registrar within one month.

The redemption of shares does not amount to a reduction of capital as the redeemed shares remain part of the nominal capital of the company and must be shown in the balance sheet.

Share warrants

A company may, if its shares are fully paid up and it is given authority by its articles, issue share warrants stating that the bearer is entitled to the shares specified therein. They are negotiable instruments and may be transferred by delivery of the warrant.

When a share warrant is issued, the member's name must be struck off the register. Certain particulars must then be entered in the register, namely that a warrant has been issued, a statement of the shares included in the warrant, and the date of issue of the warrant.

The payment of a dividend is usually made by means of a coupon attached to the warrant, which is sent to the company when a dividend is advertised. The holder of a warrant may at any time surrender his warrant, be entered in the register, and issued with a share certificate.

If the articles so provide, he may be deemed to be a member of the company for certain purposes. The articles usually provide that the holder of a warrant may not requisition a meeting, give notice of resolutions, or vote unless he first deposits his warrant with the company before a general meeting. At the conclusion of the meeting the warrant is returned to him.

A share warrant is unsuitable as a qualification share for a director, as a company would be unable to ensure that he continued to hold the warrant.

Increase and alteration of share capital

A share company or a guarantee company having share capital may alter its share capital so as to:

(a) Increase its share capital by creating new shares;

(b) Consolidate and divide its shares into shares of larger amount;

(c) Sub-divide its shares or any part of them into shares of a smaller amount. When the shares are not fully paid the proportions paid up and unpaid will remain unaltered.

(d) Convert its paid up shares or re-convert its stock into paid up shares;

(e) Cancel any unissued shares.

The articles must authorise any of these alterations which must be made by the company at a general meeting. An ordinary resolution is sufficient, unless the articles provide otherwise (section 61).

The Registrar must be informed of any alteration in the share capital. Notice of an increase of share capital must be forwarded to him within fifteen days, with a copy of the resolution authorising the increase. Notice of any of the other alterations listed above must be given to the Registrar within one month.

(a) The articles normally give authority to increase capital. Article 44 states that a company may, from time to time, by ordinary resolution increase the share capital by such sum, to be divided into shares of such amount, as the resolution shall prescribe. If the articles do not give this power they must be altered by a special resolution before a resolution to increase the capital can be passed.

(b) A company may consolidate and divide its shares and if the shares are found to be divided into unwieldy or inconvenient amounts, for example 50 000 shares of 35p each might be consolidated into 17 500 shares of £1 each.

(c) A company may sub-divide its shares if the nominal or market value of the share is so high that it restricts dealings in the shares, for example £100 shares might be sub-divided into ten £10 shares.

(d) The conversion of fully paid shares into stock offers certain advantages: e.g. stock need not be numbered; may be divided into any fraction; and may be transferred in any amounts subject to any restriction in the articles. Article 41 provides that the directors may fix the maximum amount of stock that may be transferred (e.g. stock may only be transferred in multiples of 50p or £1).

(e) Only unissued shares can be cancelled; that is, a cancellation of the authorised but not issued capital. This is sometimes known as diminution of capital, to distinguish it from a reduction of capital. It is rarely invoked, but it has been used when the capital structure of a company has been altered in an amalgamation or reconstruction, or when a company has wished to rid itself of unissued shares carrying burdensome rights.

Reduction of capital

The capital of a company may not be reduced except as permitted by the Act which provides that a limited company may, if authorised by its articles, reduce its share capital. The method is by special resolution and the Court must confirm the reduction (section 66).

If the articles do not contain the power to allow a reduction of capital, the articles must be altered so as to allow this power by special resolution, and a further special resolution must be passed to sanction the reduction. These resolutions may be passed successively at the same meeting.

Companies reduce their capital for a variety of reasons, for example:

(i)   A company having partly paid up shares may have surplus capital and may wish to relieve its members of their liability in respect of the amount not paid up (e.g. a company having a share capital of 10000 £1 shares with 50p paid on each share may wish to reduce its capital to 10000 fully paid shares of 50p each).

(ii)   A company may have capital in excess of its requirements and may wish to return some of it to its shareholders. This often happens when a company sells part of its undertaking and decides to confine its activities to the remaining section of the business (e.g. a company with a share capital of 10000 fully paid £1 shares wishes to reduce its capital to 10000 fully paid 50p shares, the remaining 50p per share to be returned in cash, to each member).

(iii)   A company may wish to cancel paid up share capital which has been lost or is not represented by available assets (e.g. a company with a share capital of 10000 fully paid £1 shares may only have assets amounting to £5000, and may seek to reduce its capital to 10000 fully paid shares of 50p each).

Where the proposed reduction involves either a diminution of the liability of shareholders, or the return of paid up capital to shareholders, the company's creditors are entitled to object. The Court then settles a list of creditors, who either consent to the reduction or are paid off by the company.

A public company may not reduce its capital below the statutory minimum under section 66, unless it first re-registers as a private company.

The Court may make the order on such terms and conditions as it thinks fit. It may also require the company to add the words 'and reduced' to its name for a period of time, and for the company to publish the reasons for the reduction and the causes which led to the reduction.

Purchase of shares

The Companies Act 1981, section 46, permits a limited company having a share capital to purchase its own shares, if so authorised by its articles. It may purchase its shares in both off-market and market transactions.

An off-market purchase is a purchase other than on a recognised stock exchange, or is a purchase on a recognised stock exchange which is not subject to a marketing arrangement on that stock exchange. The terms of the proposed contract of purchase must be authorised by a special resolution of the company, before it enters into such a contract. In the case of a public company, the authority must specify a date on which the authority is to expire. A purchase is invalid if a member, holding shares to which the resolution relates, votes in favour of the resolution, and the resolution would not have been passed without his votes (Companies Act 1981, section 47).

A market purchase is a purchase on a recognised stock exchange. The purchase must be authorised by the company in general meeting. The authority may be unconditional or subject to conditions, and must specify the maximum number of shares authorised to be acquired, the minimum and maximum prices which may be paid for the shares, and the date on which the authority expires (Companies Act 1981, section 49). A contract under which the company becomes entitled or obliged to purchase its shares (e.g. options) is termed a contingent purchase contract. The purchase of its shares by a company in these circumstances must be approved in advance by special resolution (Companies Act 1981, section 48).

Payment of the purchase price must normally be made from a company's distributable profit, and an amount equal to the nominal value of the shares purchased must be transferred to a capital redemption reserve. The reserve may be applied by the company in paying up unissued shares to be allotted to members as fully paid bonus shares.

A private company may, if authorised by its articles, make a purchase of its own shares out of capital, after exhausting any available profits and/or the proceeds of any fresh issue of shares made for the purposes of purchase. Such a payment must be approved by special resolution. The directors must also make a statutory declaration that having made a full inquiry into the company's affairs and prospects they have formed the opinion that the company will be able to meet its debts initially on purchasing its shares, and in the following year. The auditors must also append a report to the same effect.

Within the week following the resolution, the company must publish in the *London Gazette* a notice stating that it has approved the payment out of capital; the amount of capital involved; the availability for inspection of the directors' and auditors' report; and that any creditor may apply to the Court within five weeks for an order prohibiting the payment. It must also publish a notice to the same effect in an appropriate national newspaper, or give notice in writing to each of its creditors.

Any member who did not vote for the resolution and any creditor may, within five weeks, apply to the Court for the cancellation of the resolution. The Court on hearing the application may make an order either cancelling the resolution, or confirming it on such terms as it thinks fit. It may also adjourn the proceedings in order to make arrangements for the purchase of shares of dissentient members, or for the protection of dissentient creditors.

If a company having purchased its shares out of capital is subsequently wound up, within one year of the purchase, the person from whom the shares were purchased, and the directors who made the statutory declaration, will be liable to contribute to the assets of the company.

Variation of class rights

It is sometimes necessary to amend or vary the rights of one or more classes of shares. If preferential or other special rights are attached to a class of shares, the articles and the memorandum have to be examined to discover if these rights can be varied and by what procedure.

The majority of these rights relate to dividend, voting and the distribution of the assets in the winding up of the company.

The procedure to be adopted depends on whether the class rights are defined in the memorandum or in the articles. If the class rights are defined in the memorandum, which provides a procedure for variation, the rights can be varied by following this procedure. If the variation requires the consent of a specified proportion of the class, or the sanction of a general meeting, the minority shareholders can apply to the Court for the cancellation of the variation (section 72).

Section 72 provides that where the articles or memorandum authorise the variation of rights of a class of shares, subject to the consent of a specified proportion of the holders of that class, and such a variation is made, the holders of 15 per cent of the issued shares of the class who did not consent to the variation may, within twenty-one days, apply to the Court to have the variation cancelled. The variation will not become effective unless confirmed by the Court. If the memorandum does not contain any provision for the variation of class rights, these rights may be varied by the unanimous consent of all the members of the company.

If the memorandum prohibits any variation, no variation is possible other than under section 206 which permits compromises to be effected between the company and any class of member.

If class rights are attached to shares other than in the memorandum, for example in the articles or the terms of issue of the shares, and there is a clause permitting their variation (i.e. a variation of rights clause), the class rights can be varied, but only in accordance with the clause. If no provision is made in the articles for variation, class rights may only be varied with the consent in writing of the holders of three-quarters of the issued shares of the class, or with the consent of an extraordinary resolution passed at a separate general meeting of the class. In such a case the rights of the minority shareholders of that class are protected by section 72.

Where the variation of class rights is connected with the giving, varying, revoking or renewing authority to the directors to issue or reduce share capital, then three-quarters of the holders of the class must consent in writing to the variation, or an extraordinary resolution must be passed by a class meeting to sanction the variation (section 72, as amended by section 32, 1980 Companies Act).

Public notice must be given of any special rights attaching to a company's shares and of any variation of these rights. The directors must deliver to the Registrar particulars of any special rights attaching to any class of shares, unless these details are dealt with under some other filing provision – under the company's memorandum or articles, or the resolution within section 143 which deals with the filing of special resolutions (section 33, Companies Act 1980).

An increase in the number of preference and ordinary shares which dilutes the control of existing shareholders is not a variation of class rights.

In *White v. Bristol Aeroplane Company Ltd*, the issued capital of the company consisted of £600000 preference and £3300000 ordinary stock. The articles of the company provided that class rights could not be altered without the sanction of an extraordinary resolution of the class concerned. The company proposed to issue £600000 preference shares as bonus shares to the ordinary shareholders which would rank *pari passu* with the existing preference shares. It was held that the issue of new preference shares would affect the enjoyment of the rights of the existing preference stock, not the rights themselves.

In *Re John Smith's Tadcaster Brewery*, a company proposed to increase its capital by creating 280 000 new ordinary £1 shares and issuing them to the ordinary shareholders as fully paid bonus shares from the company's undistributed profits. It was held that the issue of these shares would not affect the rights or privileges of the ordinary shareholder. It would mean that a greater number of people would have similar voting rights.

12

Shares

A share represents the interest of a shareholder in a company. He does not own any of the company's assets as these belong to the company, a separate legal entity. Nevertheless, he is a proportionate owner of the company and has various rights and liabilities. For example, he has the right to vote, to a dividend (if declared), to attend meetings, and he must pay for any amount outstanding on his share.

Each share in a share company must have a nominal value (e.g. £5, £1, 50p) as the memorandum of such a company must state in its capital clause, 'the division thereof into shares of a fixed amount'. It is therefore impossible for a company to issue shares of no par value. Each share must also be distinguished by its number, unless all the issued shares, or all the issued shares of a particular class, are fully paid and rank *pari passu* (section 74).

Application for shares

An application for shares in a company will usually be in writing, although it can be made orally. Such an application, often in response to a prospectus, will be an offer by the applicant. The acceptance of the application will be a letter of allotment from the company. The application form usually reads: 'I agree to accept such shares and any smaller number that may be allotted to me.' Without this clause, a company would be making a counter offer if it allotted any applicant a smaller number of shares than he had applied for, and he could refuse to take any shares.

An application must be accepted within a reasonable time. In *Ramsgate Victoria Hotel v. Montefiore*, Montefiore offered to take shares in the company in June 1864. He did not receive a reply to his letter, but the company allotted him shares in November 1864. By that time the company was in financial difficulties and he refused to take the shares. It was held that the offer had lapsed due to the company's delay in notifying their acceptance.

If the application is subject to a collateral agreement, the acceptance of the application constitutes a binding agreement. If the collateral agreement is not carried out, the applicant's remedy is an action for damages in respect of the collateral agreement. In *Elkington's Case*, Elkington applied for shares and paid 30s (£1.50) per share on allotment. He refused to pay a further call made by the company on the grounds that the company had agreed that, until they had taken and paid for goods to the value of £3000 from him, no further calls were to be made on the shares. It was held that he must pay the call, and that his remedy lay in action against the company for breach of contract.

Acceptance

The company's acceptance must be communicated to the applicant. Notice of the allotment is generally sent by post and the contract is complete on posting the letter. This is so even if the letter is delayed or lost in the post. In *Household Fire Insurance Co. v. Grant*, Grant applied for 100 shares in a company and was allotted the shares. The letter of allotment was posted by the company, but was not received by Grant. The company went into liquidation and Grant had to pay the balance owing on the shares.

An application for shares may be withdrawn at any time before the letter of allotment is posted. The right to withdraw an offer for shares was of great inconvenience to public companies, as speculators were able to withdraw their applications for shares if they discovered that the issue was under-subscribed. The Act now provides that where a prospectus is issued generally, that is to persons other than the company's members or debenture holders, applications for shares cannot be withdrawn until the expiration of the third day after the opening of the lists (section 50). The company has usually posted its letters of allotment before this 'third day'.

Allotment of shares

Directors may not allot shares (i.e. issue shares) unless authorised to do so by the company in general meeting or by the articles. The authority must state the maximum amount of securities that may be allotted, and the date on which the authority expires. The date of expiry must not be more than five years from the date of incorporation when the authority is contained in the company's articles, or five years from the date of passing the resolution giving the authority for altering the articles (Companies Act 1980, section 14).

Public company

A public company issuing a prospectus is subject to certain restrictions in respect of the allotment of shares.

1 A company may not allot any shares unless the minimum subscription has been subscribed, and the application money has been received by the company. This is only applicable to a first allotment. (The minimum subscription is the minimum amount which in the director's opinion is required by the company to pay for the purchase of property, preliminary expenses, repayment of loans and for providing working capital.) If the minimum subscription is not received within forty days from the issue of the prospectus, all money received must be repaid within the following eight days. Any delay beyond this time will make the directors liable to repay it with 5 per cent interest (section 47). An allotment made in contravention of this section is voidable at the applicant's option.

2 It must not allot shares unless 25 per cent of the nominal value of each share, plus any premium due has been paid (1980 Companies Act, section 22).

3 No allotment may be made unless the capital is fully subscribed for, or the offer states that the shares subscribed for may be allotted in any event, or in the event of certain conditions being fulfilled. This is subject to section 22 (above).

4 A company may not allot any shares until the beginning of the third day after the issue of the prospectus, or until any later time stated in the prospectus, as the time of opening the lists (section 50). An allotment in contravention of this section is valid, but the officers of the company will be subject to penalties.

5 If a prospectus states that an application has been made or will be made for permission to deal with the shares on any Stock Exchange, any allotment is void if permission has not been applied for before the third day after the issue of the prospectus or if permission is subsequently refused (section 51).

6 The consideration for the allotment may be money, or with the company's consent, money's worth (e.g. goodwill or know how) but a public company may not accept payment by work or service for its shares. Any person who pays for shares by work or services is liable to

pay the full value of the shares in money (1980 Companies Act, section 20).

7   A public company may not make an allotment of shares, either fully or partly paid up, other than in cash if part of the payment includes an undertaking that may be performed more than five years after the date of allotment. If the consideration for an allotment of shares is the transfer to the company of a non-cash asset, it must be transferred to the company within five years of the allotment, and must be valued by a person qualified to be the company's auditor. This rule does not apply to an arrangement where the whole or part of the consideration for the allotment is the transfer to the company of shares in another company, or the cancellation of shares in another company; or to an allotment of shares in connection with a proposed merger. An arrangement in this context is any scheme or arrangement, and includes any arrangements under sections 206 or 287 of the Act (1980 Companies Act, sections 23–25, as amended by the 1981 Companies Act).

8   The directors must file with the Registrar within one month particulars of any allotment of shares whose rights are not stated in a company's memorandum or articles, or in any resolution or agreement filed with the Registrar, unless the shares are uniform with shares previously allotted (1980 Companies Act, section 33).

9   Whenever a limited company makes an allotment of its shares it must, within one month of the allotment, file with the Registrar a return of allotments, stating the number and nominal amount of the shares and the name of the allottees (i.e. individuals to whom shares have been issued). If the shares have been allotted other than for cash, the consideration for the allotment must also be stated (section 51).

Issue of shares at a discount

A company may not issue shares at a discount (1980 Companies Act, section 21), so that the issue of £1 share for, say, 75 pence is void. Any attempt to achieve an issue at a 'discount' by indirect means is prohibited. In *Moseley v. Koffyfontein Mines*, a company proposed to issue £1 debentures at a 20 per cent discount, namely at 80 pence. The holders were able to have the right to exchange the debentures for fully paid shares at any time before the debentures were repaid. The company was prevented by injunction from proceeding with the issue as there was nothing to prevent a debenture holder from exercising his rights immediately and receiving 100 £1 shares for every £80 that had been paid for the debentures.

Shares issued at a discount will be treated as paid up if payment is made of the nominal value less the discount. The allottee is then liable to pay to the company an amount equal to the amount of the discount, plus interest.

The only exception to the rule is contained in section 53 which allows the allottees of shares to deduct or be paid underwriting commission for subscribing for these shares.

Issue of shares at a premium

A company may issue shares at a premium (i.e. at a price in excess of their nominal value) so that the issue of a £1 share for £2 is in order. The Act requires that the premium must be transferred to a share premium account and details of the share premium account must be included in every balance sheet (section 56).

The share premium account may be used to pay up bonus shares to be issued as fully paid to members, to provide a premium on the redemption of shares and to write off the preliminary expenses, commissions and discounts in respect of issues of shares or debentures. Apart from these exceptions the share premiums must be treated as capital.

The Companies Act 1981 gives relief from the provisions of section 56 in certain situations. The 1981 Act (sections 36–41) provides that the premiums on shares issued in exchange for shares in another company (i.e. a merger), where the acquiring company obtains an equity holding of 90 per cent or more, do not have to be credited to the share premium account. It also provides that in certain group reconstructions, when the acquiring company issues shares at a premium, only a sum equivalent to the cost of the shares, or equivalent to the amount at which they stood in the company's records, need be transferred to the share premium account.

Bonus shares

A company makes a bonus or capitalisation issue of its shares when it issues bonus shares to its shareholders. These unissued shares are wholly or partly paid out of the company's reserves and a company may use its undistributed profits, its share premium account, and its capital redemption reserve fund to finance the issue of bonus shares. The articles must allow the capitalisation of profits.

A company does not part with its capital as the shareholders are allotted bonus shares in lieu of cash. Their issue involves an adjustment to a company's balance sheet. For example, a company has an authorised share capital of £100 000 £1 shares. 50 000 shares have already been issued. The company resolves to capitalise £50 000 from its reserves and issue the remaining 50 000 shares as bonus shares on the basis of one new share for each share previously held by the shareholder.

The adjustment is made by reducing the reserves of profit and loss account by £50000 and adding £50000 to its issued capital. As both items appear on the liabilities side of the balance sheet, the company's liabilities remain the same.

A shareholder owns the same proportion of the company's share capital as he held before the issue of the bonus shares.

Share certificates

A company must have a share certificate ready for issue within two months of allotment or of lodging a valid transfer (not being a transfer which the company is entitled to refuse), unless the terms of issue of the shares provide otherwise. In the case of an allotment of shares the terms of issue normally provide otherwise as a company rarely issues share certificates until all the shares are fully paid, which usually takes longer than two months.

If a share certificate is lost or destroyed, the articles usually provide that the company may issue a duplicate on such terms as to indemnify as the directors think fit (Article 8).

Although there is no requirement in the Act that a share certificate must be under seal, the articles usually provide this. Section 81 states that a certificate under the common seal of the company, specifying the shares held by any member, shall be *prima facie* evidence of the title of the member to the shares. It enables him if he so wishes to sell, mortgage or pledge the shares.

'The certificates are the proper (and indeed the only) documentary evidence of title in the possession of a shareholder' (Lord Selbourne). A share certificate is not therefore conclusive evidence of a member's title to the shares, and the true owner can assert his right to the shares. He can compel the company to restore his name to the register when it has been removed and to pay him any dividends that are outstanding.

A company may be estopped from denying to any person, who has in good faith relied upon the certificate, that the person named on the share certificate is the registered holder (i.e. estoppel as to title).

In *Re Bahia and San Francisco Railway*, a Miss Trittin, who held five shares in the company, left the shares with her broker. The broker sent a forged transfer to the company and the shares were transferred to Stocken and Goldberg, who were issued with share certificates. The company removed Miss Trittin's name from the register. The shares were transferred by Stocken and Goldberg to Burton and Goodburn, who were issued with share certificates by the company. The forgery was subsequently discovered and the company was compelled to restore Miss Trittin's name to the register. As the transfer had been forged no title to the shares passed to Burton and Goodburn, and they claimed damages from the company for the loss of their shares. It was held that they succeeded, for although the shares were not really theirs, the company was estopped from denying the validity of the certificates. The damages awarded were the value of the shares at the time when the company refused to recognise Burton and Goodburn as the shareholders, with interest at 10 per cent from that date.

If the certificate itself is a forgery and has been issued by an officer of the company who does not have the authority to issue certificates, there is no estoppel. In *Ruben v. Great Fingall Consolidated*, Ruben, a firm of moneylenders, lent money to Rowe, the company's secretary, on the security of a share certificate. Rowe signed his own name on the certificate, fraudulently affixed the company's seal, and forged the signature of two of the company's directors. It was held that the certificate was a forgery and the company was not bound.

If the company incurs a loss as a result of acting upon a forged transfer, it may claim an indemnity from the person who sent the forged transfer for registration, that is the transferee and his brokers, who by submitting a transfer impliedly warrants that it is genuine. In *Sheffield Corporation v. Barclay*, two individuals, Timbrell and Honeywill, were joint owners of Sheffield Corporation stock. Timbrell forged Honeywill's signature and transferred the stock to a bank as security for a loan. The bank sent the transfer to the Corporation for registration and was issued with certificates registering the Bank as a stockholder. The Bank later transferred the stock to a third party. On Timbrell's death Honeywill discovered the forgery and the Corporation replaced the stock. The Corporation successfully sued the bank for an indemnity.

A company may, in similar circumstances, be estopped from denying that the amount stated as being paid on the shares has not been paid (i.e. estoppel as to payment).

In *Bloomenthal v. Ford*, Bloomenthal lent £1000 to a company and was given 10000 shares as security for the loan. The share certificate described the shares as fully paid, although nothing had been paid on the shares. The company went into liquidation and the liquidator placed Bloomenthal's name on the list of contributories. It was held that the company was estopped from denying that the shares were fully paid and Bloomenthal's name should be removed from the list.

Transfer of shares

A shareholder has an unrestricted right to transfer his shares to any person, subject to any restriction in the articles. The articles may restrict the right to transfer shares; for example Article 24 provides that 'the directors may decline to register the transfer of a share (not being a fully paid share) to a person of whom they shall not approve'. The articles of a large number of private companies contain restrictions on the transfer of shares, while the shares of a public company must normally be free of restrictions on the right of transfer in order to obtain a Stock Exchange quotation.

The directors may be given the power to refuse a transfer of shares without giving reasons for their refusal and, unless there is evidence to the contrary, they will be presumed to have acted in good faith, and in the best interests of the company.

In *Re Smith & Fawcett*, there were only two shareholders, who were also the company's directors. Each held 4001 shares. One shareholder died and his son, as executor, applied for the shares to be registered in his name. The other shareholder refused his request (relying on the articles which gave the directors an absolute and uncontrolled discretion to refuse to register a transfer of shares), but offered to register 2001 shares if 2000 shares were sold to him at a certain price. It was held that the director was within his rights to refuse the transfer of the shares.

If the directors give reasons for their refusal, these can be challenged in the Courts, and where they have a discretion to refuse to register the transfer 'to persons of whom they do not approve', their refusal must be on grounds that are personal to the transferee.

In *Re Bede Steam Ship Co. Ltd*, the directors of the company refused to register a transfer on the grounds that the shares should not be transferred in small units to individuals with no interest or knowledge of shipping. It was held that this refusal was not on personal grounds and the transfer must be registered.

The board of directors must act positively to refuse a registration of a transfer. In *Re Copal Varnish* there were only two directors, the quorum was two and the chairman had a casting vote. His fellow director deliberately refused to attend meetings to consider transfers of shares, so that a quorum was not present. It was held that the transfers should be registered.

The power of refusal must be exercised within a reasonable time. Section 78 provides that a company must send notice of its refusal to register a transfer to the transferee within two months. It would appear that if the company does not comply with this provision it must register the transfer, as a longer period than two months constitutes unreasonable delay.

The articles of a large number of companies contain provisions that a member who wishes to transfer his shares to a person who is not already a member shall first offer them to the other members at a price ascertained in accordance with a formula set out in the articles, or at a fair price estimated by the directors or the company's auditors. A member may only transfer the shares to a proposed transferee if the other members do not wish to purchase his shares; this is known as a right of pre-emption. If the other members wish to purchase the shares, they must be prepared to purchase all the shares that are being offered for sale. The majority of pre-emption clauses provide for the sale of shares at a fair value. If agreement cannot be reached by the parties as to the value of the shares, provision is usually made for their valuation by the auditor.

Other pre-emption clauses found in the articles of companies include clauses to the effect that the transferor may select the shareholder to whom he wishes to sell; that the offer has to be made first to the directors, then to the other members; that on the death of a member, the surviving members and the directors are obliged to purchase the deceased member's shares; and that on the bankruptcy of a member, or death of a director, the shares must be offered to the other members. Pre-emption clauses are usually supplemented by an additional clause which provides that if the existing shareholders do not wish to avail themselves of these pre-emption rights, the directors may decline to register the transfer.

The 1980 Companies Act provides that a company proposing to issue equity securities for cash must first offer them to existing shareholders in proportion to their present holding or, if the articles so provide, to shareholders of a particular class. Equity securities are defined as shares having unrestricted dividend and capital rights which are not subscribers' shares, bonus shares or shares under an employee's share scheme. It also provides that a private company may alter its articles to exclude these pre-emption rights, or it may, like a public company, withdraw these pre-emption rights by passing a special resolution or relying on powers expressly granted by the articles (sections 17, 18).

Certain rights and obligations are implied in a contract for the sale of shares. The seller undertakes that he will grant the purchaser a valid transfer and will do everything necessary to enable the purchaser to be registered as a member. If the directors decline to register the transfer the purchaser has no remedy, unless he purchased the shares 'with registration guaranteed'. He will be unable to sue the seller for damages for breach of contract, for rescission of the contract, or for recovery of the purchase price from the seller.

Nevertheless, the purchaser has an equitable interest in the shares and the seller holds the shares as a quasi-trustee on the purchaser's behalf until the transfer is registered. Until that time the seller is recognised by the company as the registered owner of the shares and as such will be liable for any instalments or calls outstanding on the shares, and will be entitled to vote and receive dividends in respect of the shares. The purchaser must indemnify the seller for any calls or instalments paid by the seller after the date of the contract of sale, and the seller must vote at company meetings in accordance with the dictates of the purchaser. Shares may be purchased *cum* (with) or *ex* (without) dividend or with a specified sum paid, but if there is no such agreement the purchaser will be entitled to any dividends or benefits declared after the date of the contract.

The form of transfer

A company may only register a transfer of shares if a proper instrument of transfer is delivered to the company; that is, the transfer must be in writing. This is to ensure that stamp duty is paid on transfers. The Stock Transfer Act 1963 created a simplified method of transferring shares and this applies to the transfer of fully paid securities of companies limited by shares, statutory companies and chartered companies. Securities include stocks, shares, debentures and debenture stock.

A transfer is effected by the seller delivering to the purchaser a signed transfer, accompanied by his share certificate. The purchaser has the transfer stamped and sends the transfer, the share certificate and the registration fee to the company for registration. The company enters the purchaser's name on its register of members, cancels the old share certificate, and within two months issues a new share certificate to the purchaser. If the directors refuse to register the transfer, they must notify the purchaser of their refusal within two months.

The Stock Exchange (Completion of Bargains) Act 1976 has introduced a system called Talisman to simplify the activities connected with the completion of bargains when shares are transferred on a stock exchange. Transfers will be made initially to a stock exchange nominee known as Sepon Ltd, which will subsequently transfer the shares to the ultimate purchaser. The company whose shares are being dealt with will not issue Sepon Ltd with share certificates, but will issue share certificates to the ultimate purchaser.

If a seller is transferring part only of his shareholding he sends a signed transfer and his share certificate to the company for certification. The company certifies (or certificates) the transfer to the effect that a certificate for a particular number of shares has been lodged with the company, and returns the transfer to the seller. The seller hands the transfer to the buyer, who signs and registers the transfer with the company. The company must then issue within two months new certificates – one to the buyer and another to the seller for the balance of his holding. Certification of a transfer is also required when the whole or part of a holding is to be transferred to more than one buyer.

When the new Talisman system is fully operational, certification will no longer be necessary in stock exchange transactions as the seller's certificate will be lodged with Sepon Ltd. At a later date, the company will issue new share certificates to the respective purchasers, and in cases where the seller is not disposing of all his holding, a share certificate for the balance of his holding.

Certification is not a warranty by the company as to the title of the seller, it is a representation by the company that documents have been produced which on the face of them show that the seller has a *prima facie* title to the shares (section 79). The company is liable to any person who acts on the faith of a false certification, if the certification is made either negligently or fraudulently.

Transmission of shares
When a shareholder dies, or in some way becomes incapacitated and no longer has the capacity to contract (e.g. becomes bankrupt or of unsound mind), the power to deal with the shares passes to the person administering the estate (on death), or to the trustee in bankruptcy (on bankruptcy) or to a Receiver under a Protection Order (on becoming of unsound mind). The shares remain initially in the member's name on the company's register.

On the death of a member the shares vest in his personal representative who becomes entitled to deal with them. He may, without being registered as a member, transfer the shares as if he were a member, and does so by signing the transfer in his representative capacity. Alternatively he may choose to be registered as a member.

On the bankruptcy of a member the shares vest in the trustee or receiver in bankruptcy, who like a personal representative becomes entitled either to hold shares in his personal or representative capacity. The trustee can disclaim partly paid shares. If he does so the company may prove in the shareholder's bankruptcy for any loss it sustains. If the bankrupt's name remains on the register, the bankrupt is entitled to vote and attend meetings, but the company will pay any dividends to his trustee in bankruptcy.

Forged transfers

Such a transfer is a nullity and cannot affect the title of a shareholder whose signature is forged. If a company registers a forged transfer and removes the name of the true owner from the register, it can be compelled to restore his name to the register.

A company incurs no liability in damages by putting the transferee's name on register as a result of a forged transfer, but if it issues a certificate and any person acts on faith of it and suffers damage, the company is liable (*Re Bahia and San Francisco Railway*).

Most companies take precautions to avoid registering forged transfers. When a company receives a transfer for registration, it usually writes to the transferor informing him of the transfer and stating that unless he advises the company by return to the contrary, the transfer will be assumed to be in order and the company will act upon it. If the transferor does not reply, he can still prove the transfer is a forgery.

Companies do not usually accept a transfer for registration unless a share certificate has been surrendered, and will only issue a duplicate certificate after proper enquiry has been made and sufficient indemnity has been provided by the applicant.

Companies may in certain circumstances pay compensation under the Forged Transfer Acts 1891 and 1892. These Acts do not give any right to compensation, they merely give the company power to pay. Most companies insure against liability for forged transfers.

Calls on shares

Most companies provide that if shares are not paid in full on allotment, any sums owing shall be paid by fixed instalments at certain fixed dates. This is financially advantageous to the company and also enables the shares to be converted into stock.

If the shares are not fully paid on allotment and no provision is made for payment by instalment, the company will make a call on these shares when it requires further capital.

A call is a demand by a company, in respect of money unpaid on its shares, where the company does not stipulate a date for payment. The articles generally give the directors power to make calls, and usually provide that no call shall exceed a quarter of the nominal value of the share; that at least a month shall elapse between successive calls; and that each member be given at least fourteen days' notice of the time and place of payment (Article 15). If the articles make no provision for calls, a company may make them by passing an ordinary resolution in a general meeting.

A call must be made for the benefit of the company. If the directors, as in *Alexander v. Automatic Telephone Co.*, pay nothing on their own shares but enforce a call on the other shareholders, such a call is improperly made as it deprives the company of capital. The directors must pay a similar amount on their shares.

A company may not make a call upon one particular member without making a similar call on the other members. In *Galloway v. Hallé Concerts Society*, two members of the society, a guarantee company, were in conflict with the society committee. In addition to the guarantee clause in the memorandum, the articles contained a provision that any member should be liable to pay on demand to the company a sum not exceeding £100, termed the contribution. The committee resolved to call up the whole contribution of the dissident members, but made no corresponding call on the other members. Such a call was held invalid.

Calls and instalments are specialty debts; that is, the company can sue to recover the amounts outstanding for up to twelve years after payment is due. If payment is still not forthcoming, the directors may declare the shares forfeit. The articles generally provide that interest may be charged on overdue calls.

The articles usually provide that directors may accept calls in advance, that is accept from a member part or the whole of the amount uncalled and unpaid on his shares. This is regarded as a loan, and usually carries interest at the rate of 5 per cent per annum, which may be paid out of capital if there are insufficient profits. Capital paid up in advance ranks for repayment in a winding up in priority to capital not paid up in advance.

Mortgage of shares

A shareholder wishing to borrow money on the security of his shares may be able to effect a mortgage of his shares. Such a mortgage may be either legal or equitable.

LEGAL MORTGAGE: A legal mortgage is an out and out transfer of shares to the lender, who is registered as a shareholder in respect of those shares. He is therefore entitled to dividends and other monies in respect of the shares, and is also entitled to exercise the voting powers of those shares. An agreement is made that, on repayment of the loan, the shares will be re-transferred to the borrower.

If the loan is not repaid on the agreed date, the lender may sell the shares, or apply to the court for a foreclosure order. If the document containing the terms of the mortgage is by deed, the lender may also sell the shares if the borrower fails to pay an instalment of mortgage interest for two months after it falls due, or breaks any other covenant of the mortgage.

A legal mortgage is not suitable in all circumstances, for example for shares that are not fully paid up, or for the mortgage of shares by a director who must hold a qualification shareholding. Stamp duty is also payable on the transfer and re-transfer of the shares.

EQUITABLE MORTGAGE: An equitable mortgage may be created by depositing share certificates with the lender. The borrower usually signs a blank transfer form at the same time. There is an agreement that on the repayment of the loan, the share certificate will be handed back to the borrower.

The borrower still remains on the register of members and is entitled to dividends and to exercise his voting powers. The rights of the lender are not recognised by the company, for under section 117 the company cannot take notice of any trust or similar right over its shares. The weakness of an equitable mortgage is that if the borrower fraudulently informs the company that he has lost his certificate he can obtain a new certificate and transfer the same shares to a purchaser.

The only safe course for the lender is to serve a 'Stop Notice' on the company, which provides that the company cannot register a transfer without first notifying the lender. The lender has eight days to obtain an injunction, for after this time the company will be at liberty to transfer the shares.

If the loan is not repaid the lender may, in a case where a blank transfer has been signed, fill in his own name or that of a purchaser and complete the transfer of the shares. If the mortgage consists of share certificates not accompanied by a signed blank transfer, the lender will require a Court order before he can enforce his security.

Forfeiture and surrender

The articles of a company generally contain clauses providing for the forfeiture of shares if a member fails to pay any call or instalment (Articles 33, 39). Such a power must be given by the articles, as forfeiture for any other reason is invalid and amounts to an unlawful reduction of capital.

The power to declare shares forfeit is in the nature of a trust and must be exercised for the company's benefit, not for the benefit of any individual shareholders. In *Re Esparto Trading Co.*, Finch and Goddard were given shares in the company to induce them to become directors and paid nothing on their shares. At a later date both men asked the company to forfeit their shares and this was done. It was held invalid and they were liable to pay in full for their shares.

Its effect is that the shareholder ceases to be a member of the company and is theoretically no longer bound by his obligations as a member, such as to pay any amount outstanding on his shares. The articles, however, usually provide that despite forfeiture he shall be liable for all the money which at the time of forfeiture he owed the company, that is he becomes a debtor of the company (Article 37).

If directors are given the power to accept a surrender of partly paid shares, provision will have to be made in the articles for the surrender of shares. Neither the Act nor Table A make any provision for the surrender of shares.

Surrender is valid only in the circumstances which would justify forfeiture and is used to avoid the formalities of forfeiture. It cannot be used to cancel a member's liability for future calls, as this would amount to an illegal reduction of capital.

Any shares forfeited or surrendered become the company's property, and the articles generally give the directors power to sell such shares. They may be sold for any price they will fetch, but the purchaser will be liable to pay any amounts unpaid on forfeiture or surrender, and will not usually be allowed to vote until the arrears are paid. If the shares are not disposed of by the Company within three years, they must be cancelled (1980 Companies Act, section 38).

Lien on shares

A private company possesses a lien on the shares of its members if the articles so provide. The articles frequently provide that a company has a lien on the shares of a member for money that is owed to the company in respect of shares or as a result of any other transaction. The company is given an equitable interest in the shares which can be enforced by selling the shares (if this power is given in the articles), or by withholding dividends on the shares or by refusing to register any transfer of the shares.

If the company sells the shares, it may retain from the proceeds of the sale the amount owed to the company, but it must return the balance (if any) to the member.

Section 38 of the 1980 Companies Act provides that a lien or other charge of a public company on its own shares is void. The section does permit two exceptions: a charge on any amount outstanding on a partly paid up share is valid; as is a charge taken by a company whose ordinary business includes lending money, on its own shares, whether fully paid or not, in the ordinary course of business.

13

Dividends

A shareholder expects a return on his investment in a company. A trading company is expected to earn profits, and these profits are distributed among its shareholders as dividends. A dividend may be defined as that part of the profits of trading that is distributed to members in proportion to their shares and in accordance with their rights as shareholders.

Payment of dividend

There are two cardinal principles relating to the payment of dividends (i.e. making a distribution):

 (i) A dividend may not be paid out of capital.
(ii) A dividend may only be paid out of the profits available for that purpose.

A company does not require an express power in its memorandum or articles to pay a dividend, although a guarantee company which is allowed to dispense with Ltd in its name may not pay a dividend.

The articles usually determine the way and set out the fund from which a dividend is to be paid, and provide that 'all dividends shall be apportioned and paid proportionately to the amounts paid or credited as paid on the shares' (Article 118).

A shareholder cannot insist on a company paying a dividend, even though a company has made sufficient profits and is able to make a distribution to its members. This applies to preference shareholders, as well as to ordinary shareholders.

Declaration of dividend

The company in general meeting may declare a dividend, but no dividend may exceed the amount recommended by the directors (Article 114).

The declaration of a dividend by a company creates a debt due to its members. If the dividend is stated to be payable at some future date, a shareholder will be unable to enforce payment until the actual date for payment arrives.

Directors are usually given the power to pay such interim dividends (i.e. dividends paid in between two annual general meetings) as appear to the directors to be justified by the company's profits (Article 115). As an interim dividend does not require the approval of a general meeting it is not in the nature of a debt due from the company. If it is not paid, it cannot be sued for.

The articles often give power to the directors, before recommending a dividend, to set aside out of the company's profits such sums as they think appropriate to form a reserve fund, and to carry forward any profits which they think prudent not to divide (Article 117).

A company may, on the recommendation of its directors, capitalise any part of reserve accounts or its profit and loss account, and apply that sum in paying up in full unissued shares to be allotted as fully paid bonus shares to its members who would have been entitled to that sum if it had been distributed as a dividend (Article 128, 128A).

Unless the articles state otherwise, dividends must be paid in cash, and a shareholder can restrain a company from paying him in any other way. In *Wood v. Odessa Waterworks Co.*, the company proposed to pay a dividend by giving debentures to its shareholders in lieu of cash. It was held that the payment of a dividend meant payment in cash, and the company was prevented from paying a dividend other than in cash.

Profits available for dividend

The 1980 Companies Act (sections 39–45) imposes restrictions on the distribution of a company's assets to its members (in cash or otherwise). A public or private company (other than an investment company) may only make a distribution to its members out of the profits available for the purpose. These are its accumulated realised profits (not previously utilised by distribution or capitalisation) less its accumulated realised losses (so far as not previously written off in a reduction or re-organisation of capital). Profits and losses include profits and losses made at any time and include both revenue and capital profits and losses. Any profit or loss for an accounting period must not be treated in isolation from other accounting periods, but as a continuation. Therefore, any previous losses must be made good before a distribution can be made.

A further restriction is imposed on a public company making a distribution. It may only make a distribution if its net assets are at least equal to the aggregate amount of its share capital and undistributable reserves. (Its net assets are the total assets less its liabilities and provisions.)

The undistributable reserves are:

The capital redemption reserve fund;
The amount by which the accumulated unrealised profits exceeds its current accumulated unrealised losses;
Any of the reserve which a company is prevented from distributing.

A company may not use its unrealised profits to write off realised losses, or in paying up debentures, or any amounts remaining unpaid on its issued shares. This is to prevent profits not available for distribution being used indirectly to pay dividends. A company may apply its unrealised profits in paying up unissued shares to be issued to its members as fully paid bonus shares.

The right of a company to make a distribution and the amount it may distribute is determined by reference to the relevant items in the 'relevant accounts'.

Relevant items are any of the following: profits, losses, assets, liabilities, provisions, share capital and reserves (including undistributable reserves). Relevant accounts are normally the last annual accounts which were laid or filed in respect of the last preceding accounting reference period.

If the last annual accounts are taken as the 'relevant accounts':

(i)   The accounts must have been properly prepared;
(ii) The company's auditors must have made a report in respect of those accounts;
(iii) If the report is not unqualified, the auditors must state in writing whether the subject matter of their qualification is material in determining whether a distribution should be made.
(iv) A copy of the auditor's statement must have been laid before the company in general meeting or delivered to the Registrar.

In certain circumstances a distribution may be made on the basis of interim or initial accounts. A company, unable to make a distribution if reference were made only to its last annual accounts, may make a distribution if more recent (i.e. interim) accounts show that it is able to make a distribution. Initial accounts are drawn up when a company proposes to make a distribution during its first accounting reference period or before any accounts are filed.

Any member who knowingly receives an unlawful distribution is liable to repay it to the company. If the distribution is made other than in cash, the member is liable to pay a sum equal to the value of the distribution.

These restrictions on distributions do not apply to:

(i) An issue of fully or partly paid bonus shares;

(ii) The redemption of shares out of the proceeds of a fresh issue of shares and the payment of any premium payable on their redemption out of the share premium account;

(iii) The reduction of share capital by extinguishing or reducing liability in respect of share capital not paid up, or paying off paid up share capital;

(iv) The distribution of assets to the members on a winding up.

14

General Meetings

The will of the members of a company is normally expressed at the general meeting, when they may vote for or against any resolution that is proposed. If the appropriate majority is obtained for a resolution, the will of the majority of members usually prevails and binds every member.

In this way the majority of members are entitled to exercise the company's powers and control its operations. They are able to appoint directors of their choice and may delegate to the directors the necessary powers to operate the company's business.

The articles of a company invariably give the board of directors the power to convene a general meeting or a class meeting. They will normally do so by passing a resolution at a duly convened board meeting. The articles may provide that a resolution in writing, signed by the directors without a meeting, shall be as effective as a resolution passed at a meeting of the board.

Types of meeting

There are three types of meetings of shareholders:

(a) The annual general meeting,
(b) An extraordinary general meeting,
(c) A meeting of a class of shareholders.

The annual general meeting

Every company must hold an annual general meeting each (calendar) year in addition to any other meeting which it may hold. Not more than fifteen months may elapse between one general meeting and another. An exception is made for a newly formed company in that it may hold its first annual general meeting at any time within eighteen months of incorporation.

If default is made in holding the meeting the Department of Trade may, on the application of any member, call or direct the calling of the meeting and may give any ancillary or consequential directions as it thinks fit (section 131).

The nature of the business at the annual general meeting depends upon the articles, but the ordinary business at the meeting is generally understood to include the following:

the declaration of a dividend;
the consideration of the accounts and balance sheets;
the consideration of the directors' and auditors' reports;
the appointment of directors and auditors;
fixing the auditor's remuneration.

Any other business is to be regarded as special business (Article 52). In a notice convening an annual general meeting to transact ordinary business only, it is unnecessary to specify the ordinary business as the members will be aware of the nature of the business from the articles. Members will therefore be entitled to move resolutions without giving notice to other members in respect of ordinary business. In order to prevent a member from proposing a person as a director at an annual general meeting without giving prior warning, the articles often stipulate that any such nomination must be notified to the company not later than a specified number of days before the meeting.

Extraordinary general meeting

Any general meeting other than the annual general meeting is called an extraordinary general meeting. The articles usually give the directors power to call an extraordinary general meeting at any time they think fit. This power is used by directors to deal with matters which cannot be held up until the next annual general meeting. In non-urgent matters it is often more convenient to hold a meeting to discuss matters.

The notice convening the meeting is often accompanied by a circular giving the board of directors' views. The board is within its rights in sending out circulars, and it is proper for the company to meet this expenditure as long as the intention is to benefit the general body of members, and is not motivated by self interest (e.g. to stay in office or gain some other advantage). The board is under no obligation to send out the circulars of members who are opposed to its policy.

Members holding not less than 10 per cent of the paid up capital carrying voting rights may at any time compel the directors to call a meeting, that is, to requisition a meeting (section 132). The articles may extend this power by allowing a smaller number of shareholders (e.g. 5 per cent) to requisition the meeting, but they may not restrict this important minority right.

The requisition must state the objects of the meeting and must be deposited at the registered office of the company. If the directors do not convene the meeting within twenty-one days, the requisitionists or a majority of them in voting rights, may themselves convene a meeting. This meeting must be convened in the same manner (or as nearly as possible) as meetings convened by the directors, and must be held within three months of depositing the requisition (section 132).

Any expenses incurred by the requisitionists, due to the failure of the directors to convene a meeting, may be recovered from the company, which must withhold these sums from the fees or other remuneration of the directors who are at fault.

A public company must convene an extraordinary general meeting if there is a serious loss of capital; that is, if the net assets are half or less of the company's called up share capital, the directors must summon a meeting to consider what measures should be taken to deal with the situation (1980 Companies Act, section 34).

Class meetings

If a company has different classes of shares it must hold a meeting of the class in question when required to do so by the Act, or the articles, or the terms of the issue of shares. Any resolution passed at such a meeting will bind the members of that class only, and as the matters under discussion relate only to the members of that class, they alone may attend, vote and speak at class meetings.

Class meetings are usually held to agree to alterations in the rights of that class, or to agree to compromises or arrangements affecting the class.

Notice of general meeting

A meeting cannot be held unless proper notice of it has been given to every person entitled to receive notice.

The persons entitled to notice are *prima facie* the members of the company and the auditor. This may be modified by the articles, which often provide that members with calls in arrear cannot vote and that preference shareholders have no right to notice of meetings or to attend and vote at meetings except in certain circumstances, such as that their dividends are three months in arrear, or a resolution is proposed which affects their rights or is a resolution for winding up the company.

The articles may also provide that notice must be given to the personal representative of a deceased member, or, if a member is bankrupt, to his trustee in bankruptcy (Article 133).

An omission to give notice to any person entitled to it will invalidate a meeting, but the articles usually provide that the accidental omission to give notice of a meeting to, or the non-receipt of a notice of a meeting by, any person entitled to receive notice shall not invalidate the proceedings at that meeting (Article 51), and that notice need not be given to shareholders who have no address in the United Kingdom (Article 134).

The Act provides that no less than twenty-one days' notice must be given for an annual general meeting or for a meeting to pass a special resolution. At least fourteen days' notice is required for any other meeting. The articles can specify longer notice but cannot stipulate shorter notice of meetings (section 133).

There are instances when meetings may be called by shorter notice. An annual general meeting may be called by shorter notice if all the members entitled to attend and vote agree. In the case of any other meeting, the agreement of a majority holding 95 per cent of the shares having the right to attend and vote, will enable shorter notice to be given (section 133).

The notice must state the date, time and place of the meeting. It must also state clearly the nature of the business to be transacted. If the true nature of the business is not disclosed, such transactions passed at the meeting will be invalid.

In *Baillie v. Oriental Telephone and Electric Co. Ltd*, the directors had from 1907 to 1914 received fees from a subsidiary company. At a later date they were advised that payment of the fees should have been approved by the shareholders. They called a meeting to approve their remuneration and to alter the articles to allow directors to receive payment for serving on the boards of subsidiary companies. The notice merely stated that the directors' fees would be a small percentage of the subsidiary's profits, and did not state that the subsidiary had made very large profits, or that the total amount of directors' fees was in the region of £45000. It was held that the resolution approving the payment of these was invalid, as proper disclosure had not been made to the shareholders.

In *Kaye v. Croydon Tramways Co.*, there was a provisional agreement for the sale of one undertaking to another, with an agreement to pay a substantial sum to the directors for loss of office. The agreement was conditional upon acceptance by the shareholders of the company selling the undertaking. The notice convening the meeting described it simply as an agreement for the sale of the undertaking. It was held that proper disclosure had not been made.

Quorum

In order that a meeting may proceed to business, a quorum of members must be present. The Act provides that two members personally present shall be a quorum, unless the articles state otherwise (section 134). Proxies may only be counted towards the quorum if the articles so provide. If the articles only require a quorum to be present when the meeting proceeds to business, and if the number of members who remain present falls below the stipulated quorum, the meeting may complete its business. If only one person remains present, whether as a member or as a proxy for others, the meeting may not pass valid resolutions as one person alone cannot constitute a meeting.

There are exceptions to this rule in that if the Department of Trade calls an annual general meeting, it may direct that one member present in person or by proxy shall constitute a general meeting (section 131). The Court may make similar directions in cases where it is impractical to call a meeting or conduct a meeting in accordance with the articles or the Act. It may make the order of its own volition, or on the application of any director or shareholder who is entitled to vote (section 135).

In *Re El Sombrero Ltd*, the company had three members. Laubscher held 90 per cent of the shares, Salaman and Lewis held 5 per cent each and were the two directors of the company. Laubscher requisitioned an extraordinary general meeting to pass a resolution removing the two directors and appointing others in their place. The two directors did not attend and as there was no quorum present the meeting could not take place. Laubscher successfully applied to the court for an order that the court call a meeting, where these resolutions could be passed, and that one member should constitute a quorum.

Similarly in *Re H R Paul & Son Ltd*, a shareholder holding 90 per cent of the shares called a meeting to alter the articles. The minority refused to attend and there was therefore no quorum. It was held that the quorum provisions in the articles were not a right vested in the minority to enable it to frustrate the wishes of the majority. The court convened the meeting.

The articles usually provide that if a quorum is not present within half an hour of the appointed time, a meeting convened on the requisition of members is dissolved, but any other meeting shall be adjourned to the following week at a day, place and time to be determined by the directors. If, at the adjourned meeting, a quorum is not present within half an hour, the members present shall form a quorum (Article 54).

The chairman

The Act provides that if the articles make no provision for the appointment of a chairman to preside at meetings, the members present at the meeting may elect any member as chairman (section 134). The articles generally provide that the chairman of the board of directors shall be the chairman at general meetings (Article 55). If there is no chairman, or he fails to attend or is unwilling to act, then the directors present shall elect one of themselves to be chairman. If there is no director present or willing to act, the members present may elect one of their number to be chairman of the meeting (Articles 55, 56).

The duty of the chairman is to preserve order and to see that the meeting is properly conducted. He must see that the meeting is properly constituted and in particular that a quorum is present. He should restrain irrelevant discussion and intemperate language, and should any persons act in a disorderly manner he should ask them to desist. If they refuse, he may have them ejected, using reasonable force only. Should the meeting become disorderly, the chairman may adjourn the meeting until order is restored.

He must decide points of order and questions of procedure, for example whether a proposed amendment to a resolution should be permitted. An amendment is only allowed if it falls within the scope of the notice convening the meeting.

The chairman must give a reasonable opportunity to the members present to discuss any proposed resolution, and he must allow minority shareholders reasonable time to express their views within the time available. As soon as reasonable time has been given to airing both the views of the minority and majority, he may, with the meeting's consent, close the discussion and put the question to the vote.

In *Wall v. London and Northern Assets Corporation*, Wall and other shareholders wished to continue a discussion at a meeting regarding the proposed amalgamation of two companies. The chairman moved that the question be now put and this resolution was passed, as was a resolution that the amalgamation go ahead. It was held that the resolution was properly passed and that the minority was not entitled to discuss the matter indefinitely to obstruct the business of the meeting.

In this way he should be able to ascertain the sense of the meeting in regard to any question which is before it. After the questions have been put to the meeting, the votes are counted and the result is declared. The articles usually provide that the chairman's declaration, as to whether or not a resolution has been passed by a specified majority, is conclusive (Article 58). The chairman may have a casting vote where the votes are equal (Article 60), but in the absence of such an article he has no such vote.

He has no general power to dissolve or adjourn a meeting of his own will, unless this power is given to him by the articles. Otherwise his power of adjournment, without the meeting's consent, is limited to adjourning the meeting in case of disorder. Should he prematurely close the meeting and declare it dissolved or adjourned, the meeting may elect another chairman and proceed with the business. Unless the articles otherwise provide, the chairman is not bound to adjourn the meeting even if the members wish him to do so.

Voting at the meeting

The articles usually contain provisions as to voting and may restrict the voting rights of shares (e.g. that preference shares shall carry no voting rights unless their dividend is in arrear). Unless the articles otherwise provide, each shareholder has on a show of hands one vote, irrespective of the number of shares held by him. On a poll, a member has one vote for each share which he holds.

The articles of private companies and guarantee companies may stipulate that certain shares shall have weighted voting rights. In *Bushell v. Faith*, Bushell and his two sisters each held 100 of the company's 300 £1 shares. The articles provided that in the event of a resolution being proposed at a general meeting for the removal of a director, each share held by that director should carry three votes. It was held that such voting rights were valid.

The articles usually provide that in the event of a joint holding of shares, only the first named is entitled to vote. Therefore most joint holders have their names on the register in a different order; for example, Smith and Jones are joint holders of 100 shares, but the shares are registered as fifty shares in the names of Smith and Jones, and fifty in the names of Jones and Smith.

The votes on a resolution are usually taken on a show of hands and the chairman then declares the result. Any member or proxy may demand a poll on any question, except the election of a chairman or adjournment of the meeting, either before or on the declaration of the result.

A poll must be held if it is demanded by not less than five members, or a member or members holding 10 per cent of the voting rights, or 10 per cent of the paid up capital carrying the right to vote (section 137).

The articles may provide that a poll can be demanded by less than five members, or by the holders of less than 10 per cent of the capital.

When a poll has been properly demanded, the chairman fixes the time and place for taking it, and the result of any vote on a show of hands is nullified. The chairman is entitled to decide whether a poll shall be taken there and then, unless the articles direct otherwise. This is often the most convenient course of action where the number of votes to be counted is relatively small. He may, however, defer holding a poll until a later date.

On a poll, the votes are recorded by each person signing a paper 'for' or 'against' the resolution and adding the number of votes to which he is entitled. A member holding several shares is entitled on a poll to cast votes for and against the resolution. This provision meets the needs of a nominee (e.g. a bank holding shares on behalf of several persons) to vote in one way in respect of some shares, and in another way, or not at all, in respect of others.

Proxies

A proxy is a document authorising another person to attend meetings and vote on behalf of an absent member. The person who has been so appointed is also known as a proxy.

There are two forms of proxy in use: the ordinary proxy appointing a person to vote as he thinks fit at the meeting; and a special proxy directing the proxy before the meeting to vote for or against a particular resolution. This is known as a 'two-way proxy'. The Stock Exchange makes it a condition for permission to deal, that public companies distribute two-way proxy forms in all cases where special business is to be transacted at a meeting.

Any member who is entitled to attend and vote at a meeting of a company is entitled to appoint another person, whether a member or not, as his proxy. This does not apply to companies not having a share capital, unless the articles state otherwise.

A proxy has the right to attend a meeting of a public company, but no right to speak at the meeting except to demand or join in demanding a poll. He can only vote on a poll. A member of a public company may appoint more than one proxy, so that a nominee holding shares for various parties can appoint different persons as proxies to represent different interests. The articles of a public company may extend these basic proxy rights.

A proxy at a meeting of a private company has the same right as a member to speak at the meeting, but unless the articles provide otherwise a member of a private company can only appoint one proxy who can only vote on a poll. Presumably this restriction is to prevent a possible abuse of this privilege.

The articles may require the proxy papers to be deposited with the company before a meeting, but they cannot require such deposit more than forty-eight hours before a meeting. The articles cannot deprive a member of his right to appoint a proxy.

Directors, when sending out notices of a meeting, often include proxy forms which enable the members to appoint one or other of the directors as their proxy. It is not unusual for the directors to have in their possession, at the commencement of the meeting, proxies in their favour which will ensure the passing of any resolution supported by the directors.

As long as the directors are satisfied that their policies are in the company's interests they may, at the company's expense, print and distribute such proxy forms. The effect of this may be partially offset by the requirement that in every notice calling a general meeting there must appear with reasonable prominence a statement that any member entitled to attend and vote is entitled to appoint a proxy (section 136).

Should the directors wish to invite members to appoint a person or a number of persons as proxy, such an invitation, if sent out at the company's expense, must be sent to all the members entitled to appoint proxies, thus preventing the directors from selecting only the members who would grant them proxies of support.

It is also common to make out alternative proxies, for example in favour of one person or in his absence another, so that if the first named is prevented from attending the second named can attend and exercise the rights under the proxy.

A proxy may be revoked by informing the proxy, or if the shareholder after appointing the proxy attends the meeting, he can vote in person – thus impliedly revoking the proxy. A proxy is also automatically revoked by the death or insanity of the person giving it. The articles usually provide that the proxy shall be valid, unless the company has been notified of the member's death or insanity or revocation of the proxy (Article 73). This is necessary to ensure that resolutions have been validly passed.

If a company is a member of another company, it may appoint any person to represent it at meetings of the company of which it is a member. Such a representative is not a proxy and may exercise the same powers on behalf of the company he represents as if it were an individual shareholder.

Adjournment of general meetings

The articles usually empower the chairman, with the consent of the meeting, to adjourn the meeting. He must do so if directed by the meeting (Article 57). A poll may be taken forthwith on the question of adjournment (Article 61). However if a chairman improperly adjourns the meeting, the members who remain may appoint another chairman and continue the business.

A meeting may be adjourned for various reasons. It may be that there is no quorum present, or that the business cannot be completed on that day, or that the adjournment is to take a poll, or the meeting has to be adjourned because of disorder.

An adjourned meeting is regarded for some purposes as a continuation of the original meeting. Fresh notice of an adjourned meeting need only be given if the meeting is adjourned for thirty days or more, but only unfinished business can be transacted at the meeting (Article 57). A resolution passed at an adjourned meeting is to be treated as passed on the date on which it was in fact passed.

Resolutions

There are three types of resolutions which may be passed at a general meeting – special, extraordinary and ordinary. The nature of the business to be transacted determines the type of resolution to be used at a meeting. The Act states that certain matters must be transacted by special or extraordinary resolutions and may not be passed in any other way. All other business may be approved by ordinary resolution unless the memorandum or the articles provide otherwise.

Special resolution

A resolution passed at a general meeting by a majority of three-quarters of the members, voting in person or by proxy, of which twenty-one days' notice has been given specifying the intention to propose the resolution as a special resolution.

Less than twenty-one days' notice may be given if agreed upon by a majority of those entitled to attend and vote holding 95 per cent of the shares giving those rights.

A special resolution is required when fundamental changes are proposed by a company, and the twenty-one days' notice required gives members an opportunity to deliberate on the nature and consequences of the proposed changes.

The following are some of the changes requiring a special resolution:

Alteration of the objects (section 5);

Alteration of the articles (section 10);

Change of name (section 18);

Creation of reserve capital (section 60);

Reduction of capital (section 66);

Making director's liability unlimited (section 203);

Procuring a winding up by the court (section 222);

Initiating a members' voluntary winding up (section 278);

Sanctioning a sale to another company in consideration of shares (section 287);

Re-registration of an unlimited company as limited (section 44, 1967 Act);

Re-registration of a private company and an unlimited company as a public company (sections 5 and 7, 1980 Act);

Registration of an 'old public' company as a private company (section 8, 1980 Act);

Giving financial assistance for the acquisition of shares (section 43, 1981 Act);

Off-market purchase by a company of its own shares (section 47, 1981 Act).

Extraordinary resolution

A resolution passed at a general meeting by a majority of three-quarters of the members voting in person or by proxy, of which notice has been given to propose the resolution as an extraordinary resolution.

This type of resolution is only required for certain purposes, mainly in connection with the voluntary winding up of a company. The following require the approval of such a resolution:

Initiating a creditors' voluntary winding up (section 278);

Granting certain powers to a liquidator in a voluntary winding up (section 303);

Making an arrangement with creditors in a voluntary winding up (section 306);

Variation of class rights (section 32, 1980 Act).

Ordinary resolution

This is a resolution requiring a simple majority of those who attend and vote at a meeting. Where the Act or the articles state that the company in general meeting may do some act, this requires an ordinary resolution.

An ordinary resolution is passed initially by a majority on a show of hands. Should a poll be demanded, only a simple majority is required. It is not necessary that the majority of members present should vote in favour of a resolution, merely that a majority of those voting should support the resolution; for example, if 100 members are present and twenty vote in favour, ten against and seventy abstain, the resolution is passed.

There are certain ordinary resolutions which require special notice to be given to a company. These are resolutions for:

> Removing a director or appointing a person instead of the director who has been removed at that meeting;
> Appointing or approving the appointment of a director over 70;
> Appointing as auditor a person other than the retiring auditor;
> Removing an auditor before the expiration of his term of office;
> Filling a casual vacancy in the office of auditor;
> Re-appointing an auditor who was appointed by the directors to fill a casual vacancy.

In these cases twenty-eight days' notice must be given to the company, who must give twenty-one days' notice of such a resolution to its members at the same time and in the same manner as it gives notice of a meeting.

If it can be shown that all the shareholders with the right to attend and vote at a general meeting agree to a course of action which a general meeting could carry into effect, their assent is as binding as a resolution at a general meeting. In *Re Express Engineering Works Ltd*, a company was formed with five members, who were also the directors of the company. They sold property to the company for £15 000 which they had bought for £7000, to be paid by the issue of debentures. The articles provided that a director could not vote in respect of a contract in which he was interested. It was held that as there was no fraud, the contract could be ratified by the unanimous agreement of the members and the debentures were valid.

In *Cane v. Jones* all the shares in a company were held by members of one family. They agreed that the chairman should no longer have a casting vote, and in the case of an equality of votes an independent chairman would be appointed. Papers were signed to this effect, but no general meeting was held or special resolution passed. A dispute later arose between the members and it was held that the informal agreement was valid and binding.

Circulation of members' resolutions

Members holding 5 per cent of the total voting rights, or not less than 100 members holding shares on which there has been paid an average sum per member of not less than £100, may on giving six weeks' notice to the company require it to send to all members notice of any resolution they intend to move at the next annual general meeting.

They may also require the company, on giving one week's notice, to circulate to members a statement not exceeding 1000 words with respect to any resolution or business to be dealt with at any general meeting. This enables members who are opposed to a course of action or scheme to be submitted to the meeting, to circulate their objections to the other members before the meeting. The requisitionists must deposit a reasonable sum with the company to meet the company's expenses in giving effect to these provisions (section 140).

The directors or any other aggrieved person may apply to the court for an order that the statement should not be circularised as they consider that these rights are being abused to secure needless publicity for defamatory matter. In practice, members who are opposed to the board's policy will themselves send circulars to their fellow members. They can obtain their names and addresses by inspecting the register of members or obtaining copies of the register from the company. In this way they will not be subject to the directors' possible censorship or limited to 1000 words in their circular.

Registration of resolutions

As a rule any resolution or business transacted at a general meeting is of interest only to the members of the company. As certain resolutions and agreements may affect third party interests copies of the following must be forwarded to the Registrar within fifteen days (section 143):

(a)   Special and extraordinary resolutions.
(b)   Resolutions or agreements passed or agreed to by all the members which would otherwise not have been effective unless passed as special or extraordinary resolutions.
(c)   Resolutions agreed upon by all the members of a class of shareholders.
(d)   Resolutions requiring a company to be wound up on the effluxion of time.

The copies may be printed or in some other form approved by the Registrar.

If a special resolution alters the company's memorandum or articles, the company must send to the Registrar, with the notice of alteration, a printed copy of the altered memorandum or articles. The Registrar must then publish in the *London Gazette* notice of the receipt by him of those documents. The latest version of the company's constitution is then available for public perusal at the Registry.

Minutes of meetings

Every company must keep minutes of general meetings and directors' meetings. Any minutes signed by the chairman or by the chairman of the next succeeding meeting are *prima facie* evidence of those proceedings. There is a presumption that, if a meeting has been duly held and convened, the proceedings have been properly conducted and all appointments made at the meeting (e.g. directors, managers, liquidators) are valid (section 145).

The books containing the minutes of general meetings are to be kept at the registered office and are open to inspection by any member, without charge, for at least two hours a day. Any member is entitled, within seven days, to a copy of the minutes at a charge not exceeding 2½p per hundred words.

15

Appointment and Proceedings of Directors

As a company is an artificial legal entity it cannot exercise any of its powers in person, but must of necessity act through the medium of its agents – its directors. Although the Act now stipulates that a public company registered since 1929 must have a minimum of two directors and a private company at least one director, this has only come about since 1929. Prior to that date there was no statutory obligation on a company to have a director.

The articles of association of some companies state that a company shall be managed by a 'council' or 'managing committee', whilst the articles of other companies provide that the power of management shall be exercised by a 'governing director', 'life director', or 'permanent director'. Whatever terminology is used such persons will be regarded as directors with certain rights, liabilities and obligations. Section 455 defines a director as 'any person occupying the position of a director by whatever name called'.

The 1980 Companies Act introduces the concept of the 'shadow director'. A person, not a director, will be regarded as a shadow director if the directors of a company are accustomed to act in accordance with his instructions or directions. He will not be a shadow director if the directors so act by reason only that they do so on advice given by him in a professional capacity. Certain sections of the Act and subsequent Companies Acts are applicable to shadow directors.

Appointment of directors

The appointment of directors is usually dealt with by the company's articles of association. The first directors are usually named in the articles, but if no directors are appointed by the articles or if no articles are submitted, the first directors will be nominated by the subscribers to the memorandum. Article 75 provides that the number of directors and names of first directors shall be determined in writing by the subscribers of the memorandum of association or a majority of them.

Section 21 of the 1976 Companies Act provides that on the formation of a company a statement of the particulars of the first directors must be submitted with other relevant documents. This effectively appoints the first directors.

The articles usually fix the minimum and maximum number of directors that a company may have. Should the number of directors fall below the minimum set by the company, the remaining directors cannot act unless they are given specific powers in such a situation. Directors are usually given the power to appoint new directors so that the numerical requirements are satisfied. If not, their powers are limited to summoning a general meeting of the company so that new directors can be appointed. Any new directors appointed solely by the board will only hold office until the next annual general meeting when the members may re-elect them if they so wish.

A company can appoint a person a director for life. Such an appointment may be revoked by altering the articles. If such an appointment was made before 18 July 1945, then the director cannot be removed from office.

A director may, if the articles so provide, appoint a person to act for him in his absence. This 'alternate' director will normally be granted the same powers as the director that he represents. The appointment is usually subject to the approval of the majority of the directors. In all probability the alternate director will be a fellow director, and in that case will be able to cast two votes at board meetings. This appointment can be terminated by the original director.

Outside bodies are sometimes given power to appoint directors to the board of an independent company. It is often a condition of a loan made to a company that the lender shall have the power to appoint a certain number of directors to the board to safeguard his interests. A director does not have to be a natural person and so a holding company will nominate the directors of its subsidiary company.

If the articles permit, a director can assign his office, that is transfer his rights and liabilities as a director, to another person. This must be approved by a special resolution of the company. If a director of a private company has been given the power by the articles to nominate his successor, this is not an assignment and will not require the formality of a special resolution.

Although no qualification by law is required for a director, the articles frequently provide that aliens shall not be appointed to the board of directors. This is often the case with shipping companies where it is sought to preserve British control of the company.

Every company must keep a register of its directors which includes the name, address and business occupation of each director. It must also include details of other directorships currently held by a director, and any other directorship held in the past five years.

Restriction on the appointment of directors

The Act prohibits certain individuals from acting as directors.

(i) An undischarged bankrupt cannot act as such unless he is authorised by the Court.

(ii) A person cannot be appointed a director of a public company if at the time of his appointment he has reached the age of 70. This provision can be excluded by the articles, and such an appointment may be approved by the majority of members at a general meeting.

(iii) If a person is disqualified by the Court for fraud or breach of duty in connection with the promotion, formation, management or liquidation of a company, the Court may make an order that he shall not act as a director or be directly or indirectly concerned in the management of a company for up to fifteen years. A magistrates court may disqualify a director for these offences for a period of up to five years.

Qualification shares

An individual may also be prevented from acting as a director unless he holds a certain number of shares in a company. These are known as qualification shares. The reasoning behind this shareholding is that a director should be prepared to have a financial interest in a company whose affairs he is directing. It is not obligatory to have a qualification shareholding, and Article 77 states that the shareholding qualification for directors may be fixed by a company in general meeting, or unless or until so fixed no qualification shall be required. The share qualification is now so small as to be meaningless, or can be a disadvantage in that too high a share qualification can deter suitable persons from becoming directors. Indeed if a director holds a substantial number of shares this could influence his decisions with regard to dividends, or in relation to his tax position.

If a company does specify a share qualification for directors, this must be obtained within two months, or such shorter time as the articles specify. If a director does not obtain the requisite number of shares within the time, he must vacate office and cannot be re-appointed director until he has obtained the shares. The articles frequently state that qualification shares must be held in the director's own name, so that bearer shares or shares held jointly with another person are not suitable.

The power of management

The management of the company may be exercised by the members in general meeting or it can be delegated by the shareholders to the board of directors. The articles of the majority of the companies delegate this power in words similar to that of Article 80: 'The business of the company shall be managed by the directors, who . . . may exercise all such powers of the company as are not . . . required to be exercised by the company in general meeting.'

The shareholders, having given these powers to the directors, cannot then over-ride the directors' discretion. In *Scott v. Scott*, the shareholders passed a resolution at their general meeting that certain payments in respect of dividends should be made to preference shareholders. The resolution was invalid as it was an attempt by the shareholders to usurp the directors' powers of financial control. Directors have been held to have powers to sell a company's undertaking, to declare an interim dividend, and to sue on behalf of a company without the concurrence of the shareholders.

Board meetings

If the articles vest the power of management collectively in the directors, they must exercise this power only at board meetings. Control of board meetings is in the hands of the chairman of the board. Directors should not take decisions outside meetings unless allowed to do so by the articles. The articles normally provide that the board may delegate its powers to the managing director or a committee of one or more of its directors (Article 102). It is frequently impracticable for all matters to be dealt with at board meetings, and articles such as Article 106 usually provide that if all the directors sign a resolution, it will be as effective as a resolution passed at a board meeting. In practice, a minute is circulated and after each of the directors has signed, it is inserted in the minute book.

The articles usually provide that 'the directors may meet together for the despatch of business, adjourn and otherwise regulate their meetings as they think fit'. Large companies hold board meetings at regular intervals, while small companies tend to hold meetings only where there is a sufficient agenda to justify summoning the board of directors. Unless there are regular meetings at fixed intervals, directors will be entitled to reasonable notice of meetings, but this need not specify the nature of the business to be transacted. If the directors are all present and agree, the formalities of summoning a meeting can be dispensed with and a meeting can be called at any time.

If a director is abroad notice need not be given to him, but if the company inadvertently fails to inform a director of a proposed board meeting, the meeting is irregular. This is a mere technicality as the articles usually declare that a meeting shall be properly constituted, despite an accidental omission to inform a director of a meeting. Even if there were no such article, a later properly constituted board meeting could ratify what had been done irregularly.

The articles generally fix the quorum for a board meeting; this is the number of directors who must be present to enable them to exercise their power as a board. Article 99 states 'The quorum necessary for the transaction of the business of the directors may be fixed by the directors and unless so fixed shall be two'. However, it can be one. The quorum must be a disinterested quorum, as the directors present must not have a personal interest in the matters to be voted on, and are therefore by the terms of the articles unable to vote on that particular issue.

Directors exercise their powers at board meetings by passing resolutions approved of by the majority. The articles may provide that in the case of an equality of votes the chairman shall have a second or casting vote (Article 98).

Directors may delegate any of their powers to committees if the articles permit them to do so. A committee may consist of one member; for example, if the board delegates powers to the managing director, he is in effect a committee of one. Regulations are usually embodied in the articles which govern the proceedings of such committees.

The managing director

Larger companies normally appoint a managing director or indeed a number of managing directors to deal with various aspects of the company's business. The powers of such a director are derived solely from the articles. The managing director of a company, to which Table A applies, will initially have to be a director of the company as Article 107 states that 'the directors may from time to time appoint one of their body to the office of managing director'. Such an appointment may be for such a period as his fellow directors think fit, and may even be an appointment for life, although this can be revoked at a general meeting of the company, and he can be removed from office in the same manner as any other director. The articles which delegate this power to a managing director will give the board of directors the right to 'revoke, withdraw, alter or vary such powers'.

In *Harold Holdsworth and Co. Ltd (Wakefield) v. Caddies*, Caddies acted as the managing director of the major company and its subsidiary. A disagreement arose between him and the board of Harold Holdsworth and Co. Ltd, the parent company, and he was informed that his activities would be solely confined to the subsidiary company. Caddies sued for damages for breach of contract. It was held that the directors had acted within their powers, and Caddies was unable to succeed in his action.

The remuneration of the managing director will be decided upon by his fellow directors, and this may include salary, participation in profits or commission.

A prudent managing director will have a contract of service which clearly states that he is an employee of the company. In *Lee v. Lee's Air Farming Ltd*, Lee was the holder of 2999 shares out of the company's total 3000 shares. He was the managing director of the company and drew up a contract between the company and himself for his services as a pilot, where he was described as an employee of the company.

A managing director or any other director may be removed from office, despite having a service contract with the company. Southern Foundries Ltd appointed Shirlaw their managing director in 1933 on a ten year contract. In 1935 the company merged with other companies and in 1937 Shirlaw was removed from the board of directors. He had to relinquish the post of managing director as the articles stated that only a director could be a managing director. He sued Southern Foundries for breach of contract and recovered damages of £10000 (*Southern Foundries Ltd v. Shirlaw*).

A director who is both an employee and managing director will be given all the protection granted to employees under the Employment Protection Consolidation Act 1978 which covers redundancy payments, contracts of employment specification and provisions for unfair dismissal.

Remuneration of directors

The amount of a director's remuneration is usually stated in the director's service contract. The article may make provision for payment of directors' fees, and Article 76 stipulates that the remuneration of the directors shall from time to time be determined by the company in general meeting.

If provision is made in the articles for directors' remuneration, it becomes a debt due from the company to the directors and may be recovered, even though a company has not made any profit; that is, it may be paid out of capital.

It is unlawful for a company to pay a director a fee which is free of income tax (section 189). If a director is paid a sum in excess of that permitted by the company's regulations, he is liable to repay the excess amount to the company. However, a company in general meeting may vote a gratuity which exceeds the director's normal fees.

If a director vacates office during the currency of the year, the articles must be examined to determine the amount, if any, of his remuneration. Article 76 states that the director's 'remuneration shall be deemed to accrue from day to day', and in such a case he will be able to claim. If there is no such article, then the position is not clear. It has been held that to express a director's salary at the 'rate of £1000 per annum' entitles a director to be paid for the period he has served as a director. If his salary is expressed as £1000 per annum, or a yearly sum of £1000, it would appear that a director will only be paid if he completes a full year's service. The Apportionments Act 1870 should apply in this situation, as it states that all annuities and other periodical payments in the nature of income should be apportionable. As annuities include salaries and pensions, it would seem that directors' fees would be covered by this provision.

Vacation of office

The articles of the majority of public companies provide that at the first annual general meeting of a company all the directors shall retire from office. They are eligible for re-election, which is usually a mere formality. Article 89 provides for the retirement by rotation of one-third of the directors who have been longest in office in each year. They are eligible for re-election. If the number of directors is not exactly three, or a multiple of three, then the number nearest one-third will retire. In compiling this number the managing director is not included, nor are the directors appointed by the board to fill any casual vacancies which have occurred since the last annual general meeting. These directors only hold office until the next annual general meeting at which meeting they must submit themselves for re-election. An example of the working of the formula would be as follows. A company has seven directors (including a managing director). Of the other six directors, two were appointed by the board during the year. These two directors plus one other must stand for re-election. These provisions are rarely found in the articles of private companies.

A retiring director who offers himself for re-election will be deemed to be re-elected unless it is decided at the meeting not to fill the vacancy, or it is resolved at the meeting that the director be not re-elected.

Section 184 provides that a director can always be removed from office by a resolution of members passed by a simple majority. This resolution requires special notice. The director concerned may then require the company to circulate a statement to all the members outlining his defence. If the company fails to do so, or is unable to do so, the director may have the statement read out at the meeting. The company can apply to the Court to be excused from publishing the statement, if it considers that the director is merely making the statement to secure needless publicity for defamatory matter. Additionally, the director is entitled to address the meeting, whether he is a member or not. Section 184 applies to all companies and all directors, with one exception. It does not apply to a director of a private company who was appointed a director for life, on or before 18 July 1945.

Should a director be removed from office in consequence of section 184, the company may appoint another person to take his place. This may be filled by the board as a casual vacancy or there may be an appointment at the same meeting. If an appointment is made at the same meeting, special notice must be given of the intention to fill the vacancy. Such a director holds office only for the unexpired period of office of his predecessor. If the deposed director has a service contract with the company, he may claim compensation and damages for loss of office. The articles may provide that on a resolution to remove a director the shares held by that director shall carry additional voting rights (*Bushell v. Faith*).

The articles of most companies provide that a director shall vacate office if he:

(i) Ceases to be a director by virtue of not having obtained his share qualification.

(ii) Ceases to be a director on attaining the age of seventy. This provision only applies to directors of public companies and the age limit may be removed or amended by a company's articles. Alternatively the company in general meeting may re-appoint him director after reaching the age of seventy, as long as his age has been disclosed to the members.

(iii) Is made bankrupt, or makes any arrangement with his creditors generally (i.e. with all his creditors, not with one or more).

(iv) Is prohibited from being a director by reason of any of the following:

(a) if he is convicted of an offence in connection with the promotion, formation, management or liquidation of a company;

(b)   if he is found guilty of fraudulent trading;

(c)   if he is guilty of any fraud or breach of duty to the company whilst an officer of the company;

(d)   if he has persistently defaulted in relation to delivery of documents to the Registrar.

The Court may in these cases order that he shall not, for a period of up to fifteen years, be a director or take part in the management of a company without the Court's leave.

(v)   Becomes of unsound mind.

(vi)   Resigns his office by notice in writing to the company.

(vii)   Is absent, without permission, from board meetings for more than six months. In *Re London and Northern Bank, Mack's Claim* a director who lived in Northern Ireland was unable to travel to London for board meetings over a period of time. It was held that he had not 'absented himself' so as to be disqualified, as his prolonged illness was an involuntary reason for his absence.

Articles frequently provide that a director shall vacate office if he becomes directly or indirectly interested in any contract entered into by the company. On completion of the contract the director may be validly re-appointed.

Compensation for loss of office

Compensation may be paid to a director for loss of his office. Such payment is lawful as long as it is disclosed to the members of the company and approved by the company in general meeting (sections 191–3).

It may arise in three situations:

(i)   Compensation paid by the company on his retirement, whether voluntary or enforced.

(ii)   Compensation paid on retirement following the sale of a company's undertaking. Usually the payment will be made by the purchaser.

(iii)   Compensation paid on retirement in connection with an offer for the share capital of the company. If the offer is for one-third or more of the capital, or is conditional on acceptance to a given extent, the approval of the shareholders must be obtained.

If a director does not disclose payments made to him as compensation, he will hold such payments in trust for the company in situations (i) and (ii). In situation (iii) he will hold the money in trust for the shareholders who have sold their shares as a result of the offer. Money will also be held on trust for shareholders if a director receives a higher price for his shares than is paid to the other shareholders, and this fact is not disclosed.

If there is a scheme of reconstruction providing compensation for displaced directors, any payment made to such a director must be disclosed to members when seeking their approval for the reconstruction. If proper disclosure is not made, the scheme is invalid.

16

Duties of Directors

Directors must act honestly and in the best interests of the company. If a transaction entered into by the directors is not in the best interests of the company – for example, the power to issue shares being used to retain control (*Piercy v. Mills & Co.*) – it is not binding. In *Re Roith Ltd*, the memorandum and articles of a company were altered to allow pensions to be paid to dependants of the company's employees. Shortly afterwards a director, in poor health, was appointed general manager for life under a service agreement which provided, *inter alia*, that his widow would be paid a pension for life on his death. It was held that the agreement was not binding, as it was not for the Company's benefit.

A director must account to the company for any profit made by him by virtue of being a director, unless the members give their consent in general meeting. In *Boston Deep Sea Fishing Co. v. Ansell*, a director of the company entered into contracts for constructing fishing smacks, and was paid a commission on the contract by the shipbuilders. He also owned shares in an ice-making company which paid, in addition to dividends, a bonus to shareholders who were owners of fishing smacks and who purchased ice from the ice company for use in their ships. Neither of these transactions was disclosed to the company and Ansell had to account for the bonus and the commission to the company, even though the company could not have qualified for the bonus.

In *Regal (Hastings) Ltd v. Gulliver*, a company which owned a cinema in Hastings proposed to acquire two other cinemas in order to sell the three cinemas together. It formed a subsidiary company to purchase the cinemas. The subsidiary company was unable to provide all the required capital, so the directors bought some shares in the subsidiary company to enable it to provide the necessary capital. The subsidiary company acquired the two cinemas and the shares of Regal Ltd, and the subsidiary was sold at a profit. It was held that the directors must account to the Regal Company for the profit they had made, as it was only through the knowledge and opportunity they had gained as directors of Regal Ltd that they were able to obtain the shares.

(The directors of Regal Ltd could have obtained ratification of the action by the company in general meeting, but it did not occur to them to do so as they believed their actions were legal and proper.)

A director who, in the course of his employment, obtains a contract for himself, must account to the company for the profit, even though it is debatable whether the company could have obtained the contract.

In *Industrial Development Consultants Ltd (IDC Ltd) v. Cooley,* IDC Ltd, provided construction consultancy services for gas boards. Its managing director was an architect named Cooley. The Eastern Gas Board offered tenders for building four depots, and Cooley was informed that it was unlikely that IDC Ltd would be given the contract. He realised that he had an excellent opportunity of obtaining the contract for himself and represented to IDC Ltd that he was ill. IDC Ltd released him from his contract with them and he then obtained the benefit of the contract for himself. IDC Ltd successfully sued Cooley for the profit he made on the construction of the depots.

Directors as trustees

Directors may be compared to trustees in that they stand in a fiduciary relationship to the company in the performance of their duties. They have possession or control of the company's money and property, and therefore hold these on trust for the company. If these are misapplied, this constitutes a breach of trust.

In *Allen v. Hyatt*, the directors entered into negotiations for the amalgamation of the company with other companies. They informed a number of shareholders that it was necessary to grant the directors an option to purchase their shares at par in order for the amalgamation to take place. The directors then exercised the option and made a substantial profit. It was held that they must account for this profit to the shareholders.

Directors are trustees of the powers entrusted to them; for example, the power to issue shares is granted to directors to enable them to raise capital, when it is required by the company. In *Piercy v. Mills & Co.*, the company's two directors made an allotment of shares although the company did not require further capital. The aim of the directors was to maintain control of the company and prevent the appointment of other directors. It was held that the allotment was invalid and void.

In *Howard Smith Ltd v. Ampol Petroleum Ltd*, the directors of Millers Ltd (a company in which Ampol Petroleum Ltd and another shareholder held 55 per cent of the issued share capital) allotted shares to Howard Smith Ltd in order to destroy the majority holdings of Ampol Ltd and the other shareholders (this was to enable Howard Smith Ltd to make an offer for the shares of the minority shareholders). It was held that the allotment was invalid and void.

The directors of a company are trustees for a company and not for the individual shareholder. In *Percival v. Wright*, the directors of a company purchased shares from Percival at a price based on his valuation. At this time the directors were negotiating for the sale of the company to a third party. If successful, the price realised for each share would have been greater than that paid for Percival's share. The negotiations proved abortive. It was held the directors were not trustees for the individual shareholders and could purchase their shares without disclosing any pending negotiations for the sale of the company.

If it is discovered that the directors have acted from improper motives, they can nevertheless make full disclosure to the shareholders and obtain their approval. Provided their acts are not *ultra vires* the company, they can be ratified by a general meeting (*Bamford v. Bamford*).

The Limitation Act 1939 applies to the acts of directors, as it applies to trustees. The Limitation Act bars any rights against a director for negligence or breach of trust, where the proceedings are commenced more than six years after the alleged wrong or omission.

Directors as agents

As agents of a company directors are limited by the contractual powers of the company, as set out in its objects clause. As long as they contract within the scope of their authority, they incur no personal liability on any contracts made by them. If an agent exceeds his authority when entering into a contract, the agent becomes personally liable for breach of warranty of authority; that is, he is liable as he warrants that he has authority that he does not possess. If the directors make a contract which is beyond the board's power to make, they become personally liable on the contract.

Should a contract be beyond the powers of the directors, but within the power of the company – that is, *ultra vires* the board but *intra vires* the company – the company can in a general meeting ratify the board's actions. This occurred in *Bamford v. Bamford* where the directors of Bamford Ltd, manufacturers of agricultural machinery, allotted unissued shares to a third party to forestall a takeover bid. Although the articles provided that the unissued shares were at the directors' disposal, they exceeded their powers by issuing them for this reason. Nevertheless, it was held that the shareholders, at a meeting one month later, could ratify and validate the directors' actions as they approved of these actions.

A third party can still enforce a contract against the company, entered into by its board of directors, even though the contract is *ultra vires* the company, as long as he can show that he acted in good faith (European Communities Act 1972, section 9(1)). The third party need not inquire as to the company's capacity to enter into a contract or the power of the directors to bind the company for as long as he is unaware of any limitations he can enforce the contract.

If directors hold themselves out as agents to the shareholders in transactions involving the shareholders, they must account for any profit made by them in the course of the transactions (*Allen v. Hyatt*).

Duties owed to employees

Part of a director's fiduciary duty is to have regard to the interests of a company's employees, as well as the interests of the members. This duty is owed to the company and is enforceable by the company in the same way as any other duty owed to it by a director (1980 Companies Act, section 46).

A company is given power to make provision for employees and former employees of the company or its subsidiaries on the cessation or transfer of the business, even though it is not in the best interests of the company. This reverses the decision in *Parke v. Daily News Ltd*, where a company was prevented from distributing £1500000 of its assets of £2000000 among its employees to compensate them for loss of pension rights and provide them with redundancy payments. The Court held that such payments were *ultra vires* as they were not made for the company's benefit.

The position of the creditors is safeguarded, as provision may only be made out of such sums as would otherwise have been available for distribution amongst its members as a dividend.

The power to provide for employees is given by section 74 of the 1980 Companies Act and may be implemented by an ordinary resolution, unless the memorandum or the articles provide that a resolution by the directors is sufficient, or that the exercise of the power requires a resolution other than an ordinary resolution.

The degree of skill to be shown by a director

A director must exercise a degree of skill and diligence in the perform-ance of his duties. The degree of skill will vary with the size and complexity of the company. The position of a director of a company carrying on a small retail business is vastly different from that of a director of a multi-national company. The duty owed by a director has been described as the care that an ordinary man might be expected to take in the circumstances.

In *Re City Equitable Fire Insurance*, the directors entrusted the company's investments to its managing director, Bevan, who was also a senior partner in a firm of brokers which handled the company's investments. Some £1200000 was lost due to Bevan's fraud and incompetence, including £350000 left with the brokers. It was held that although the other directors had acted honestly, they had been negligent in not establishing how the company's funds were invested.

In *Re City Equitable Fire Insurance*, Romer J. laid down the following propositions:

1 A director need not exhibit in the performance of his duties a greater degree of skill than may reasonably be expected from a person of his knowledge and experience. (A director of a life insurance company, for instance, does not guarantee that he has the skill of an actuary or physician.)

2 A director is not bound to give continuous attention to the affairs of his company. His duties are of an intermittent nature to be performed at periodical board meetings, and at meetings of any Committee of the board upon which he happens to be placed. He is not however bound to attend all such meetings, though he ought to attend whenever, in the circumstances, he is reasonably able to do so.

3 In respect of all duties that, having regard to the exigencies of business and the articles of association, may properly be left to some other official, a director is, in the absence of grounds for suspicion, justified in trusting that official to perform such duties honestly.

These are general propositions, and outline the minimum standards to be expected from non-executive directors. A far greater degree of skill and commitment will be expected of an executive director and managing director.

A director is not liable for the wrongful acts of his co-directors of which he has no knowledge and in which he has not taken part, but may become liable for the acts and misdeeds of his fellow directors if he habitually abstains from attending board meetings.

A director is not liable for errors of judgement. Brett L.J. stated in *Lagunas Nitrate Co. v. Lagunas Syndicate* that: 'A director must be guilty of such negligence as would make liable in an action. Mere imprudence is not negligence: want of judgement is not. It must be such negligence as would make a man liable in point of law.'

In *Re New Mansholand Exploration Co.*, the directors of a company had power to lend mõney and promote other companies. They passed a resolution to lend Green a sum of money on his giving security. The company's solicitor handed a cheque for £250 to Green without obtaining any security. Later another cheque for £1000 was handed to Green without security being obtained, as Green was bringing out a company which the directors believed would benefit their own company. It was held that the directors were not liable for breach of trust or misfeasance as they had exercised their judgment and discretion honestly.

Remedies for breach of duty

The following remedies may be available against a director in breach of his duties:

(i) The other party to the agreement may apply for rescission of the contract if a director has contravened the rules relating to contracts in which he is interested. This is only possible if the parties can be restored to their former positions and third parties have not acquired rights under the contract.

(ii) Damages may be awarded if the other party has suffered loss as a result of the director's actions.

(iii) An injunction may be granted to restrain a breach which is threatened but which has not yet occurred, for example to prevent the board from taking action which is beyond its power.

(iv) Action may be taken for the restoration of the company's property where the property has remained under the director's control, or it is possible to trace it to a purchaser who was aware of the director's breach of duty.

(v) A director is liable to account for any profit made by him in his capacity as director, which has not been disclosed to the company.

(vi) A director who is an employee of the company (e.g. a managing director) may be summarily dismissed.

(vii) A director (or any other person) may be criminally liable for fraudulent trading, whether or not the company has been or is in the course of being wound up (section 96, 1981 Act).

It may also be possible to take action against a director by a misfeasance summons. Such a summons may be applied for by the liquidator, any creditor or contributory when the company is in the course of being wound up. Section 333 provides that the Court may order a director to repay or restore money or property, or compensate a company, where he has misapplied or retained the company's property or money, or has been guilty of any misfeasance or breach of trust.

A director may escape liability if the company in general meeting validly ratifies the breach. In *Pavlides v. Jensen*, it was alleged that the directors had been negligent in selling an asbestos mine owned by the company for £182000, whereas its true value was in the region of £1000000. The company resolved that no proceedings should be taken against them.

Any article of the company seeking to exempt a director from liability for negligence, default, breach of duty or breach of trust in relation to the company is void (section 205). A company may provide in its articles that it shall indemnify any director against any liability incurred by him in successfully defending any civil or criminal proceedings, or in connection with an application under Section 448 in which relief is granted to him by the Court (Article 136).

Relief may also be granted by the Court. Section 448 provides that if in proceedings for negligence, default, breach of duty or breach of trust against a director of a company, it appears that he has acted honestly and reasonably, and having regard to all the circumstances he ought fairly to be excused, the Court may relieve him, wholly or partly, from liability on such terms as it thinks fit.

17

Disclosure of Directors' Business Interests

As directors' interests often coincide with those of a company, the various Companies Acts have progressively insisted upon a greater degree of disclosure.

Contracts with the company

As a general rule a director cannot make a contract with a company, as he should not place himself in a situation where his personal interests might conflict with his duty to the company. Such a contract is voidable at the company's option.

In *Parker v. McKenna*, the directors of the National Bank of Ireland increased the capital of the Bank by issuing 20 000 £50 shares. Any shares not taken up were to be disposed of by the directors at a £30 premium. Stock entered into agreement to purchase 9778 shares for £30, placing a deposit of £5 on each share, the balance to be paid by instalments. As Stock was unable to take all the shares, the directors took a considerable number of these shares and afterwards disposed of them at a profit. It was held that the directors must account to the Bank for the profits made by them by the sale of the shares.

A director may enter into a contract to take up shares or debentures in a company.

The articles may provide that a director may enter into a contract with the company or have an interest in such a contract. In this situation, the Act imposes certain conditions and provides that if a director has such an interest he must declare the nature of his interest at the first meeting when the contract or proposed contract is considered. If at that time he had no interest but later becomes interested, he must disclose his interest at the next meeting after he becomes interested. If he fails to do so, the contract is voidable at the company's option (section 199). This section is now extended to require disclosure of arrangements with directors and connected persons, as defined in the next paragraph.

A person 'connected with a director' includes his spouse (if not a director); his children under eighteen; an associated company in which the director and any person connected with him together are interested in more than one-fifth of the equity share capital or control more than one-fifth of the voting power; and any trustee for, or partner of, the director, or his spouse, children or associated company. A contract entered into in contravention of this section is voidable at the company's option, unless restitution is not possible, or innocent third parties have acquired rights, or the contract is ratified by the company within a reasonable period of time.

A director may give a general notice that he is to be regarded as having an interest in any contract made with a specified company or firm or specified person (1980 Companies Act).

A general meeting must approve of any contract to transfer to, or acquire from, a director or a person connected with a director, a non-cash asset whose value at the time of the transaction exceeds £50000 or 10 per cent of the net assets, provided it is not less than £1000 (1980 Companies Act, section 48).

The 1981 Companies Act, section 110, relaxes this prohibition in three circumstances:

(a) an arrangement by a holding company and any of its wholly owned subsidiaries, or between two wholly owned subsidiaries of the same holding company.

(b) an arrangement entered into by a company which is being wound up (other than in a members' voluntary winding up).

(c) obtaining an asset from a company in the capacity of a member (e.g. the issue of bonus shares).

The articles may contain a provision which prohibits a director from voting on a contract in which he is interested (Article 84), but the articles of the majority of private companies do not contain this prohibition. Even if prohibited from voting at a directors' meeting, such a director is entitled to vote on the same question at a general meeting.

Section 184 provides that a company in general meeting may, by ordinary resolution, remove a director before the expiration of his period of office, notwithstanding anything in its articles or any agreement between the company and the director. The director's remedy is a claim for damages (*Southern Foundries v. Shirlaw*).

Loans to directors

The general rule is that a company may not make a loan to a director of the company or to a director of its holding company. Neither may a company enter into a guarantee or provide any security in connection with a loan made by any person to such a director (1980 Companies Act, section 49).

Additionally, a relevant company (i.e. a public company and any subsidiary or holding company of a public company) may not make a quasi loan or enter into a guarantee, or provide security for a director of the company, or its holding company, or for any person connected with the director, that is his immediate family and any associated company.

A quasi loan is a transaction between a company and the director whereby the company pays or promises to pay a third party on terms that the director will reimburse the company, for example the use of credit cards by a director, where the company is the cardholder and promises to pay a third party on the terms that the director will reimburse the company.

Certain exceptions are allowed and include:

(i)   Loans or quasi loans or guarantees made to a member of a group of companies (even though a director of one member of the group is associated with another).

(ii) A quasi loan of up to £1000 if it is agreed that it is to be repaid within two months.

(iii) The provision of funds for expenses incurred by a director for the purposes of the company or in connection with his duties. In the case of a relevant company there is a ceiling of £10000 for each director.

(iv) Credit transactions made with directors in the normal course of business on commercial terms.

(v)   Credit transactions where the 'relevant amount' (i.e. the value of all outstanding transactions made with director and connected persons) does not exceed £5000.

(vi) Loans made by a money lending company in the ordinary course of business and on normal commercial terms. If the company is not a bank there is a £50000 limit per director.

(vii) Loans made by a money lending company for house purchase and house improvement. This is subject to a limit of £50000 and is applicable to all companies.

(viii) A loan to a director of the company or its holding company, if the aggregate of the relevant amounts does not exceed £2500 (1981 Act, section 110).

Option dealings

It is an offence for a director, or the spouse or infant children of a director, to deal in options to buy or sell quoted shares or debentures of the company of which he is a director or to deal in securities of associated companies.

A director who buys a right to call for, make delivery of, or at his election a right to call for, or make delivery of a specified number of shares, or a specified amount of debentures within a specified time is liable to a fine and/or a term of imprisonment (1967 Companies Act, section 25.30).

The aim of this prohibition is to prevent a director and his immediate family using inside information to speculate in the securities (i.e. shares or debentures) of companies with which he is closely associated.

A director may acquire an option to buy the securities of a private company, or the unquoted securities of a public company and it is lawful to buy a right to subscribe for shares or debentures directly from the company, or to buy debentures which carry a right to subscribe for or convert into shares.

A director's spouse or infant child, who is accused of contravening these sections, may submit that she (or he) had no reason to believe that the spouse (or parent) was a director of the company in question.

Directors' service contracts

Every company must make available for the inspection of its members the terms of its service contracts with its directors. If the contract is in writing, a copy of the contract must be retained. If it is not in writing, a written memorandum setting out the terms must be available for inspection. Any variations in the terms of the contract must also be shown. The details of a service contract of a director with a subsidiary company must also be available for inspection.

A service contract may contain a provision that a director's employment cannot be terminated by notice, or (only in specified circumstances) for a period exceeding five years. Unless the consent of the general meeting is obtained, such a provision will be void (1980 Companies Act, section 47). The aim of this section is to prevent directors from entering into long term service contracts in anticipation of moves to remove them. A breach of contract in these circumstances would entitle them to large sums as compensation.

Register of directors' interests

A director is under an obligation to notify a company of his interest in its shares or debentures existing at the time of his appointment. He must notify the company in writing of the number and class of shares in which he has an interest, and the amount and class of debentures involved. This obligation extends to notifying the company of any interest of his spouse or infant children.

A director is deemed to have an interest in the following situations:

(i) if he is the holder of shares;

(ii) if he enters into a contract for the purchase of shares;

(iii) if he exercises, or is entitled to exercise, rights conferred by the shares (and he is not the holder of the shares);

(iv) if a company is interested in the shares and that company or its directors are accustomed to act in accordance with his directions, or he is entitled to exercise or control a third or more of the votes at that company's general meeting. If that company controls a third or more of the voting power at another company's general meeting, he is regarded as having an interest in that other company;

(v) if he has an option to take shares or debentures;

(vi) if any interest in shares is comprised in trust property and he is a beneficiary of that trust. A person is also interested if his spouse, or infant child or step-child is so interested.

He must also inform the company if he ceases to be so interested; or if he makes a contract to sell any shares or debentures; or if he assigns a right to subscribe for the company's shares or debentures; or if a related company grants him a right to subscribe for its shares and debentures.

A company must keep a register of directors' interests which must be open during business hours for inspection by any member of the company. Whenever a company grants a director a right to subscribe for its shares or debentures it must inscribe in the register against his name the date on which the right is granted, the period during which it is exercisable, and the consideration for the grant. When a director exercises such a right, the company must inscribe in the register against his name the fact that the right has been exercised, the number of shares or debentures involved, and the name of the person in whose name they were registered (Companies Act 1967, as amended by the Companies Act 1981).

Insider dealing

The 1980 Companies Act makes it a criminal offence for an individual to deal on a recognised stock exchange in the securities of a company if he has inside information relating to those securities which, if known, would be likely to affect the price of those securities.

An individual who is, or at any time in the previous six months has been, connected with a company shall not deal in that company's securities on a recognised stock exchange if he has information which he holds by virtue of his connection with the company, which he would not be expected to disclose as he is aware that it is unpublished price sensitive information relating to those securities.

This prohibition also extends to dealings in the securities of another company, if the information relates to any transaction, actual or contemplated, involving that company and the company with which he is connected. This also applies to any transaction involving one of those companies and the securities of the other company.

An individual contemplating, or who has contemplated, making a takeover bid for a company in a particular capacity is prohibited from dealing on a recognised stock exchange in the securities of that company in any other capacity, such as through a nominee.

An individual who is prohibited from dealing by these provisions must not counsel or procure any other person either to deal in those securities or communicate information, if he knows that such information will be used for the purpose of dealing on a stock exchange.

An individual is connected with a company if he is a director, officer or employee of that company or a related company. A person having a professional or business relationship with the company or related company is connected with the company if this relationship gives him access to unpublished price-sensitive information, which he would not be expected to disclose except in the proper performance of his work.

The prohibition on insider dealings also applies to stock exchange dealings by Crown servants, obtained in their official capacity.

Certain exceptions are permitted to these prohibitions:

(i) Any person using the information other than with a view to making a profit or avoiding a loss.
(ii) Any person entering into a transaction in good faith while acting as liquidator, receiver or trustee in bankruptcy.
(iii) Receiving the information in the course of business as a jobber (1980 Companies Act, sections 68, 69, 73).

The penalty for insider dealing is a maximum of two years' imprisonment and a fine of £1000. The transactions entered into in breach of the prohibitions on insider dealing are valid, despite the contravention of the Act.

The prohibition on insider dealing does not apply to share transactions in a private company and to other private deals, or to certain dealings in international bonds.

18

Majority Rule and Minority Protection

Every member of a company is by virtue of the articles contractually bound to the company and to his fellow members. As such he undertakes to accept as binding the decisions of the majority as expressed at a general meeting of the company, when a member may attend, put forward his views and (with certain exceptions) vote. If a sufficient majority support a resolution to which he is opposed, he must abide by the majority decision. The majority, who have control of the company, are thus able to formulate policy and appoint the directors of their choice.

Even if a wrong is alleged to have been committed against a company, the members may, by ordinary resolution, validly resolve that no proceedings be taken in respect of the act. The shareholder cannot complain, as he has agreed to the course of action, even if he does not approve of it. A minority shareholder failed in his attempt to prevent a company selling a mine valued at £1 000 000 for £182 000, as no fraud on the minority was alleged (*Pavlides v. Jensen*).

The rule in Foss v. Harbottle

The minority shareholders may be able to rely on the exceptions to the rule in *Foss v. Harbottle*. In this case the minority shareholders attempted to sue the directors, alleging that the losses incurred by the company were due to the directors' mismanagement. The action was dismissed and the Court formulated two propositions:

1 The proper plaintiff in respect of a wrong alleged to be done to a company is, *prima facie*, the company itself – so preventing a multiplicity of suits.

It is implicit in the rule that the matter relied on as constituting the cause of action shall be a course of action properly belonging to the general body of corporator or members of the company or association, as opposed to a cause of action which some individual member can assert in his own right.

The company alone can sue, or be sued; and it matters not whether the dissentients comprise a lone voice or a full 49 per cent minority of the equity voters. (Jenkins L.J. in *Edwards v. Halliwell*.)

2   The Court will not interfere if the irregularity is capable of being confirmed by the majority, so that it is futile to litigate except with the consent of the majority.

Exceptions to the rule
There are exceptions to this rule and the majority cannot:

1   Sanction an act which is *ultra vires* the company or is illegal (*Ashbury Railway Carriage and Iron Co. v. Riche*).

2   Take advantage of a resolution passed by means of a trick (*Baillie v. Oriental Telephone and Electric Co.*).

3   Commit a fraud on the company. In *Menier v. Hooper's Telegraph Works*, the company brought an action against one of its directors, claiming that he had taken the benefit of a contract which belonged to the company. The majority shareholders persuaded the company to drop the action and proposed that the company should be wound up voluntarily. This would have enabled the majority shareholders to obtain the benefit of the contract for themselves. It was held that the company could be prevented from following this course of action.

In *Daniels v. Daniels*, the minority shareholders brought an action against the company and two of its directors alleging that the company had, on the instructions of the directors (a husband and wife who were the majority shareholders), sold land to one of the directors for a figure (£4250) well below its real value. The land was sold four years later for £120000 and the court held that the minority could bring an action for fraud. Although the transaction was not fraudulent, the directors' use of their power was a fraud on the minority.

4   Take advantage of an act passed by a simple majority vote which requires a special resolution.

5   Exercise their rights merely to discriminate against the minority. In *Clemens v. Clemens Bros Ltd*, Clemens held 45 per cent of the company's share capital and her aunt held 55 per cent and was one of its

five directors. The aunt and her fellow directors wished to alter the articles. She proposed to increase the share capital by issuing 200 shares to herself and 850 shares to be held on trust for the benefit of the company's employees. The appropriate resolutions were passed approving these measures. The effect of this issue of share capital would be to reduce Clemens' percentage holding to less than 25 per cent, and she would be unable to oppose the passing of any special or extraordinary resolution. It was held that the majority's actions were oppressive and discriminatory and the resolutions should be set aside.

6   Use their influence in such a way as to defeat the 'interests of justice'. A company, Thomas Poole and Gladstone China Ltd, was in severe financial difficulties. Two of its directors conceived a scheme whereby it would sell its assets to Newman Industries Ltd. The two directors were also directors of Newman Industries Ltd. In return, Newman Industries Ltd would take over Thomas Poole and Gladstone China Ltd's debts and pay its shareholders £325 000. This figure was arrived at by a valuation of the assets, based on misleading information supplied by the two directors. Further incorrect information was given by the directors at Newman Industries Ltd's meeting to approve the transaction. The Prudential Assurance Company, a shareholder, successfully brought an action on its own behalf, and on behalf of all the other Newman shareholders, for damages against the two directors for breach of their fiduciary duties to the company (*Prudential Assurance Co. Ltd v. Newman Industries*).

If the rule in *Foss v. Harbottle* is not applicable, the minority shareholders can sue in the company's name. In practice, the minority shareholders make use of a representative action in which they sue the company (and usually the directors or majority shareholders) on their own behalf.

A shareholder bringing a representative action may do so at the ultimate expense of the company. In *Wallersteiner v. Moir*, a minority shareholder took a series of actions against the controlling director of a group of companies for the misapplication of £230 000. Although he obtained judgement, he had exhausted his own and other shareholders' finances as the litigation had dragged on for more than ten years. It was held that when the wrongdoers were in control of the company the Court had power to indemnify a shareholder in a representative action, whether he was successful or not.

Statutory protection of the minority

1980 Companies Act, section 75

The minority may always petition the Court to wind up the company on the grounds that it is just and equitable to do so, because of the oppressive conduct of the majority. It is often not in the minority's interest that the company should be wound up, and they may petition the Court for an order under Section 75 of the Companies Act 1980 for relief against the company, on the grounds that the affairs of the company have been conducted in a manner prejudicial to some members.

This section provides that any member may petition the Court on the grounds that 'the affairs of the company are being or have been conducted in a manner which is unfairly prejudicial to the interests of some part of the members, or any actual or proposed act or omission of the company is or would be so prejudicial'.

If the Court is satisfied that the petition is well founded it may make such order, as it thinks fit, for giving relief with regard to the matters complained of.

It may also make an order:

(i)   Regulating the conduct of the company's affairs in the future;
(ii) Requiring the company to do, or to refrain from doing, any act;
(iii) Authorising civil proceedings to be brought in the company's name or on behalf of the company by such person and on such terms as the Court may direct;
(iv) Providing for the purchase of any shares and, if appropriate, any consequent reduction in the company's capital.

If an order requires the company not to make any alteration to either its memorandum or its articles, the company has no power to make any alteration without leave of the Court.

If the Secretary of State has received an inspector's report, or has exercised his powers to inspect a company's books and papers under the Companies Act 1967, and it appears to him that a member would have grounds for applying under section 75, he may himself petition for an order under this section.

Section 75 of the 1980 Act replaces section 210, which provided that the Court could impose a just and equitable solution as an alternative to winding up, where a member complained of oppression.

Re Harmer Ltd and *Scottish CWS Ltd v. Meyer* are examples of situations which have been dealt with under the provisions of section 210.

In *Re Harmer Ltd*, the eighty-eight year old founder of a company dealing in stamps held the majority of the company's shares. He was, with his wife, able to control general meetings and pass special and extraordinary resolutions. He was the chairman of the board and consistently ignored the other shareholders' wishes and the views of his co-directors and even appointed directors without consulting his fellow directors. His two sons, both directors, petitioned the Court for relief. It was held that he should not interfere in the company's affairs (except in accordance with the board's decisions), and should be given the honorary title of President of the company.

In *Scottish CWS Ltd v. Meyer*, both parties had joined forces in forming a subsidiary company to manufacture rayon and cloth. The Scottish co-operative spun the yarn at their mill and Meyer provided the necessary knowledge and expertise to make up the cloth. The co-operative society held 4000 £1 shares and appointed three directors, while Meyer and his associates held 3900 £1 shares and appointed two directors. The co-operative society wished to acquire further shares in the subsidiary at par, although the shares were then valued at £6 each. When this was refused, they adopted a policy of deliberately running down the subsidiary by withholding supplies of yarn, so that the subsidiary's shares became almost worthless. The minority petitioned the Court, and an order was made under Section 210 ordering the Scottish co-op to buy out the minority shareholders at a price of £3.15s (£3.75) per share.

Other sections protecting minorities

The holders of not less than 10 per cent of the paid up capital carrying a right to vote may at any time compel the directors, by a signed requisition, to call an extraordinary general meeting (section 132).

The holders of not less than 5 per cent of the company's paid up capital, or 100 members who have paid an average of £100 on their shares, may compel a company to give notice of a resolution to be moved at a meeting and circulate statements to members (section 140).

The holders of not less than 15 per cent of any shares affected by a variation of class rights may apply to the Court to have the variation cancelled (section 72).

The holders of not less than 15 per cent of the issued share capital may apply to the Court to cancel a special resolution altering the company's objects (section 5).

The holders of at least 10 per cent of the issued shares of a company, or 200 shareholders whatever their shareholding, may apply to the Department of Trade to appoint inspectors to (i) investigate the company's affairs (section 164), or (ii) investigate the company's ownership (section 172).

Minority shareholders may apply to the Court when a company proposes to acquire their shares on a reconstruction of the company (section 287).

In a takeover bid, the dissenting shareholders may compel the company to acquire their shares if the company has not chosen to do so (section 209).

Minority shareholders have the right to demand a poll (section 137).

The holders of not less than 5 per cent of the issued share capital, or 5 per cent of the members (if no share capital) or fifty members can apply to the Court to cancel a resolution for re-registering a public company as a private company (1980 Companies Act, section 11).

The holders of not less than 10 per cent of the issued share capital of a private company may apply to the Court to cancel a special resolution for giving financial assistance for the purchase of shares (1981 Act, section 44).

The holders of not less than 10 per cent of the issued share capital may requisition a company to investigate the ownership of its shares, and may ask the Court to impose restrictions in respect of shares where replies are not received or are unsatisfactory (1981 Act, sections 74, 76).

Investigations by the Department of Trade

Occasions may arise which may make it desirable for an investigation to be made into various aspects of a company's affairs. Various Companies Acts have given the Department of Trade powers of investigation and inspection.

Investigation into a company's affairs

1   The Department of Trade may appoint inspectors to investigate a company's affairs if requested to do so by 200 members or members holding 10 per cent of the issued shares, or on the application of the company. The application must be supported by evidence showing that the applicants have good reason for requiring the investigation. They may be required to provide security, not exceeding £5000, for payment of the costs of the investigation.

2   The Department may investigate a company's affairs if it appears that a company's affairs are being or have been conducted (i) with intent to defraud its creditors or the creditors of any other person; or (ii) for a fraudulent or unlawful purpose; or (iii) in a manner unfairly prejudicial to some part of its members. (This covers any actual or proposed act or omission.)

The Department may also investigate if there is evidence of misfeasance, or other misconduct, or if it appears that a company was formed for any fraudulent or unlawful purpose.

3　The Department must appoint inspectors if the Court, by order, declares that the company's affairs ought to be investigated.

An inspector is given the powers to investigate any related company if he deems it necessary for the purpose of his investigation.

An inspector may examine on oath past and present officers and agents (including bankers, solicitors and auditors) of the company or related company, and require them to produce all books and documents in their custody. If an officer or agent refuses to co-operate with an inspector he may be punished by the Court as if he had been guilty of contempt of court. An inspector may also require any other person, who may be in possession of any information relating to the company's affairs, to produce any books or documents in his custody relating to the company. Such a person is also required to give an inspector every assistance in connection with the investigation. An inspector also has power to examine a director's bank accounts if he has reason to believe that such accounts have been used in connection with certain offences under the Companies Acts (e.g. the payment of undisclosed emoluments).

An inspector may make an interim report to the Department, and at the conclusion of his investigation he must submit a final report to the Department. If an inspector was appointed as a result of an order of the Court, the Secretary of State must furnish the Court with a copy of the inspector's report. He may, if he thinks fit, publish the report and make the report available to the company and to other interested parties.

If as a result of the inspector's report it appears to be in the public interest that a company should be wound up, the Department may present a petition for winding up on the grounds of 'just and equitable'.

If the report indicates that civil proceedings ought, in the public interest, to be brought by any company, the Department may bring proceedings on the company's behalf and in the company's name (sections 164–168, as amended by sections 86–88, Companies Act 1981).

Investigation of the ownership of a company

The Department of Trade may also appoint an inspector to investigate and report on the membership of a company to determine the identity of the persons who have been financially interested in a company's success or failure, or who are able to control or materially influence the company's policy.

An application may also be made to the Department by shareholders holding 10 per cent of the issued shares of the company, or 200 shareholders for an investigation into the company's ownership.

If the Department believes there is good reason to investigate the ownership (though unnecessary to appoint an inspector) they may require any person they have reasonable cause to believe to be, or to have been, interested in a company's shares or debentures to give information of past and present members. If it appears that the difficulty in finding out the relevant facts about any shares is due to the unwillingness of the parties concerned to assist the investigation, the Department may order that:

Any transfer of the shares shall be void;
No voting rights shall be exercisable;
No further shares are to be issued in respect of these shares;
Any sums due on those shares shall not be paid, except in a liquidation.

If the Department makes such an order, any person aggrieved by it may appeal to the Court for an order that the shares shall not be subject to these restrictions.

Investigation of directors' share dealings and interests in shares

The Department may appoint an inspector to determine whether sections 25 and 27 of the Companies Act 1967 have been contravened.

Section 25 penalises a director or his immediate family from dealing in options to buy or sell listed shares or debentures of a company or its related company.

Section 27 imposes a duty on a director of a company to notify the company of his interests in its shares or debentures or those of a related company. An interim report may be made to the Department in relation to these matters, and a final report must be made at the conclusion of the investigation (Companies Act 1967, sections 25, 27, 30).

Inspection of a company's books and papers

The Department may at any time, if it thinks there is good reason to do so, direct a company to produce such books or papers as may be specified, or authorise any officer of the Department to require their production forthwith.

Copies of extracts may be taken from the books and papers and any past or present officer of the company may be required to provide an explanation of them.

An application may be made to a Justice of the Peace for a warrant to search premises, when there are reasonable grounds for suspecting that there are books and papers on those premises which have not been produced as requested by the Department (Companies Act 1967, sections 109, 110).

19

Borrowing Powers

Every trading company has an implied power to borrow for purposes that are incidental to its business. Nevertheless most trading companies include in their objects clause an express power to borrow, and the clause may limit the amount which may be borrowed.

A company's articles usually give the directors authority to borrow on a company's behalf. It may be a general authority to exercise all the powers of the company that are not required to be exercised by the company in general meeting (Article 80), or a specific authority. Specific authority is found in Article 79 which provides that 'the directors may exercise all the powers of the company to borrow money', but limits the amount to the nominal amount of the share capital. Any borrowing in excess of this sum requires the consent of a general meeting. A company seeking a Stock Exchange quotation must include an article limiting the directors' borrowing powers.

Ultra vires borrowing

1   If a company's memorandum imposes a limit on the amount that a company can borrow, and a loan is made to a company in excess of this limit, such a transaction is void. The company may not be sued for the repayment of the loan and is under no contractual liability to the lender. Any security given in respect of the loan will also be void. The company may repay the loan if it so wishes.

The lender may be able to claim the benefit of section 9(1) of the European Communities Act 1972 which provides that a person dealing with a company in good faith shall be able to reply upon a company's capacity to enter into a transaction decided upon by its directors. If a lender acts in good faith, that is without knowledge or suspicion that the company is exceeding its powers on a transaction decided upon by the directors, he can enforce a contract against a company.

2   The articles may impose a limit on the directors' borrowing powers; for example, the directors may be given authority to borrow up to a certain sum, with any borrowing in excess of this amount requiring the approval of a resolution. If the directors borrow in excess of this amount, without obtaining the company's approval, such borrowing is *ultra vires*. The company may ratify such an act by passing an appropriate resolution or altering its articles and so validating the transaction.

In these circumstances the lender may be able to rely on the rule in *Royal British Bank v. Turquand*.

The rule in Royal British Bank v. Turquand

This rule provides that if a transaction is within a company's powers and within the ostensible authority of the directors, a person contracting with the company is entitled to assume that all the necessary internal procedures have been complied with. In *Royal British Bank v. Turquand*, the directors of a company were empowered to issue bonds if authorised by a general resolution of the company. The company borrowed £2000 from the Royal British Bank and, when sued on the bond, claimed that no resolution had been passed. It was held that the Bank had a right to assume that a resolution had been passed and the bond was binding on the company.

A person contracting with the company may be able to rely on the rule if it later transpires that the directors did not have the authority or were not properly appointed as directors. In *Freeman and Lockyer v. Buckhurst Park Properties*, an individual named Kapoor acted as managing director, even though he was not appointed as such. He appointed architects to act on the company's behalf and they successfully sued the company for their fees. It was held that as Kapoor had acted with the board's acquiescence – he had been held out as having authority – the company was liable.

The rule has certain limitations and does not apply in the following circumstances:

(i)   If the transaction is known to be irregular. In *Howard v. Patent Ivory Manufacturing Co.*, the articles provided that the directors could borrow up to £1000 without the shareholders' approval, but any borrowing in excess of this amount required a resolution. The directors lent the company £3500 without a resolution being passed, and debentures were issued to them for that amount. The company was later wound up, and the debentures were held valid for £1000 only as the directors were aware that a resolution had not been passed sanctioning the borrowing.

(ii)   If the transaction is so unusual that the person should be put on enquiry as to its regularity. In *Underwood (AL) Ltd v. Bank of Liverpool and Martins Ltd*, the sole director of a company paid cheques drawn in favour of the company into his own bank account in order to pay his debts. A debenture holder brought an action against the bank for conversion of the cheques. It was held that the bank could not rely on the rule, as the payment of a company's cheques into a private account was unusual and should have put the bank on enquiry.

(iii) If the transaction requires a special or an extraordinary resolution as copies of these resolutions are filed with the Registrar.

(iv)   If the person relies on a document which turns out to be a forgery (*Ruben v. Great Fingall Consolidated*).

3   A lender who is unable to sue the company, or invoke the European Communities Act, or the rule in *Royal British Bank v. Turquand* may have recourse to other remedies. If the money borrowed has not been spent, or it can be identified (e.g. specific investments have been purchased with the money) the lender may apply to the Court for a tracing order to recover the money or the investments. If the money has been used to pay legitimate debts, the lender may be subrogated to the rights of the creditors paid off; that is, he stands in the shoes of the creditors that have been paid off and may sue the company to the extent of their debts. If the money cannot be identified, but it can be shown that the assets of the company have increased, the lender may claim repayment out of such an increase. The lender may also bring an action against the directors for a breach of an implied warranty of authority.

The securities offered

A company may offer one or several of the following as security for a loan:

(a)   A legal mortgage of specific parts of its property.
(b)   An equitable mortgage created by depositing title deeds with a lender.
(c)   A mortgage of chattels.
(d)   A bill of exchange or a promissory note.
(e)   A bond.
(f)   A charge on uncalled capital if allowed by the memorandum or the articles.
(g)   Debentures and debenture stock.

A company usually borrows by means of debentures.

20

Debentures

Definition

There is no precise legal definition of a debenture as the Act merely states that debenture 'includes debenture stock, bonds and other securities of a company whether constituting a charge on the assets of a company or not' (section 455). In *Levy v. Abercorris Slate and Slab Co.*, it was defined as 'a document which creates or acknowledges a debt'.

It is a document which sets out the terms of a loan and is normally issued under a company's seal. It provides for the repayment of the loan at some future specified date and for the payment of interest to the debenture holder at a specified rate at fixed intervals.

A document which is not in this format may nevertheless be a debenture. In *Lemon v. Austin Friars Investment Trust Ltd*, a company issued 'income stock certificates' as an acknowledgement of a debt. The certificates did not create a charge, no date was fixed for repayment, and they were not issued under the company's seal. They provided that three-quarters of the company's profits were to be applied in redeeming the certificates, and that a register of certificate holders was to be kept by the company. It was held that the certificates were debentures.

It is an attractive form of security to the lender as he is given certain rights in the event of a company not meeting its obligations under the terms of the debenture, and it also offers a degree of flexibility to the company.

A debenture holder is not a member of the company, and as a creditor is entitled to interest on his debentures whether a company earns profits or not. A company may issue 'income debentures', which provide that payment of interest or the repayment of capital is dependent on the company earning sufficient profits.

Issue of debentures

A debenture may be issued at a premium or at a discount and the prohibition imposed on the issue of shares at a discount does not apply to debentures as they do not form part of the company's capital. A debenture may be issued which allows the holder, within a certain period of time, to convert the debenture into shares. Such a debenture may not be issued offering an immediate option to convert, as this would be in effect issuing shares at a discount (*Moseley v. Koffyfontein Mines*).

Debentures issued to the public are normally issued in a series and are said to rank *pari passu* (i.e. equally), otherwise they would take priority as to security and payment in the order of their serial numbers or date of issue. A single debenture may be issued privately and is usually of a high nominal value, providing security for a bank loan or overdraft.

The usual form of debenture creates a floating charge over the company's undertaking, with or without a fixed charge on its freehold property. A debenture not secured by a charge is termed a naked or unsecured debenture, and offers no more than an unsecured promise by the company to repay a loan.

Most debentures issued to the public stipulate that they are redeemable on or before a certain date (e.g. 1990–4). This means that a company will redeem the debentures within those years. The redemption may be financed out of a sinking fund, a sum set aside annually to provide for redemption out of a new issue of debentures. A partial redemption may be accomplished by 'drawings', when a company draws lots and redeems an agreed number of debentures. The drawings may be at the company's option, or it may be stated in the terms of issue of the debentures that drawings will take place at fixed intervals.

A company may purchase its debentures in the market. It is clearly to the company's advantage if the debentures stand at a discount in the market as it may extinguish part of its liability in this way. It may redeem debentures at their issue price or at a higher price. They may be re-issued unless the company is prohibited from doing so.

Types of debentures

A debenture may be classified as *irredeemable* in that no date is fixed for its redemption. It may only be redeemed if the company is wound up, or there is a breach of a condition of its issue (e.g. default in the payment of interest).

A perpetual debenture is similar, in that no time is fixed for redemption, but the company does have the right to redeem the debenture at its option.

A debenture may be registered, in that the lender is entered in the register of debenture holders. This register must be kept at the registered office of the company, or at any other office of the company where it is made up, and must be open for the inspection of debenture holders and other persons for not less than two hours each day (section 86, 87).

A bearer debenture may be issued by a company. It is similar to a registered debenture, except that it is stated to be payable to bearer. It is a negotiable instrument which may be transferred by mere delivery. Coupons are attached to bearer debentures and these are submitted to the company when interest is payable.

Companies also issue *debenture stock*. This may be transferred in fractional amounts, although the terms of issue or the articles may specify that stock may only be transferred in minimum amounts. The lender is issued with a stock certificate.

Fixed and floating charges

A debenture may be secured by a fixed charge or a floating charge or a combination of both.

Fixed charge

A fixed charge or mortgage is expressed to cover specific assets of the company, such as land or interests in land or ships. Although the company normally remains in possession of such property, it may not dispose of the property, free from the charge, without the prior consent of the holders of the charge. A debenture holder secured by a fixed charge ranks as a secured creditor in a winding up of a company.

Floating charge

A floating charge is a charge on a company's undertaking which allows a company to offer as security assets that are constantly changing (e.g. stock, cash, book debts).

In *Re Yorkshire Woolcombers Association*, Romer L.J. stated that a floating charge has three characteristics:

(i) It is a charge on a class of assets present and future;
(ii) Which is changing from time to time in the ordinary course of business;

(iii) A company can carry on its business in the ordinary way until steps are taken to enforce the charge.

A floating charge 'crystallises' (i.e. becomes a fixed charge) when the company ceases to carry on business, or is wound up, or on the occurrence of some event specified in the terms of issue of the debenture; for example, if a company defaults in the payment of interest or fails to redeem the debentures, the debenture holders may take steps to enforce their rights.

Disadvantages of floating charges

1 A floating charge has certain disadvantages and is deferred to the following:

(i) To a fixed charge. As a fixed charge is a legal mortgage of a specific asset it will have priority over a floating charge which is equitable. This is so even if the fixed charge is created after the floating charge, with one exception. If the individual taking the fixed charge is aware of a clause in the floating charge prohibiting the creation of any fixed or floating charge ranking before it, the holder of the fixed charge will not rank before the floating charge.

(ii) To a landlord who distrains for rent; that is, if the rent is in arrear the landlord can seize goods on the tenant's premises and sell them.

(iii) To the interests of a judgment creditor; that is, a person obtaining judgment in the Court against the company, and the goods have been seized and sold by the sheriff.

(iv) To preferential debts for wages, taxes and rates.

(v) To owners of goods supplied to the company under a hire purchase agreement.

2 A floating charge created within twelve months of the commencement of the winding up of a company is invalid, unless the company was solvent after creating the charge, except as to the amount of any money paid to the company at or after the time of creating the charge, and in consideration of it (section 322). This is to prevent an insolvent company from creating a floating charge to secure past debts and thereby prejudice its unsecured creditors.

3 Any charge created by a company within six months of winding up is void if it is a fraudulent preference, voluntarily preferring one creditor at the expense of another (section 320).

4 A charge must be registered with the Registrar within twenty-one days of its creation. Failure to register renders the charge void against

the liquidator and any creditor of the company. The holder of such a void charge is relegated to the position of an unsecured creditor (section 95).

Registration of charges

Charges created by a company must be registered in two registers:

At the Companies Registry,
In the company's register of charges.

(a) The Companies Registry

Particulars of charges created by a company must be registered with the Registrar within twenty-one days of creation (section 95). This section relates to, amongst others:

floating charges;
charges on land;
charges on book debts;
charges on uncalled capital;
charges on goodwill, patents and trade marks; and
charges to secure any issue of debentures.

The following particulars must be submitted to the Registrar when a debenture is secured by a charge:

The total amount secured by the whole series.
The date of the resolution authorising the issue.
A general description of the property charged.
The names of the trustees for the debenture holders.

The trust deed must be forwarded with these particulars. If there is no trust deed, one of the debentures in the series must be submitted instead. The Registrar will then issue the company with a certificate of registration of the charge, which is conclusive that all the requirements of registration have been satisfied. A copy of this certificate must be endorsed on every debenture, or debenture stock certificate before it is issued.

If a company does not register such a charge it is void against the liquidator and creditors of the company. The debt is nevertheless valid and is immediately repayable. The debenture holders become unsecured creditors.

If a company purchases property, subject to an existing charge, the charge must be registered within twenty-one days. Failure to do so does not make the charge void.

The Court may extend the time for registration if it is satisfied that it was an accidental omission, or was due to some other sufficient cause, or that it is just and equitable to grant relief and that in so doing no creditor or shareholder would be prejudiced. The Court usually imposes a condition that such a charge will be postponed to any other charge registered in the meantime.

When the debt is paid, or the property subject to the charge is released, the Registrar enters a 'memorandum of satisfaction' on the register. The company is entitled to a copy of this memorandum.

The company's register of charges

Every limited company must keep at its own registered office a register of charges containing particulars of any property of the company that is subject to a charge; the amount of any charge; and the names of the chargees. If there is a trust deed the names of the trustees are entered as chargees.

Failure to register a charge does not affect the validity of the charge, but renders the defaulting officers liable to a fine.

The trust deed

Debentures and debenture stock are often secured by a trust deed, which conveys the company's property to trustees in favour of debenture holders.

Whether a trust deed is appropriate depends on the circumstances of the loan. If the loan is short term (e.g. issued to a bank to secure an overdraft or to the directors of the company) it is generally dispensed with. When debentures are offered for sale to the public in a large scale borrowing, a trust deed is invariably drawn up appointing trustees (e.g. a trust corporation to safeguard the interests of the debenture holders).

A trust deed usually contains provisions dealing with:

(i) The amount and terms of issue of the debentures.
(ii) The date and method of redemption and details of any sinking fund set up by the company to provide for redemption.
(iii) The nature of the charge, which is usually a fixed charge on the land and buildings and a floating charge on the undertaking and assets of the company.
(iv) The powers of the trustees to act if the company defaults in the payment of interest or other major breach of conditions (e.g. to enter into possession and sell, to appoint a receiver or manager).

(v) Covenants for insurance and repair of property by company.
(vi) The remuneration of trustees.
(vii) The exemption of the trustees from liability.
(viii) Meetings of debenture holders. Sometimes a clause is included providing for the modification of rights, if approved by a majority, at a meeting of debenture holders. All debenture holders are then bound.

The appointment of trustees is advantageous to the company and to its debenture holders. A company is able to deal directly with the trustees instead of a number of individual debenture holders. The title deeds and company investments are in the safe custody of the trustees. The trustees may authorise the company to deal with the property charged, thus enabling the company to carry on the business. The trustees may also allow a company to create mortgage of specific assets.

The interests of debenture holders are better served by the employment of a professional trust corporation which acts for the benefit of all the debenture holders. The trustees can ensure that a legal mortgage is created over the company's property so that any charges created at a later date cannot gain priority. This is also accomplished by having custody of the title deeds. The trustees can ensure that the company observes the various covenants contained in the trust deed, for example to repair and insure property. If a company defaults, the trustees may take immediate steps to protect the interests of the debenture holders, as a trust deed usually gives the trustees various powers to sell the property, to appoint a receiver or manager, and to carry on the company's business.

Any provision in a trust deed which exempts a trustee from liability for breach of trust, if he fails to show the required degree of care and diligence, is void. However, the deed may provide that he should be excused in respect of specific acts or omissions, or on ceasing to act, or on his death, if three-quarters in value of the debenture holders so resolve at a meeting called for the purpose (section 88).

Remedies of debenture holder

(a) *If a debenture is not secured by a charge* and the company defaults in the payment of interest or in the repayment of capital, the debenture holder has two remedies only available to him. He is in a similar position to any other trade creditor of the company.

(i) He may sue for the principal and interest that are owed by the company and obtain judgment from the Court. If the company does not pay the judgment debt he may levy execution against the company's property.

(ii)   Alternatively he may petition for the winding up of the company by the Court on the grounds that the company is unable to pay its debts, so that he may prove for his debt in the winding up.

    If the company is already being wound up, he can prove in the winding up for the amount that is owed to him.

(b)   *If a debenture is secured by a charge*, the holder of the debenture is in a far stronger position than an unsecured debenture holder. He may petition for the winding up of the company, but usually the deed creating the charge (i.e. the debenture or the trust deed) contains remedies for enforcing the security without having to seek the Court's aid, such as the power of sale and appointment of a receiver.

The remedies available to the secured debenture holder are:

(i)   *A debenture holder's action*. Any debenture holder may bring an action against the company when the company defaults in the payment of interest or repayment of capital. He sues on behalf of himself and the other debenture holders. The Court usually appoints a receiver (and manager) and either orders a sale of the property or gives permission to apply for a sale of the property.

(ii)   *Valuation of security*. If a company is insolvent and is being wound up, a debenture holder may value his security and prove for the balance of the debt, or he may surrender his security and prove for the whole debt.

(iii)   *Foreclosure*. He may apply to the Court for a foreclosure order. This is rarely applied for, as all the debenture holders must be parties to the action. Its effect would be to vest the title in the property in the debenture holders, free from the company's equity of redemption (i.e. the company's right to repay the loan and recover its property free from the charge).

(iv)   *Sale*. The power to sell the property is usually found in a trust deed and may be exercised without the Court's consent. The power of sale may also be sought in a debenture holder's action where the trust deed or debenture does not give this power. If a debenture is a single debenture, with a charge over the company's assets, it will usually contain an express power of sale, but even in the absence of an express power the holder may be given an implied power of sale under section 103 of the Law of Property Act 1925.

(v)   *Receiver*. The usual remedy is to appoint a receiver. The debenture or trust deed usually provides for the appointment of a receiver. If no such provision exists, application may be made to the Court in a debenture holder's action for such an appointment.

The receiver

A company may not be appointed receiver, nor may an undischarged bankrupt, except by the Court. A receiver is normally an accountant or a member of an accountant's staff.

A receiver appointed by the debenture holders is an agent of the debenture holders and they are liable on his contracts, unless the terms of issue provide otherwise. The debenture or trust instrument usually provides that he is to be the agent of the company. He is entitled to the same indemnity and subject to the same personal liability as a receiver appointed by the Court. He is paid by the debenture holders, but if the company is wound up the Court may review the payments made to the receiver and reduce the amount, if considered excessive. He may apply to the Court for directions in connection with the performance of his duties.

An application may be made to the Court for the appointment of a receiver when:

(i) The principal or interest is in arrear.
(ii) The company is being wound up.
(iii) The security is in jeopardy, that is when there is a risk of the security being seized and used to pay claims which do not rank in priority to the claims of the debenture holders.

In *Re London Pressed Hinge Co. Ltd* the debenture holders had a floating charge on the company's undertaking and sought the appointment of a receiver and manager of the company. Default had not been made in the payment of interest or principal, but a creditor had obtained judgement against the company and was in a position to issue execution. The appointment of a receiver would mean that the debenture holders, to whom nothing was due, would be paid in priority to the creditor who was owed money. It was held that a receiver should be appointed.

A receiver appointed by the Court is an officer of the Court and any interference with him is a contempt of Court. No proceedings may be commenced against him or in respect of the property, without the Court's consent. Since the Court cannot be liable, he is personally liable on any contracts entered into by him, although he is entitled to an indemnity out of the company's assets in priority to the debenture holders.

When a company is being wound up by the Court, the Official Receiver may be appointed receiver.

A manager may be appointed if the debentures give a charge over the 'business' or undertaking of the company. Usually the person appointed as receiver will also act as manager.

He is appointed to sell the business as a going concern and so his term of office will be for a comparatively short period of time.

On the appointment of receiver (and manager):

(i)   The floating charges crystallise and so become fixed.

(ii)   The powers of the directors are suspended.

(iii)   If the receiver is appointed by the Court, the company's employees are automatically dismissed. If appointed by the debenture holders there is no dismissal, unless the business is sold.

(iv)   Other contracts bind the company but not the receiver. He must not refuse to carry out current contracts if such a refusal would injure the company's goodwill.

(v)   Every invoice, order and business letter issued by the company must contain a statement that a receiver has been appointed.

(vi)   Where a receiver or manager of all or substantially all of the company's property is appointed, on behalf of debenture holders secured by a floating charge, he must notify the company forthwith of his appointment. The company must submit a statement of affairs to the receiver within fourteen days of notification.

Within two months of receiving a statement of affairs the receiver must submit the statement, with his comments, to the Registrar and the Court. He must also send a summary of both to the Registrar. He must send the company a copy of his comments, or a notice that he makes no comments. A copy of the summary must also be sent to the debenture holders and to the trustees.

Within two months of each anniversary of his appointment or of ceasing to act, the receiver or manager must submit an abstract of receipts and payments to the Registrar, the debenture holders, and the trustees (section 372).

Where (vi) is not applicable, the receiver or manager if appointed by debenture holders must file with the Registrar a similar abstract at intervals of six months and within one month of ceasing to act (section 374)

Distribution of assets

If a receiver realises the company's assets, and they are insufficient to meet all the company's debts, he must apply them in the following order:

The costs of realising the property.

The costs of the receiver, including his remuneration.

The costs and remuneration of the trustees for the debenture holders.

The costs of the plaintiff in a debenture holder's action.

The claims of the preferential creditors, if the debentures are secured by a floating charge.

Any sums due to debenture holders in respect of principal and interest.

21

Accounts

Every company must keep proper accounting records which will be sufficient to show and explain the company's transactions. They must disclose at any time, with reasonable accuracy, the financial position of the company at that time, and thus enable the directors to ensure that any balance sheet or profit and loss account complies with the Act. The accounts must be prepared in accordance with generally accepted accounting principles. Companies may adopt either historical cost accounting or current cost accounting in the compilation of their accounts.

A company must prepare a balance sheet, profit and loss account, group accounts (if applicable), auditors' report and directors' report. Certain other information must also be given to supplement the balance sheet and profit and loss account. The accounts must be laid before the general meeting and copies of the documents must be delivered to the Registrar within a specified time.

An unlimited company need not file its accounts, or the directors' report, or the auditors' report.

Various exemptions are granted to small and medium-sized companies. A small company need only file an abbreviated version of its balance sheet, and is not required to file a profit and loss account or directors' report. A medium-sized company must file a full balance sheet and directors' report, but only a modified profit and loss account. These companies will have to prepare full accounts for their shareholders.

In particular the accounting records must contain:

(i) Entries from day to day of all money received and expended by the company and the matters in respect of which the receipt and expenditure take place;

(ii)   A record of all the company's assets and liabilities;

(iii)   In the case of a company dealing in goods:

   (a)   Statements of stock held by the company at the end of each financial year;

   (b)   Statements of stocktaking;

   (c)   Statements of all goods purchased and sold (except by way of ordinary retail trade) and the buyers and sellers of these goods.

These records must be kept at the company's registered office or at such other place as the company's directors think fit, and must be open to inspection at all times to the company's officers.

They must be preserved for six years by a public company and for three years by a private company. If a company fails to comply with these requirements any officer of a company in default is guilty of an offence, unless he shows that he acted honestly and that in the circumstances in which the business was carried on the default was excusable.

The balance sheet

The directors of every company must prepare a balance sheet as at the date to which any profit and loss account is made up. It must give a true and fair view of the state of a company's affairs as at the end of its financial year. Companies (other than banking, insurance and shipping companies) must adopt format 1 or 2 in the presentation of their balance sheets. (Most United Kingdom companies will probably adopt format 1, as this closely resembles current United Kingdom practice.)

The formats are as follows:

Format 1

A.   *Called up share capital not paid*

B.   *Fixed assets*

   I   Intangible assets

   1   Development costs

   2   Concessions, patents, licences, trade marks and similar rights and assets

   3   Goodwill

   4   Payments on account

   II   Tangible assets

   1   Land and buildings

   2   Plant and machinery

   3   Fixtures, fittings, tools and equipment

   4   Payments on account and assets in course of construction

 III Investments
  1 Shares in group companies
  2 Loans to group companies
  3 Shares in related companies
  4 Loans to related companies
  5 Other investments other than loans
  6 Other loans
  7 Own shares

C. *Current assets*
 I Stocks
  1 Raw materials and consumables
  2 Work in progress
  3 Finished goods and goods for resale
  4 Payments on account
 II Debtors
  1 Trade debtors
  2 Amounts owed by group companies
  3 Amounts owed by related companies
  4 Other debtors
  5 Called up share capital not paid
  6 Prepayments and accrued income
 III Investments
  1 Shares in group companies
  2 Own shares
  3 Other investments
 IV Cash at bank and in hand

D. *Prepayments and accrued income*

E. *Creditors: amounts falling due within one year*
  1 Debenture loans
  2 Bank loans and overdrafts
  3 Payments received on account
  4 Trade creditors
  5 Bills of exchange payable
  6 Amounts owed to group companies
  7 Amounts owed to related companies
  8 Other creditors including taxation and social security
  9 Accruals and deferred income

F. *Net current assets (liabilities)*

G. *Total assets less current liabilities*

H. *Creditors: amounts falling due after more than one year*
  1 Debenture loans
  2 Bank loans and overdrafts
  3 Payments received on account
  4 Trade creditors

     5   Bills of exchange payable
     6   Amounts owed to group companies
     7   Amounts owed to related companies
     8   Other creditors including taxation and social security
     9   Accruals and deferred income

I.   *Provisions for liabilities and charges*
     1   Pensions and similar obligations
     2   Taxation, including deferred taxation
     3   Other provisions

J.   *Accruals and deferred income*

K. *Capital and reserves*
   I   *Called up share capital*
  II *Share premium account*
 III *Revaluation reserve*
 IV *Other reserves*
     1   Capital redemption reserve
     2   Reserve for own shares
     3   Reserves provided for by the articles of association
     4   Other reserves

  V *Profit and loss account*

Format 2
ASSETS

A. *Called up share capital not paid*

B. *Fixed assets*
   I *Intangible assets*
     1   Development costs
     2   Concessions, patents, licences, trade marks and similar rights and assets
     3   Goodwill
     4   Payments on account
  II *Tangible assets*
     1   Land and buildings
     2   Plant and machinery
     3   Fixtures, fittings, tools and equipment
     4   Payments on account and assets in course of construction
 III *Investments*
     1   Shares in group companies
     2   Loans to group companies
     3   Shares in related companies
     4   Loans to related companies
     5   Other investments other than loans
     6   Other loans
     7   Own shares

C.   *Current assets*
>   I   *Stocks*
>   >   1   Raw materials and consumables
>   >   2   Work in progress
>   >   3   Finished goods and goods for resale
>   >   4   Payments on account
>   II   *Debtors*
>   >   1   Trade debtors
>   >   2   Amounts owed by group companies
>   >   3   Amounts owed by related companies
>   >   4   Other debtors
>   >   5   Called up share capital not paid
>   >   6   Prepayments and accrued income
>   III   *Investments*
>   >   1   Shares in group companies
>   >   2   Own shares
>   >   3   Other investments
>   IV   *Cash at bank and in hand*

D.   *Prepayments and accrued income*

LIABILITIES

A.   *Capital and reserves*
>   I   *Called up share capital*
>   II   *Share premium account*
>   III   *Revaluation reserve*
>   IV   *Other reserves*
>   >   1   Capital redemption reserve
>   >   2   Reserve for own shares
>   >   3   Reserves provided for by the articles of association
>   >   4   Other reserves
>   V   *Profit and loss account*

B.   *Provisions for liabilities and charges*
>   1   Pensions and similar obligations
>   2   Taxation including deferred taxation
>   3   Other provisions

C.   *Creditors*
>   1   Debenture loans
>   2   Bank loans and overdrafts
>   3   Payments received on account
>   4   Trade creditors
>   5   Bills of exchange payable
>   6   Amounts owed to group companies
>   7   Amounts owed to related companies
>   8   Other creditors including taxation and social security
>   9   Accruals and deferred income

D.   *Accruals and deferred income*

The following information is required to supplement the information given in the balance sheet, or is otherwise relevant to assessing the company's affairs in the light of the information so given:

1 The authorised share capital, and the issued share capital (if the company has allotted shares of more than one class).
2 Details of any allotment of shares, or the issue of any debentures during the financial year.
3 Where part of the allotted share capital consists of redeemable shares – the dates of redemption, whether the redemption is optional, and details of any premium due on redemption.
4 Particulars of any shares for which anyone has an option to subscribe.
5 The amount of any fixed cumulative dividends and the period for which they are in arrears.
6 Particulars of valuations of fixed assets and total amounts acquired and disposed of during the financial year.
7 Particulars of any charges on the company's assets on behalf of others.
8 The general nature of contingent liabilities.
9 Future capital expenditure under contract or authorised by the directors.
10 Details of investments.
11 The nature of the reserves and provisions during the year, and the amounts (if any) transferred.
12 The amount set aside for taxation.
13 Details of any creditor's future indebtedness.
14 Details of guarantees and any other financial commitment, entered into by the company on its own behalf or on behalf of its holding company or subsidiary, (which is not included in the balance sheet) which is relevant to assessing the company's state of affairs.

The following documents must be annexed to the balance sheet:

(i) The profit and loss account
(ii) Any group accounts.

The profit and loss account

The directors of a company must prepare a profit and loss account in each accounting reference period of a company. The period in respect of which the account is prepared must be a financial year of the company, and must show the amount of the company's profit or loss on ordinary activities before taxation.

Every profit and loss account of a company shall give a true and fair view of the profit or loss of the company for the financial year, and must show the items listed in one of the four profit and loss formats set out in the Companies Act 1981.

Format 1

1 Turnover
2 Cost of sales
3 Gross profit or loss
4 Distribution costs
5 Administrative expenses
6 Other operating income
7 Income from shares in group companies
8 Income from shares in related companies
9 Income from other fixed asset investments
10 Other interest receivable and similar income
11 Amounts written off investments
12 Interest payable and similar charges
13 Tax on profit or loss on ordinary activities
14 Profit or loss on ordinary activities after taxation
15 Extraordinary income
16 Extraordinary charges
17 Extraordinary profit or loss
18 Tax on extraordinary profit or loss
19 Other taxes not shown under the above items
20 Profit or loss for the financial year

Format 2

1 Turnover
2 Change in stocks of finished goods and in work progress
3 Own work capitalised
4 Other operating income
5 (a) Raw materials and consumables
   (b) Other external charges
6 Staff costs:
   (a) wages and salaries
   (b) social security costs
   (c) other pension costs
7 (a) Depreciation and other amounts written off tangible and intangible fixed assets
   (b) Exceptional amounts written off current assets
8 Other operating charges
9 Income from shares in group companies
10 Income from shares in related companies
11 Income from other fixed asset investments

12 Other interest receivable and similar income
13 Amounts written off investments
14 Interest payable and similar charges
15 Tax on profit or loss on ordinary activities
16 Profit or loss on ordinary activities after taxation
17 Extraordinary income
18 Extraordinary charges
19 Extraordinary profit or loss
20 Tax on extraordinary profit or loss
21 Other taxes not shown under the above items
22 Profit or loss for the financial year

Format 3

A. *Charges*
1 Cost of sales
2 Distribution costs
3 Administrative expenses
4 Amounts written off investments
5 Interest payable and similar charges
6 Tax on profit or loss on ordinary activities
7 Profit or loss on ordinary activities after taxation
8 Extraordinary charges
9 Tax on extraordinary profit or loss
10 Other taxes not shown under the above items
11 Profit or loss for the financial year

B. *Income*
1 Turnover
2 Other operating income
3 Income from shares in group companies
4 Income from shares in related companies
5 Income from other fixed asset investments
6 Other interest receivable and similar income
7 Profit or loss on ordinary activities after taxation
8 Extraordinary income
9 Profit or loss for the financial year

Format 4

A. *Charges*
1 Reduction in stocks of finished goods and in work in progress
2 (a) Raw materials and consumables
   (b) Other external charges
3 Staff costs:
   (a) wages and salaries
   (b) social security costs
   (c) other pension costs

4 (a) Depreciation and other amounts written off tangible and intangible fixed assets
   (b) Exceptional amounts written off current assets
5 Other operating charges
6 Amounts written off investments
7 Interest payable and similar charges
8 Tax on profit or loss on ordinary activities
9 Profit or loss on ordinary activities after taxation
10 Extraordinary charges
11 Tax on extraordinary profit or loss
12 Other taxes not shown under the above items
13 Profit or loss for the financial year

B. *Income*
1 Turnover
2 Increase in stocks of finished goods and in work in progress
3 Own work capitalised
4 Other operating income
5 Income from shares in group companies
6 Income from shares in related companies
7 Income from other fixed asset investments
8 Other interest receivable and similar income
9 Profit or loss on ordinary activities after taxation
10 Extraordinary income
11 Profit or loss for the financial year

Formats 1 and 2 are closest to current United Kingdom practice and it is envisaged that most companies will adopt either of these formats, with most large companies adopting format 1, and most small companies choosing format 2.

In addition, every profit and loss account must show separately as additional items:

(a) Any amount to be carried or proposed to be carried to the reserves, or withdrawn or proposed to be withdrawn from reserves.
(b) The aggregate amount of any dividends paid and proposed.

The following information is required either to supplement the information given in the profit and loss account, or to provide particulars of income or expenditure or of the circumstances of the items shown in the profit and loss account:

1 The amount of the interest on loans made to the company, including long term loans, bank loans and overdrafts.
2 The amount provided for the redemption of the share capital or loans.

3   The amount of income from listed investments.
4   The amount of rent received from land (if material).
5   The amount paid for hire of plant and machinery.
6   The amount of the auditor's remuneration.
7   The basis on which the charge for corporation tax is computed and the amount of the charge.
8   If the company has carried on two or more classes of business which in the directors' opinion differs substantially from each other, a statement of:
  (i)   the proportions in which the turnover for that year is divided amongst these classes:
  (ii) the extent to which the carrying on of the business of that class contributed to or restricted the profit or loss of the company for that year, before taxation.
9   Particulars of turnover where the company has supplied different markets during the course of the year.
10 The average number of persons employed by the company in each week in the year and the aggregate remuneration paid to them in the year.
11 Details of any extraordinary income or charges arising in the financial year.
12 The effect of any transactions that are exceptional by virtue of size or incidence, although within the company's ordinary activities.

Group accounts

The contents of the balance sheet and profit and loss account will vary according to whether the company is an ordinary company with normal shareholders or whether it is a holding or a subsidiary company.

Where a company has subsidiaries it must prepare, at the end of its financial year, group accounts dealing with the state of affairs and profit or loss of the company and its subsidiaries. The group accounts must give a true and fair view of the state of affairs and profit and loss of the company and its subsidiaries so far as it concerns members of the company.

Group accounts will normally be prepared as consolidated accounts, comprising a consolidated balance sheet and a consolidated profit and loss account of the company and its subsidiaries.

Where the group accounts are not prepared as consolidated accounts, they must give the same or equivalent information as consolidated accounts. The financial year of each subsidiary should normally coincide with that of the holding company, but where it does not the group accounts must deal with that subsidiary's state of affairs as at the end of the financial year, ending with the last before that of the holding company, and with the subsidiary's profit or loss for that financial year (section 152 as amended by the Companies Act 1981).

Group accounts may be prepared in accordance with the exemptions granted to small and medium-sized companies, if the group satisfies the criteria laid down for these companies.

A holding company must deliver full individual accounts, if its group accounts do not qualify for exemption. If the holding company's accounts permit it to be treated as a small company, but its group accounts qualify the group to be treated as a medium-sized company, it must submit its accounts as a medium-sized company.

Group accounts are not necessary if:
  (i)   The holding company is a wholly owned subsidiary of another company; or
 (ii)   if the directors are of the opinion that such accounts would be impracticable, or of no real value in view of the insignificant amounts involved or expenses or delay to the members; or
(iii)   the result would be misleading, or harmful to the business of the company or its subsidiaries; or
(iv)   the business of the holding company and that of its subsidiaries are so different that they cannot reasonably be treated as a single undertaking.

The approval of the Department of Trade is required for not dealing with group accounts in (iii) and (iv).

Additional information to be given in the accounts

1   A statement of the aggregate amount of the following:

  (a)   directors' emoluments;
  (b)   directors' or past directors' pensions;
  (c)   compensation paid to directors or past directors for loss of office.

2   The chairman's emoluments.
3   The emoluments of the highest paid director, if greater than those of the chairman's.
4   The number of directors who received no emoluments.
5   A scale dividing directors' emoluments into bands of £5000 showing the number of directors whose emoluments fell within each band.

(The disclosure of items 2–5 is only required if item 1 exceeds £40000.)

6   The number of directors who waived the right to receive emoluments.

7   The number of employees who received salaries in excess of £20000 divided into bands of £5000, commencing at £20000.

8   Where particulars of directors' emoluments or employees' salaries are shown, the corresponding amounts for the previous year.

9   (a)   Any loan, quasi loan or credit transaction or arrangement, made by a public company with its directors, or directors of its holding company or persons connected with directors. Disclosure is not required if the aggregate amount does not exceed £5000.

(A credit transaction involves the supply or lease of goods, services or land on deferred terms.)

     (b)   Any agreement to enter into such a transaction or arrangement.

     (c)   Any other transaction or arrangement with the company and its subsidiary in which a director of the company or its holding company has a material interest, e.g. property transactions, consultancy agreements. Disclosure is not required if the aggregate amount does not exceed £1000 or in a company whose assets are £100000–£500000 and the aggregate amount does not exceed 1 per cent of the company's net assets (Companies Act 1980, section 54).

10   Any loans, quasi loans, or credit transactions or arrangements made by a company with its officers (other than its directors) which are in excess of £2500 (Companies Act 1980, section 57).

11   Where the company has subsidiaries, the names of the subsidiaries, the country of incorporation, particulars of the shares of the subsidiary held by the company, the aggregate amount of the capital and reserves of the subsidiaries, and the amount of their profit or loss.

12   Where the company is a subsidiary, the name and country of incorporation of its holding company.

13   Where a company holds 20 per cent of the allotted share capital of another company, it must state the aggregate amount of the capital and reserves of that company and must provide the amount of the profit or loss of that company.

14   Where the company holds 10 per cent of the allotted share capital of another company which is not a subsidiary, particulars of these

shares and the identity and place of incorporation of such a company.

The auditors' report

The auditors of a company must make a report to the members on the accounts examined by them, and on every balance sheet, every profit and loss account and all group accounts of which a copy is laid before the company in general meeting during their tenure of office.

The auditors' report shall be read before the company in general meeting and must be open to inspection by any member. The report must state whether, in the auditors' opinion, the balance sheet and profit and loss account and (if it is a holding company submitting group accounts) the group accounts have been properly prepared in accordance with the provisions of the Companies Acts 1948 to 1981. They must also consider whether the information given in the directors' report relating to the financial year is consistent with the accounts. If they do not consider it so, they must state that fact.

The report must also state whether in their opinion a true and fair view is given:

(a)   In the case of the balance sheet, of the state of the company's affairs as at the end of its financial year;

(b)   In the case of the profit and loss account (if not framed as a consolidated profit and loss account), of the company's profit or loss for its financial year;

(c)   In the case of group accounts submitted by a holding company, of the state of affairs and profit or loss of the company and its subsidiaries.

It is the auditors' duty in preparing the report to carry out such investigations as will enable them to form an opinion as to whether:

(i)   Proper accounting records have been kept by the company and proper returns adequate for their audit have been received from branches not visited by them; and

(ii)   The company's balance sheet and (if not framed as a consolidated profit and loss account) profit and loss accounts are in agreement with the accounting records and returns.

If the auditors are of the opinion that (i) and (ii) have not been complied with they must state that fact in their report.

If the auditors fail to obtain all the information and explanations which, to the best of their knowledge and belief, are necessary for their audit, they must also state that fact in their report.

If the directors do not disclose any loan, quasi loan, credit transaction or arrangement made between themselves with the company as required by the Companies Act 1980, the auditors must include in their report (as far as they are able to do so) a statement giving these particulars.

Directors' report

Every company must attach to the balance sheet a report by its directors which must give:

1 A fair review of the development of the company's business and those of its subsidiaries during the financial year.
2 The names of the persons who at any time during the financial year were directors of the company.
3 The principal activities of the company and its subsidiaries in the course of the financial year, and any significant change in the activities.
4 Particulars of any important events affecting the company or any of its subsidiaries which have occurred since the end of that financial year.
5 An indication of likely future developments in the business of the company and of its subsidiaries.
6 An indication of the activities (if any) of the company and its subsidiaries in the field of research and development.
7 Any significant change in the fixed assets of the company or its subsidiaries.
8 The extent of a directors' shareholding or acquisition of debentures in the company at the end of the financial year, according to the register of director shareholding.
9 Information regarding health, safety and welfare provisions in respect of the company's employees.
10 If a company has 250 or more employees, a statement as to the company's policy for employment, training, career development and the promotion of disabled persons.
11 Particulars of contributions exceeding £200 given for political or charitable purposes.
12 Particulars of the acquisitions by a company (or its nominee) of its own shares.

Every member of the company, every debenture holder and any other person who is entitled to receive notices of general meetings of a company, must be sent a copy of the directors' report.

A company which has not entered into any significant accounting transaction during the relevant period (i.e. a dormant company) is not required to appoint an auditor. The accounts, however, must contain a director's declaration that the company was dormant throughout the financial year. This concession is only applicable if the company is eligible to be treated as a small company.

22

The Auditor and the Company Secretary

The auditor

Appointment

The articles usually provide for the appointment of an auditor and the auditing of a company's accounts. The first auditor of a newly created company may be appointed by the directors. Unless removed mid-term he will hold office until the conclusion of the first general meeting of the company, before which annual accounts are laid. If the directors fail to appoint the first auditor, the general meeting may do so.

Every company (except a dormant company) must, at every general meeting of the company at which accounts are laid, appoint an auditor to hold office from the end of that meeting until the end of the next general meeting at which accounts are laid. A retiring auditor may be re-appointed, but only if a resolution is passed for his re-appointment.

If the meeting fails to appoint an auditor, the Department of Trade may appoint an auditor on the company's behalf.

Special notice must be given of a resolution to appoint anyone other than a retiring auditor. The company must then notify the retiring auditor of the proposal. He may make representations to the company in writing and request that the company notify these representations to each member. The company must then send notice of the resolution to the members, accompanied by the auditor's representations. If the company does not send a copy of the representations to the members, the auditor may request that they be read out at the meeting.

Qualifications

An auditor must be qualified in one of the following ways. He must be either:

(a)   A member of a recognised body of accountants, or
(b)   Authorised by the Department of Trade as having similar quali-
      fications obtained outside the United Kingdom, or as having
      adequate knowledge and experience, or
(c)   Authorised by the Department to act as the auditor of certain
      types of companies as he was as an auditor in 1966.

The following may not act as an auditor of a company:

(i)   An officer or servant of the company, for example any director,
       manager or secretary;
(ii)   Any partner, or person in the employment of an officer or
       servant of the company;
(iii) Any body corporate;
(iv)   The officer or servant, or the partner, or the employee of the
       officer or servant of a related company.

Duties of an auditor

Lord Denning, in *Fomento (Sterling Area) Ltd v. Selsdon Fountain
Pen Co. Ltd*, observed that: 'An auditor is not to be confused to the
mechanics of checking vouchers and making arithmetical computa-
tions. He is not to be written off as a professional "adder-upper and
subtractor". His vital task is to take care to see that errors are not
made, be they errors of computation, or errors of commission or
downright untruths. To perform this task properly, he must come to it
with an enquiring mind – not suspicious of dishonesty, I agree – but
suspecting that someone may have made a mistake somewhere and
that a check must be made to ensure that there has been none.'

He has a right of access at all times to the company's books, accounts
and vouchers and is entitled to require from the officers of the
company such information and explanation as he thinks necessary for
the performance of his duties.

1   His principal duty is to make a report to the members on the
accounts examined by him and on every balance sheet, profit and loss
account and all group accounts laid before the company during his
tenure of office. The report must state whether in his opinion the
balance sheet, profit and loss, and (if applicable) group accounts have
been properly prepared in accordance with the provisions of the
Companies Acts.

The auditor must also state whether proper returns have been kept
by the company; whether the accounts are in agreement with the
accounting records and returns; whether he has obtained all the
information and explanations necessary for the purposes of the audit.

The report must be annexed to the balance sheet and must be read before the company in the general meeting. It must also be open to inspection by any member. The auditor fulfils his duty to members by sending his report to the company secretary. He is not responsible if the report is not placed before the members.

An auditor is also required to append a report to a statutory declaration made by the directors of a company which proposes to purchase its own shares out of capital, or to give financial assistance for the acquisition of its shares. The auditors must endorse the directors' opinion as to the company's ability to meet its financial obligations after adopting either of these courses, and must state that having inquired into the company's affairs they are not aware of any matter which would render the directors' opinion unreasonable in the circumstances.

2   It is also his duty to ascertain the company's true financial position as shown by the company's books. He is not responsible for matters that are concealed from him, but if there are suspicious circumstances he must fully investigate them.

In *Re Thomas Gerrard and Son Ltd*, the managing director had falsified the accounts in various ways. The auditors noticed that invoices had been altered, but failed to investigate the matter further and gave a favourable view of the company's profits. It was held they were liable for the dividends and tax that had been paid by the company as a result of their negligence.

In *Re London and General Bank*, the greater part of the capital of the bank was advanced to companies and a few select customers upon securities which were insufficient and difficult to realise. The auditors pointed this out to the directors in a confidential report, but their report to the shareholders merely stated that the value of the assets was dependent on realisation. As a result of this, dividends were declared which were in effect paid out of capital. It was held that the auditors had failed in their duty to ascertain the true financial position of the company, by not reporting to the shareholders, and were liable to make good the dividend declared.

The auditor must not confine himself to checking the mere arithmetical calculations, but must ensure that the books show the correct financial position. He is not responsible for tracking ingenious and skilful schemes of fraud when there is nothing to arouse his suspicion.

3   He must satisfy himself that the company's securities exist and are in safe custody. This should be done by personal inspection, but if the securities are in the possession of a trustworthy individual who normally holds securities in the ordinary course of business, a certificate given by such a person that they are in his custody is sufficient. In *Re*

Kingston Cotton Mill, an auditor accepted the certificate of the company's manager as to the value of the company's stock in trade. As a result dividends were paid out of capital. It was held that the auditor was not liable, as he was entitled to rely on the manager's certificate.

It is not part of an auditor's duties to take stock, but if he forms the opinion that the stock is overvalued he should report this to the shareholders. It is generally accepted that an auditor should carry out a check on some sample items in the audit.

4   An auditor may have to value a company's shares, as the articles of a private company often contain pre-emption clauses (e.g. a member selling his shares must first offer them to the existing members at a price to be determined by the auditor). An auditor need not give the reasons for his valuation, and the burden of proving that it is unfair or improper lies on the person objecting to it. It can only be challenged by showing that the auditor made a fundamental mistake; or materially misdirected himself in the course of his valuation, for example by making a serious computational error; or that he was negligent in his valuation. Where a company is in a poor financial condition he may rightly value the shares on the basis of the break up value of the company. If the shares concerned constitute a controlling block he need not value the shares on the basis of the control of the company, if there is no reason to assume that the shares will be purchased as one block.

In *Arenson v. Arenson*, it was held that an auditor owes a duty of care to a shareholder when valuing shares. Arenson, the controlling shareholder and chairman of a private company, took his nephew into the business and gave him a parcel of shares in the company. The nephew agreed that in the event of terminating his employment with the company he would sell his shares to his uncle at their 'fair value' that is the value of the shares as determined by the auditors 'acting as experts and not as arbitrators'. His employment ceased in 1970 and he transferred the shares to his uncle for £4916 – the auditors' valuation. A few months later the company 'went public', and the shares were seen to be worth six times that amount. It was held that the auditors had been negligent in their valuation.

Liability of an auditor

If an auditor fails to discharge his duties he is liable to a company for any loss resulting from his negligence or default. Any provision in the company's articles or in any contract with a company exempting him from liability, is void.

A company may indemnify him against any liability incurred by him in defending any civil or criminal proceedings in which judgment is given in his favour, or in which he is acquitted, or in which relief is granted by the Court under section 448 or section 36 of the Companies Act 1980.

Removal and resignation

Although an auditor is appointed to hold office until the next general meeting at which accounts are to be presented, a company may at a general meeting pass an ordinary resolution removing an auditor before the expiration of his term of office, notwithstanding the terms of his contract with the company. An auditor who is removed in this manner may be entitled to compensation for loss of his position as auditor, or for the loss of any other office with the company he held as a result of being its auditor, and which he also loses on his removal. The Act specifically reserves this right. Whether such compensation is payable, and its assessment, will depend on the terms of the auditor's contract with the company and his ability, if any, to mitigate the loss.

An auditor may resign his appointment by depositing written notice to that effect at the company's registered office. His resignation will take effect on the date of the notice or on such later date as the notice specifies. The auditor's notice will not take effect unless it contains a statement that there are no circumstances connected with his resignation which he considers should be brought to the attention of the company's members or creditors; or if there are any such circumstances, a statement of them.

Where an auditor's notice of resignation contains a statement that there are circumstances which should be brought to the attention of the members or creditors, he may deposit a requisition with the company calling on the directors to convene an extraordinary general meeting to consider these matters. The directors must comply with his request.

He is also entitled to receive notice to attend any general meeting at which it is proposed to fill the vacancy caused by his resignation, or at which his term of office would have otherwise expired. He may there speak on any part of the business of the meeting which concerns him as the company's former auditor.

The secretary

Appointment

Every company must have a secretary, but a sole director cannot be secretary. The secretary may be another company, but a company may not be the secretary if its sole director is also the sole director of the company (sections 177, 178).

Qualifications

The 1980 Companies Act (section 79) requires the secretary of a public company to have the requisite knowledge and experience to discharge the functions of secretary of the company. The qualifications laid down are that he should be a person who:

(a) On the appointed day held the office of secretary or assistant or deputy secretary of the company; or

(b) For at least three of the five years immediately preceding his appointment as secretary held the office of secretary of a company other than a private company; or

(c) Is a member of one of the following bodies: The Institute of Chartered Accountants in England and Wales; The Institute of Chartered Accountants of Scotland; The Association of Certified Accountants; The Institute of Chartered Accountants in Ireland; The Institute of Chartered Secretaries and Administrators; The Institute of Cost and Management Accountants; The Chartered Institute of Public Finance and Accountancy; or

(d) Is a barrister, advocate or solicitor called or admitted in any part of the United Kingdom; or

(e) Is a person who, by virtue of his holding or having held any other position or his being a member of any other body, appears to the directors to be capable of discharging those functions.

Duties

A secretary's duties vary with the size of the company and his terms of employment with a company. He is an officer of the company and as such is liable to penalties if he fails to comply with certain requirements of the Act.

Until recently it was thought that a secretary had a very 'humble role' to play in a company's activities (*Whitechurch v. Cavanagh*). However, in *Panorama Developments (Guildford) Ltd v. Fidelis Furnishing Fabrics Ltd*, it was held that 'times have changed'. Lord Denning stated that: 'A company secretary is a much more important person than he was in 1887.' (In *Barnett, Hoares and Co. v. South London Tramway Co.*, it was stated that 'He (the secretary) is a mere servant . . . no one can assume he has any authority'.) He is an officer of the company with extensive duties and responsibilities. This appears not only in the modern Companies Acts, but also by the role which he plays in the day-to-day business of companies. He is no longer a mere clerk. He regularly makes representations on behalf of the company and enters into contracts on its behalf which come within the day-to-day running of the company's business. So much so that he may be regarded as held out as having authority to do such things on behalf of the company. He is certainly entitled to sign contracts connected with the administrative side of a company's affairs, such as employing staff, and ordering cars, and so forth. All such matters now come within the ostensible authority of a company's secretary.'

In this particular case, Bayne, the company secretary of Fidelis Furnishing Fabrics Ltd, ordered cars from Panorama Developments, ostensibly for business purposes. He told the car hire firm that the cars were required to carry important customers of the firm. Bayne wrote on the company's paper ordering the cars and signed himself 'Company Secretary'. He gave references for the company which showed that the company was of good standing. The car firm sent hiring agreements naming Bayne as the hirer. Bayne used the cars himself. It was held that the Fidelis Furnishing Fabrics were liable for the hire of the cars as Bayne had ostensible authority to enter into contracts for the hire of cars.

Certain statutory duties are imposed upon a secretary, for example his signature is required on the Annual Return, and he must also certify any copy of the accounts sent with the Annual Return. His other duties include the maintenance of the company's registers, dealing with share transfers and the issue of share certificates, registration of charges, preparation of returns, preparation of notices and agendas for meetings and subsequent action after meetings.

23

Compulsory Liquidation

A company's existence can only be terminated if it is struck off the register as a defunct company, or it is dissolved as a result of winding up proceedings. A company may be wound up in one of three ways: by the Court making a winding up order; by the members passing a resolution for voluntary winding up; or by a voluntary winding up being continued subject to the supervision of the Court.

Striking off the register

If the Registrar has reason to believe that a company is not carrying on business or is not in operation he may send a letter of inquiry to the company. If no reply is received within one month, he may send a registered letter to the company stating that unless an answer is received to the second letter within one month, a notice will be published in the *London Gazette* with a view to having the company struck off the register. If he receives no answer within one month after sending the second letter, or if he is informed by the company that it is no longer carrying on a business, he may publish in the *London Gazette* a notice that, unless cause is shown to the contrary, the company will be struck off the register and dissolved within three months (section 353).

Similar notices may be sent by the Registrar if the company is in liquidation and he has reasonable cause to believe that the liquidator is no longer acting; or if he has reason to believe that the company's affairs have been fully wound up, but the liquidator has failed to submit the returns required by the Act.

This is a simple and relatively inexpensive method of dissolving a company. It does, however, deprive creditors and members of the safeguards provided for by the normal procedures of winding up, and the Act makes certain provisions for this type of dissolution. The liability of every director, officer of the company and member shall continue as if the company had not been dissolved, and the Court can wind up a company despite the fact that the company has been struck off the register. Any property of the company, including land, which remains after its dissolution becomes vested in the Crown (or the Duchy of Cornwall or the Duchy of Lancaster) as *bona vacantia*.

The Court may also within twenty years of the dissolution, order a company to be restored to the register on the application of a company or any member or creditor. Any property which had vested in the Crown (or Duchies of Cornwall or Lancaster) may be sold by the Crown, even though orders reviving the company have been made, provided the Crown pays the company an amount equal to the amount received by it for the sale of the property. This provision deals with the situation where a company was carrying on business when it was struck off, and also allows a company to be revived to take advantage of any monies or assets that subsequently come to light (section 353). In *Re Vickers and Bott*, a company was restored to the register to enable it to take advantage of £700 that became payable to the company as a result of a dividend being declared in the bankruptcy of a debtor.

Winding up by the Court

An order for the compulsory winding up of a company is obtained by presenting a petition to the appropriate Court. The petition must contain the company's name, the date of its incorporation, the amount of its nominal and paid up capital, the company's objects, and the grounds on which the petition is made. It concludes with the prayer 'that the company may be wound up by the Court under the provisions of the Companies Act 1948'.

The petition is normally initiated in the County Court if the company's paid up share capital does not exceed £120 000, otherwise the petition will be heard in the Companies Court.

A copy of the petition must be served on the company, and at least seven days before the petition is heard it must be advertised in the *London Gazette* and in one local newspaper.

The petitioners
The petition may be presented by the company itself. Such a petition is rare as it is far quicker and convenient and less expensive to pass a special resolution to wind up voluntarily. If the company passes an

ordinary resolution that it should be wound up by the Court, the directors may present a petition for a winding up order.

A creditor may petition for a compulsory winding up whatever the amount of his debt, whether his debt is secured or unsecured, and whether payable immediately or at some future date or time. An order will not be made if the debt is less than £200, unless the petitioner is able to join with other creditors and their total debts exceed £200. Should the company appear to have a substantial defence, no order will be made. It is advisable for a creditor to obtain judgement on a debt before presenting such a petition. Should a creditor satisfy these conditions the Court may nevertheless pay regard to the wishes of the other creditors, and if the majority in value of creditors object with good reason to a winding up order, the Court has a discretion to refuse the order. If the debt is disputed on some substantial grounds, the creditor cannot generally obtain a winding up order.

Any contributory may petition for winding up if the number of members has fallen below the statutory minimum, or if the shares were originally allotted to him, or have been held by him for at least six out of the last eighteen months, or have devolved on him through the death of a former holder.

A contributory in this context not only includes 'every person who is liable to contribute to the assets of the company in the event of its being wound up', that is the holders of partly paid up shares and those who were the holders of such shares in the last twelve months, but also the holders of fully paid shares and persons who ceased to be members more than a year before the commencement of the winding up.

The Court will only make an order on the petition of a contributory if he has an interest which can only be protected by winding up the company. A holder of partly paid up shares, a member of an unlimited company, a member of a guarantee company – all of these would have an interest in preventing a company from incurring further debts towards which they would have to contribute. If a company is insolvent, or is a guarantee company, the contributory is entitled as of right to a winding up order, but in other cases the Court has a discretion whether to make an order.

The Official Receiver may also petition for a winding up order where the company is already being wound up voluntarily, or under the supervision of the Court. An order will only be made if the Court is satisfied that the existing winding up cannot be continued with due regard to the interests of the creditors or contributories. In *Re Ryder Installations*, the liquidator had on five occasions failed to submit reports to the Registrar. His accounts, when audited, were unsatisfactory. It was held that the Official Receiver's petition should be granted.

The Department of Trade may present a petition for winding up if, as a result of information or documents obtained from an inspection of the company's books or papers or from an inspector's report, it appears to be in the public interest that the company should be wound up.

The Attorney General may also petition in the case of a company which has been formed for a charitable purpose.

The grounds for winding up

A company may be wound up by the Court if one or several of the following grounds exist (section 222):

(i) The company has passed a special resolution that it should be wound up by the Court.

(ii) As an 'old' public company it has failed to re-register under the provisions of the Companies Act 1980 (Companies Act 1980).

(iii) The company does not commence business within a year of its incorporation, or suspends its business for a year.

If there are prospects of commencing business in the future and the majority of members do not wish the company to be wound up the Court will not grant the order. In *Re Middlesbrough Assembly Rooms Co*, the company suspended building operations for three years during a trade recession. It intended to resume operations as soon as trading prospects improved. The petition was opposed by 80 per cent of the shareholders and it was held that it should be dismissed.

(iv) The number of members is reduced below two.

(v) The company is unable to pay its debts. This is the most common ground for a petition. As it would be extremely difficult for a petitioner who had no access to a company's books to prove that a company is unable to pay its debts, a presumption of inability arises in the following circumstances:

(a) A creditor, to whom the company owes £200 or more, has served on the company a demand for payment, and the company has for three weeks thereafter neglected to pay the sum or compound for it to the reasonable satisfaction of the creditor.

(b) An execution or judgment remains unsatisfied.

(c) If it is proved to the Court's satisfaction that the company is unable to pay its debts, taking into account its contingent and prospective liabilities, as well as the debts which are immediately payable.

(vi)   If the Court is of the opinion that it is just and equitable that the company should be wound up.

If a petition is presented on this ground, the Court may grant relief to the petitioner by some other means (e.g. section 75 of the Companies Act 1980 provides an alternative remedy for an oppressed minority on the grounds of unfair prejudice).

There are numerous instances of companies being wound up under this provision.

In *Re German Date Coffee Co*, it was held that the company should be wound up as the sub-stratum of the company had gone. The company was formed to work a German patent to extract coffee from dates. It never obtained this patent, but purchased a Swedish patent, and successfully manufactured coffee in this way. It was held that the company should be wound up as it was formed basically to work a German patent in Germany.

In *Re T. E. Brinsmead and Sons Ltd*, it was held that as the company's objects were illegal it should be wound up. The company was formed to trade on the goodwill of a similarly named company. It had no capital of its own and was hopelessly embarrassed by numerous actions brought by its shareholders on the grounds of fraud.

In *Re Yenidje Tobacco Company Ltd*, it was held that as there was deadlock in the company's affairs, the only course open to the Court was to wind up the company. The company's two director shareholders held equal voting power and were not on speaking terms due to a disagreement. Despite the fact that substantial profits were being made by the company, it was wound up.

In *Loch v. John Blackwood Ltd*, a company was wound up because of mismanagement in its conduct towards its minority shareholders. The company was formed to carry on John Blackwood's business and to divide the profits amongst the members of his family. The managing director was the majority shareholder. He omitted to hold meetings and failed to submit accounts or recommend a dividend. His purpose was to keep the shareholders in ignorance of the company's affairs so as to acquire their shares at an undervaluation.

The petition and its effect
The petition is heard in open court and the evidence consists of affidavits filed in support of and against the petition, unless the Court allows oral evidence to be given.

The Court may dismiss the petition, or adjourn the hearing, or make an interim order (e.g. adjourning the hearing and appointing a provisional liquidator), or make any other order that may be just.

A provisional liquidator is often appointed before the hearing in cases where there is likely to be a lengthy period of time between the presentation of the petition and the hearing, in order to preserve the company's assets.

If a winding up order is made, the Official Receiver becomes the provisional liquidator and continues to act in this capacity until he or another person is appointed liquidator. The Official Receiver in this context is one of the Official Receivers attached to the Bankruptcy Court. The Court has the power to appoint another officer to act as Official Receiver in the winding up of a particular company.

The Court usually limits the provisional liquidator's powers to taking possession of the company's assets and protecting them. In *Re Union Accident Insurance Co. Ltd*, it was held that a provisional liquidator was entitled to terminate loss-making contracts, for by doing so he was preserving the company's assets for the benefit of its creditors and shareholders. He can apply to the Court for the appointment of a special manager to manage the company's business.

On the appointment of a liquidator the powers of the directors cease and the company's employees are dismissed. No action can be commenced, or proceeded with, against the company except by leave of the Court. All dispositions of the company's property and executions on the company's property are void. There can be no transfer of shares or alteration in the status of any member without leave of the Court.

The statement of affairs
Within fourteen days of the Court making a winding up order, or appointing a provisional liquidator, the Company must deliver to the Official Receiver a statement of its financial affairs. This gives particulars of the company's assets, debts and liabilities, its creditors, the securities held by them and the dates when such securities were given, and any further information which the Official Receiver may require. This statement must be verified by affidavit by one or more of the directors and the secretary of the company.

Official Receiver's report
As soon as possible after receiving the statement of affairs, the Official Receiver submits a preliminary report to the Court on the company's affairs, the causes of failure and whether any further inquiry is desirable into the company's promotion, formation, failure or the conduct of its business. The Official Receiver may make a further report and if he states that in his opinion fraud has been committed, the Court may order the public examination of the individual(s) referred to.

The Court may also examine on oath, in private, any officer of the company or person known or suspected to have in his possession any property of the company or supposed to be indebted to the company, or any person thought by the Court to be capable of giving any information relating to the company's affairs or property.

Meetings of creditors and contributories

The Official Receiver must also summon separate meetings of the creditors and contributories. These meetings decide whether an application should be made to the Court for the appointment of a liquidator in place of the Official Receiver, and if so, whether to appoint a committee of inspection to act with the liquidator. If the meetings fail to decide upon an appointment, it may be made by the Court.

Committee of inspection

The committee of inspection consists of creditors and contributories and its function is to assist the liquidator and to supervise his activities. It acts by a majority and meets at least once a month, or at such times as the committee may determine. The liquidator or any member may summon a meeting. No member of the Committee may purchase the company's assets either directly or indirectly, or profit in any way out of the winding up transactions.

The liquidator

If a liquidator is appointed by the Court, he must notify the Registrar of his appointment and give security to the satisfaction of the Department of Trade. The Official Receiver then hands over the company's property and books to the liquidator. Such a liquidator's remuneration is determined by the Court.

The liquidator's powers and duties

A liquidator is usually an accountant of at least five years' standing. His duties are to collect and realise the company's assets, to settle a list of contributories and creditors, to pay the company's debts and liabilities, and to divide the surplus (if any) among the members of the company in accordance with their rights.

In order to achieve this, he may sell and transfer the company's property and borrow money on its security. He may also execute any documents in the name of the company; appoint an agent to undertake business which he is unable to do himself; prove in the bankruptcy of a contributory; take out letters of administration to the estate of a deceased contributory; and do anything necessary for winding up the company's affairs and distributing its assets.

With the sanction of the Court or of the committee of inspection, he can also bring and defend actions on the company's behalf, carry on the company's business, appoint a solicitor, pay any class of creditors in full and compromise with creditors, contributories and debtors.

He therefore takes custody or control of all the property to which the company is or appears to be entitled. This consists of property belonging to the company at the commencement of the winding up; property against which execution and attachment has been commenced but not completed before the commencement of the winding up; and any property used by the company to give fraudulent preference to any of its creditors.

Fraudulent preference

A fraudulent preference is any transaction made by the company, preferring one creditor to the detriment of the other creditor(s), within six months of the commencement of winding up, when the company was unable to meet its debts as they became due. In *Re M. Kushler Ltd*, a director of a company personally guaranteed the company's overdraft with a bank. When he realised that the company was insolvent, he arranged for the company to make payments to the bank which extinguished the company's overdraft and his personal liability. Other creditors who were pressing for payment received nothing. It was held that it was a fraudulent preference, and the money paid to the bank must be returned to the liquidator.

Any conveyance or assignment of the company's property to trustees for the benefit of all its creditors is also deemed a fraudulent preference. Such a transfer would only benefit the creditors and would be detrimental to the interests of other interested parties, such as the shareholders.

The liquidator will also require payment by the contributories of the amount, if any, uncalled on their shares. A contributory is any person liable to contribute to the assets of the company in the event of its being wound up.

In a company limited by shares, a member holding partly paid up shares is liable for the amount which remains unpaid on his share and is placed on the 'A' list of contributories. A past member, who was a member within a year of the commencement of winding up, is placed on the 'B' list. Such a member is only liable where the existing holder of the shares fails to pay the amount due. The 'B' list is only prepared if it appears that the present members are unable to meet the calls made on them. The liability of a past member only extends to the debts incurred by the company while he was still a member.

A member of a company limited by guarantee is liable to the extent of his guarantee. If the company has a share capital he is also liable for the amount which remains unpaid on his shares. The liability of past members is similar to that of past members of companies limited by shares. A member of an unlimited company is liable to contribute to the company's assets in proportion to his interest in the company.

The liquidator informs each contributory of the amount of his liability and appoints a day for hearing any objections. A contributory has a further right to appeal to the Court. Before the liquidator makes a formal call, he must obtain the consent of the committee of inspection, or if there is no committee, the Court.

A liquidator may be able to augment the company's assets by avoiding certain liabilities and by receiving compensation from individuals who have been guilty of fraudulent trading or misfeasance.

A floating charge created by a company within twelve months of winding up is invalid, unless it can be proved that the company was solvent immediately after creating the charge. Any cash paid to the company on, or subsequent to, the creation of the charge and in consideration of the charge is binding on the liquidator.

A liquidator may also with leave of the Court disclaim onerous property in those instances where certain assets of the Company are found to be a liability and burdened by onerous covenants, for example shares or stocks in other companies, unprofitable contracts and property not easily saleable as the possessor has to perform some onerous act or pay money. All these may be disclaimed within twelve months of the commencement of winding up, or of the liquidator becoming aware of their existence.

If any person suffers financial loss as a result of a disclaimer he may prove in the winding up for the extent of the loss.

If, in the course of a winding up, it appears that a company's business has been carried on with the intention of defrauding creditors, or for any other fraudulent purpose, the Court may declare that the individuals responsible, usually the directors, shall be personally liable for all or any of the company's debts. In *Re Leitch*, a company continued trading and incurring debts when the directors knew that there was no reasonable prospect of the creditors ever being paid. It was held that the business of the company was being carried on with intent to defraud.

Application may also be made to the Court if in the course of the winding up it appears that a promotor, director, liquidator or officer of the company has misapplied or retained property of the company or has been guilty of misfeasance, that is a breach of duty involving the misapplication of a company's assets. Examples of misfeasance are where directors sold their own property to the company or used a company's property to make a profit for themselves, and where an auditor sanctioned the payment of dividends out of capital.

The liquidator must keep a record book of all the minutes and resolutions of the meetings of creditors, contributories and the committee of inspection. He must also keep a cash book showing all receipts and payments. This must be submitted to the committee of inspection for audit every three months. If a company carries on in business, a trading account must be kept which is submitted for audit to the committee of inspection every month.

All money received by the liquidator on account of the company must be paid into the Insolvency Services Account at the Bank of England, unless, upon the recommendation of the committee of inspection, leave is given by the Department of Trade to open an account at a local bank. A liquidator may not retain a sum exceeding £100 for more than ten days without the authority of the Department of Trade. If he does so, the Department may remove him from office and disallow part of his remuneration. He is also liable to pay interest to the company at 20 per cent per annum on the excess retained over £100.

The creditors

A creditor must submit proof of his debts. He does so by delivering or sending through the post to the liquidator an affidavit giving details of the debt, the amount claimed and whether the debt is secured. The creditor's remedy is solely against the company and the debts for which he can prove are specified in the Act. If the company is solvent, then all debts are provable, including sums payable on a contingency, sums payable in the future and claims in respect of unliquidated damages for which a just estimate can be made. If the company is insolvent, the same rules apply, except that debts incurred with knowledge of the winding up cannot be paid, and unliquidated damages arising out of breach of trust or contract are provable.

When the company is insolvent, the liquidator may set off against any debt owed by the company a debt due to the company from the creditor and only the balance is proved or paid.

The creditor who is the most favoured is the secured creditor. As he holds some security for the debts owed to him by the company, such as a mortgage, charge or lien, he has four courses open to him. He can rely on his security and not prove in the winding up. If the security covers part only of the debt, he can realise the security and prove for the balance. Alternatively, he can surrender the security to the liquidator and prove for the whole debt, or he can value the security and prove for the balance, in which case the liquidator may redeem at the assessed value.

The payment of debts

If the company is solvent, the liquidator can settle the company's debts in any order he wishes, but if the company is insolvent he must follow a strict order for the payment of debts.

The assets are applied first in paying the cost, charges and expenses properly incurred in the winding up. This includes the remuneration of the liquidator.

The next group of debts to be paid are the preferential debts. They all rank equally and must be paid in full, unless there are insufficient assets when they abate in equal proportions. The main classes of preferential debts are listed in section 319. They are:

Income tax, corporation tax and other assessed taxes for any one year of assessment;

Value added tax for the twelve months before the relevant date;

Rates falling due within the twelve months before the relevant date;

Wages or salaries of an employee during the four months preceding the relevant date, up to £800, and all accrued holiday remuneration;

Contributions payable in respect of national insurance during the twelve months before the relevant date and certain other claims under Social Security legislation.

The relevant date in a compulsory winding up is usually the date of the winding up order.

If a person such as a bank, has advanced money to a company to enable the wages, salaries or holiday remuneration of the employees to be paid, that person is regarded as a preferential creditor to the same extent as an employee would have been.

Preferential debts have priority over a floating charge created by the company.

After the preferential debts have been paid, the claims of the ordinary creditors are met. These debts also rank equally among themselves, and if there are insufficient assets to meet their claims in full, they will abate equally. The payment to a member of any unclaimed dividend will be deferred until the ordinary creditors have been paid.

Should there be a surplus, the liquidator must repay any calls on shares which have been paid in advance, followed by the repayment of capital to the shareholders. Any further surplus will be distributed amongst the shareholders according to the rights set out in the articles.

Termination of office of liquidator

A liquidator who wishes to resign his office must summon meetings of the creditors and contributories to obtain their consent. If his resignation is accepted, the liquidator files a memorandum with the Registrar of the Court and informs the Official Receiver. His resignation then takes effect. If either of the meetings refuses to accept his resignation, or if no resolutions are passed, either the liquidator or the Official Receiver may apply to the Court, and the Court may make such an order in respect of the acceptance of the resignation, as it thinks fit.

A liquidator may be removed from office by the Court if good cause is shown. Should a receiving order in bankruptcy be made against a liquidator, then he will be removed from office. When the liquidator has completed winding up the company's affairs, he may, after giving notice to every creditor who has proved, and to every contributory, apply to the Department of Trade for a report on his accounts to be prepared. The Department of Trade will consider the report and any objections made by any creditor or contributory, and will either grant or withhold the liquidator's release.

A release relieves the liquidator from liability for any breach of duty committed in the course of the winding up. A release can be revoked if it is shown that it was obtained by fraud or by the concealment of some material fact.

Neither resignation nor removal releases a liquidator from liability, and he must follow a similar procedure in applying to the Department of Trade for his release.

The completion of the winding up

The process of winding up may be lengthy and it may take a liquidator several years to complete the winding up of a large and complex company. If a winding up is not completed within one year from its commencement, the liquidator must send to the Registrar twice yearly a statement giving particulars as to the position of the liquidation.

When the company's affairs have been completely wound up the liquidator may apply to the Court for an order that the company be dissolved. The Court will make such an order and the company will be dissolved from that date. A copy of the order must be sent to the Registrar, who minutes the dissolution of the company.

In practice such orders are rarely applied for. Instead, the liquidator applies to the Department of Trade for his release and the company is dissolved under the provisions relating to defunct companies.

The Court may, within two years, declare the dissolution void on the application of the liquidator or any other interested person. This makes possible the distribution of any asset which was overlooked when the company was dissolved (section 352).

24

Voluntary Liquidation

Procedure

A company may resolve to wind up voluntarily. This is the usual method of winding up a company and there are fewer formalities to be complied with, as compared to a compulsory winding up. The services of the Official Receiver are not required; a provisional liquidator is not appointed; the liquidator does not have to give security to the Department of Trade; the liquidator is appointed by the company or the committee of inspection, and not by the Court.

A voluntary winding up is initiated by passing one of the three types of resolutions.

An *ordinary resolution* is required if the articles specify that the company shall be wound up after a certain period of time, or on the occurrence of a certain event. Such articles are rarely found in practice, and a company is not automatically dissolved on the occurrence of either of these events. The Court is not bound to make a winding up order in these circumstances.

The company may pass a *special resolution* to wind up voluntarily. No reason need be given for the passing of such a resolution as it is sufficient that a 75 per cent majority at a meeting of the company has resolved upon a winding up. Should the voluntary liquidation be the first step towards an amalgamation or reconstruction of the company, a special resolution is required. Such a resolution can only be challenged on the grounds that it is unfairly prejudicial to the minority, or that it is not in the interests of the members as a whole.

If the company decides that it cannot continue its business by reason of its liabilities, it will pass an *extraordinary resolution* to wind up voluntarily. Usually such a resolution signifies that the company is insolvent. This is not necessarily so, as a company may decide that the payment of its debts will leave it with insufficient working capital to continue in business.

The resolution must be advertised in the *London Gazette* within fourteen days of its being passed. A voluntary winding up dates from the passing of the winding up resolution. There are two kinds of voluntary winding up:

- A members' voluntary winding up.
- A creditors' voluntary winding up.

A members' voluntary winding up

A members' voluntary winding up takes place where the company is solvent. The liquidation will be under the control of the members themselves and they will appoint the liquidator. As the creditors will be paid in full they have no role to play in the winding up.

The first step is for the directors to make and file a declaration of solvency to the effect that they have made a full inquiry into the affairs of the company, and having done so have formed the opinion that the company will be able to pay its debts in full, within a period not exceeding twelve months from the commencement of winding up. This declaration must be made within the five weeks immediately preceding the passing of the winding up resolution, and must include a statement of the company's assets and liabilities. The declaration must be filed with the Registrar within fifteen days of passing the resolution.

At the subsequent extraordinary general meeting, two resolutions are passed: a resolution to wind up; and a resolution to appoint a liquidator. The winding up resolution and the notice of the liquidator's appointment must be advertised in the *London Gazette*, and filed with the Registrar.

If in the course of the winding up the liquidator forms the opinion that the company will not be able to pay its debts in full, within the specified time, he must summon a meeting of the creditors and lay before them a statement of the company's assets and liabilities. Summoning the meeting does not convert the winding up into a creditors' voluntary winding up, it merely ensures that the creditors are given information relating to the company's financial position so that they may, if they so wish, petition for a compulsory winding up order. Otherwise the voluntary winding up continues, with the liquidator summoning annual and final meetings of creditors, as in a creditors' voluntary winding up.

If the winding up continues for more than a year the liquidator must summon a general meeting of the company at the end of the first and each successive year, and lay before it an account of his acts and dealings and the progress of the winding up during the preceding year.

As soon as the company's affairs are fully wound up the liquidator calls a final meeing of the company, which must be advertised in the *London Gazette*, and submits his final account. A copy of this account, and a return of the meeting, must be filed with the Registrar within one week before the meeting. The company is automatically dissolved three months after the registration of the return.

Creditors' voluntary winding up

If the directors are unable to file a declaration of solvency, the winding up proceeds as a creditors' voluntary winding up. In addition to summoning an extraordinary general meeting of the company to pass a resolution for winding up (a minimum of seven days' notice to be given) the company must also summon a meeting of its creditors. The notice of the creditors' meeting must be sent to each creditor at the same time as notices convening a general meeting.

The creditors' meeting must be held either on the same day as the extraordinary general meeting, or on the following day, and will be presided over by one of the directors. The directors must lay before the meeting a full statement of the company's affairs, together with a list of creditors and the estimated amounts of their claims.

At the company's meeting a resolution may be passed to nominate a liquidator. The creditors likewise have the right at their meeting to nominate a liquidator. Should different persons be nominated, the nomination of the creditors will prevail, subject to any order made by the Court. The creditors may also appoint a committee of inspection of up to five persons to act with the liquidator.

The company may then nominate up to five persons to act as members of the committee, but the creditors may disallow the company's nominations, subject to appeal to the Court.

If the winding up continues for more than one year, the liquidator must not only summon a general meeting of the company, but also a meeting of the creditors at the end of the first and each successive year, and lay before the meetings an account of his acts and dealings and the progress of the winding up during the preceding year.

As soon as the company's affairs are fully wound up, the liquidator calls final meetings of the company and creditors and submits his final accounts to both meetings. The meetings are advertised in the *London Gazette*. The liquidator sends to the Registrar a copy of the accounts and a return of the meetings within one week after the date of the later meeting.

The company is automatically dissolved at the end of three months from the registration of the return.

The effect of a voluntary winding up

When the company resolves to wind up voluntarily it ceases to carry on its business except in so far as it is necessary for its beneficial winding up. It still retains its corporate personality until it is dissolved. Shares can only be transferred with the sanction of the liquidator and any alteration in the status of the members is void. The employees of the company are dismissed only if the company is insolvent. The powers of the directors cease on the appointment of the liquidator, unless their continuance in office is sanctioned.

The liquidator's duty is to pay the company's debts and adjust the rights of the contributories among themselves.

He applies the company's property, first in paying preferential debts, and then in discharging the company's liabilities *pari passu*. Any surplus will be distributed amongst the members according to their rights.

In order to achieve this he may, without sanction, make calls, settle a list of contributories, summon general meetings and exercise most of the powers of a liquidator in a compulsory winding up.

With the sanction of an extraordinary resolution in a members' voluntary winding up, or the sanction of the Court, committee of inspection, or the creditors (if there is no committee of inspection), the liquidator may make any compromise or arrangement with creditors, pay any class of creditors in full, and compromise any calls, debts or liabilities. For example, a compromise could be sanctioned if a contributory was unable to pay the full amount of a call or a debt.

Supervision order

Where a company has resolved to wind up voluntarily and the creditors or contributories are dissatisfied with the conduct of the liquidator, the Court may make an order that the winding up shall continue under the supervision of the Court. The winding up continues for the most part as a voluntary winding up. Such an order is rare as the creditors in a voluntary winding up will usually ask the Court to determine any questions and exercise any of the powers which it could exercise in a compulsory winding up.

If applied for, a supervision order fulfils a useful function. All proceedings against the company are stayed and the court can appoint another liquidator to act with, or replace, the existing liquidator.

Arrangement with creditors

A company which is about to be, or is in the course of being, wound up voluntarily may come to a binding arrangement with its creditors. Such an arrangement requires an extraordinary resolution of the company and the approval of 75 per cent in number and value of its creditors.

Any creditor or contributory may within three weeks appeal to the Court against the arrangement. The Court may confirm or vary the arrangement.

25

The Reconstruction and Amalgamation of Companies

These are commercial terms, which are widely used, but are not given any legal definition in the Act. The term 'reconstruction' is used to describe a scheme which involves the re-organisation of a company's capital structure. It is also used to describe a scheme in which a company transfers its whole undertaking and property to a newly formed company, in exchange for shares in that company.

An amalgamation occurs when the undertakings of two or more companies are brought under single control.

A reconstruction or an amalgamation, as the case may be, may be achieved in one of four ways: by sale under the memorandum, by reconstruction under section 287, by scheme of arrangement or by takeover.

Sale under the memorandum

A company may sell the whole of its undertaking and property to a new company in return for shares in that company. Although a company has no implied power to dispose of its undertaking in this way, most companies reserve such a power in their objects clause. A company may decide upon this course of action when it does not require further capital from its shareholders. It can be used if no arrangement or composition is to be made with the company's shareholders, creditors, or debenture holders.

The old company sells its undertaking to the new company in exchange for shares in the new company. The old company is then wound up. The shares in the new company are distributed amongst the members of the old company, in accordance with their rights. If a member dissents he obtains the same protection as a member is given under section 287.

In this way it is possible to extend the objects, reduce capital, obtain new capital and perform other operations which might otherwise be difficult to accomplish.

Reconstruction under section 287

Section 287 gives a company the power to effect a reconstruction by means of a voluntary liquidation. If a company is not already in liquidation, it will circulate details of the scheme to its members, convene a general meeting, pass the necessary resolutions to wind up, and appoint a liquidator.

If the company is in liquidation, the procedure laid down by the section can be carried out at any time. Should the liquidation be a creditors' voluntary winding up, the liquidator must also obtain the Court's sanction, or that of the committee of inspection to a reconstruction.

The liquidator will invariably seek the Court's approval in a members' voluntary winding up, for without its approval the special resolution for the sale of the company's assets will be void, if a winding up order or supervision order is made within a year of passing the resolution.

This form of reconstruction is often used when a company requires further capital from its existing shareholders. The liquidator transfers the whole of the old company's undertaking to a new company for shares in the new company, credited as partly paid. The shares of the new company are distributed to the members of the old company *pro rata* to their holdings. The amount unpaid on the new shares is then called up to provide the additional capital. As the shareholders have the right to refuse or dissent, it is usual to arrange the underwriting of the new capital.

It has also been used for altering a company's objects. A company may wish to extend its activities, but finds that the alteration of its objects clause would not be permitted under section 5. It may form a new company with the desired objects, and by proceeding under section 287 transfer its undertaking to the new company.

Section 287 is also an effective method of varying shareholders' rights, where these are set out in the memorandum and are stated to be unalterable.

An amalgamation can be conveniently achieved under section 287. An existing company can sell the whole of its undertaking to another company. The shareholders of the first company become shareholders of the second company. The business and property of both companies become amalgamated into one company.

An amalgamation of two or more companies may be effected by transferring their undertakings to a new company formed for the purpose. The new company issues shares credited as fully paid to the shareholders of the old companies, in exchange for their shares. The old companies are dissolved and the new company usually assumes the name of one of the old companies to complete the amalgamation.

Rights of dissenting shareholders

A member who is opposed to the scheme may express his dissent by serving written notice on the liquidator at the company's registered office within seven days, requiring him either to refrain from proceeding with the scheme or to purchase his shares. As the liquidator is bound to carry out the resolution, he must purchase the shares. This provision only applies to a shareholder who did not vote in favour of the scheme.

If the parties agree on the purchase price the shares will be purchased at that price. Should they be unable to agree, the matter will be referred to arbitration. In determining the purchase price, regard must be had to the value of the shares before the reconstruction. Any increase in value as a result of the reconstruction should be disregarded. The purchase money must be paid to the member before the company is dissolved.

A shareholder who has not dissented, or required the liquidator to purchase his shares, may not wish to become a shareholder in the new company. He cannot be compelled to do so. Should he refuse to become a member, he will not be entitled to compensation and he may lose all rights to his shares. The scheme usually provides that the liquidator may sell the shares of such a member and the amount received for the shares will be paid to the member.

A company may not deprive a member of his right to dissent. In *Payne v. Cork Co. Ltd*, the articles of a company provided that a dissenting shareholder should not have the power to require the liquidator to purchase his shares. It was held that such an article was void.

Rights of creditors

The sale of the old company's assets by the liquidator is binding on the creditors. The transfer agreement will usually provide that the new company will take over the old company's debts, or that the old company will retain sufficient funds to cover its debts. If a creditor accepts the liability of the new company for his debts there is a novation – a substitution of a new debtor for an old debtor – and his claim against the old company will cease.

A company will pay off a creditor who is unwilling to accept a novation, as a dissatisfied creditor may within a year petition the Court for a compulsory winding up order, or a winding up under supervision. If such an order is made, any arrangement under section 287 is invalid until approved by the Court.

Scheme of arrangement

The third method of achieving a reconstruction or amalgamation is by a scheme of arrangement under section 206. This section facilitates compromises or arrangements between a company and its creditors, or between a company and its members, or both its creditors and members. It requires the approval of a specified majority of creditors and/or members and the sanction of the Court.

It can be used whether the company is a going concern or is being wound up, and unlike section 287 the company need not be wound up to carry out any scheme of arrangement. It has an advantage over section 287, in that the decision of a specified majority will over-rule the minority, unless the Court rules otherwise. It will not be necessary to purchase the interests of any shareholder or creditor who dissents from the scheme.

It has been used for a wide variety of schemes involving compromises or arrangements with creditors. Creditors and debenture holders have accepted shares in discharge of their debts; other creditors have accepted part shares and part cash in lieu of their debts; secured creditors have given up their security or agreed to the creation of prior charges; while debenture holders have agreed to forego their interest for a stated period.

It has also been used to vary the rights of members. Preference shareholders have agreed to the cancellation of arrears of dividend and a reduction in the fixed rate of dividend. Ordinary shareholders have agreed to surrender part of their holdings to preference shareholders, who in turn have agreed to accept ordinary shares in lieu of arrears of dividend.

Other schemes sanctioned by the Court under section 206 have involved the re-organisation of the capital structures of companies. These have included the reduction of a company's share capital and the cancellation of deferred shares carrying a high rate of dividend. Amalgamations involving the re-organisation of the capital structures of the companies involved have also been approved by the Court.

It has been used to alter the class rights of shares where the rights were conferred by the memorandum which made no provision for any variation of class rights.

As the scheme requires the Court's approval the first step is to ask the Court to convene the necessary meetings of the parties affected by the scheme. The application is usually made by the company or its liquidator, but it can be made by any member or creditor.

Notices of the meetings are sent out to the members and creditors explaining the effect of the proposed scheme and in particular how it would affect the interests of the directors. If the scheme involves a compromise with the debenture holders, it must show its effect on the interests of the trustees for debenture holders.

If only a certain class of members or creditors is affected, meetings need only be summoned for that particular class; for example, if the rights of ordinary shareholders are to be altered but not those of preference shareholders, only class meetings of ordinary shareholders need be summoned. There are three classes of creditors – secured, unsecured and preferential – and each class must be dealt with separately. The holders of shares paid in advance are a different class from ordinary shareholders. If there are persons who belong to different classes, they may attend and vote at meetings of each class in which they have an interest.

The various meetings are then held. Voting is by poll, and three-quarters in value of the creditors or class of creditors, or members or class of members, present in person or by proxy, must sanction the scheme. This is to prevent a majority of members or creditors with a minor interest in the company out-voting a minority with a large stake in the company.

The scheme is then submitted to the Court for its approval. Before the Court grants its approval it must be satisfied that the necessary statutory requirements have been complied with: that the requisite majority of members and/or creditors have given their approval at the necessary meeting or meetings; that the meetings fairly represented the class interest and that the scheme is one which a prudent business-man would approve.

When the Court has approved the scheme it binds all the parties concerned. The order sanctioning the scheme is not effective until a copy has been registered with the Registrar. A copy of the order must be attached to every copy of the memorandum subsequently issued.

Where, as part of a scheme, the whole or part of the undertaking of a company (the transferor company) is to be transferred to another company (the transferee company) the Court may make ancillary orders to facilitate the scheme. These have included:

The transfer of the property or liabilities of the transferor company to the transferee company;

The allotment of shares and debentures;

The dissolution; without winding up of the transferor company;

Provision for dissentients similar to that provided under section 287.

Takeovers

The fourth method of achieving an amalgamation is to acquire sufficient shares in another company so as to exercise control over that company. This can be effected by purchasing all the shares of the other company or sufficient shares to acquire a majority of the voting power.

The number and classes of shares to be acquired will vary according to the degree of control which the acquiring company seeks. It may desire total ownership, or it may require sufficient control to be able to pass extraordinary or special resolutions. In some cases the acquiring company may be satisfied with a degree of control which allows it to pass ordinary resolutions. This will enable it to secure the appointment of the directors of its choice.

The voting rights of the different classes of shares is another factor to be considered. If the preference shares do not carry votes, or only have voting powers when their dividend is in arrears, a company may regard it as sufficient to acquire control of the ordinary shares.

A takeover bid is an obvious way of merging two or more companies which are similar or complementary businesses. There are a variety of factors which may prompt a takeover bid.

The object of the bid may be to secure a particular asset, or to acquire an asset and use it more profitably, as in the Savoy Hotel case where the object of the bid was to acquire a hotel and convert it into offices.

The transferee company may wish to diversify its interests. In recent times many large companies have sought to stimulate growth by expanding into other fields.

The transferor company may have pursued a conservative dividend policy, or it may not have revalued its fixed assets. Consequently its shares are quoted at a price which is well below the actual or potential value of the business.

The transferee company may feel that the management of the transferor company is ineffective or inefficient.

Any one of these factors or a combination of them would make a company an attractive target for a takeover bid.

There are various ways in which the transferee company may acquire the shares necessary to give it the degree of control it seeks. It may be possible to purchase the shares on the open market, or (if there is agreement on the merger between the two companies) the shares may be acquired by negotiation with the principal shareholders, or by arrangement between the boards of directors of both companies. The usual method is to make a public offer to the shareholders to buy their shareholding for a combination of cash, debentures or shares in the transferee company.

There is often resistance to a takeover bid from the directors of the transferor company, who may not wish to relinquish control of the company, or who believe that the offer is totally inadequate.

The offer is usually stated to be open for acceptance for a fixed time and is made conditional on acceptance by the holders of a specified percentage of shares. Once a shareholder has accepted he is bound to sell the shares, but the transferee company is not bound to purchase the shares unless the conditions in the offer have been fulfilled (i.e. the acceptance of a given percentage of the shares in question).

The consideration offered to the shareholders of the transferor company may be cash, or an allotment of shares or debentures in the transferee company or one of its associated companies. If a cash offer is made, the price offered will be in excess of the current quoted price of the share, so as to induce the shareholders to accept the bid, rather than sell their shares on the market. The same consideration will apply to an offer of an allotment of new shares or debentures, with or without cash.

If debentures are offered as new securities, they will ensure a fixed income and grant greater security, but the holder will have no right to vote at general meetings or to share in any future in the value of the ordinary shares. Companies often offer convertible debentures as an inducement.

Section 209

The interests of the majority and minority are protected by section 209. This provides that where the holders of nine-tenths of the shares involved have within four months accepted the scheme, the transferee company may, within two months, give notice to any dissenting shareholder that it wishes to acquire his shares. The company is then bound to acquire the shares on the same terms as those given to approving shareholders, unless the dissenting shareholder appeals to the Court within one month and the Court directs otherwise.

The Court rarely intervenes to prevent the compulsory acquisition of shares but did so in the case of *Re Bugle Press* where two shareholders held 90 per cent of the issued shares in a private company. They offered to buy the third shareholder's 10 per cent shareholding for £14.50 per share, but he refused their offer. They then formed a new company in which they held all the issued share capital and this new company offered to buy the first company's shares for £10 each. The two shareholder accepted the offer and the second company sought to acquire the third shareholder's shares under section 209. It was held that this was an abuse of section 209 as the transferee company was the same as the majority in the transferor company. For such a compulsory purchase to be approved it would have to be shown to be fair. Having already offered far more for the shares on the first occasion, it was impossible to justify such action.

The power to compulsorily acquire shares is a useful provision that allows the transferee company to avoid the management and administrative problems which can occur where subsidiary companies are not wholly owned.

Section 209 also grants concessions to a dissenting shareholder in the situation where the transferee company has acquired nine tenths of the shares in the transferor company, and has not chosen to acquire his shares compulsorily. Within one month of the transferee company acquiring nine tenths of the shares it must notify the fact to the dissenting shareholders. Any dissenting shareholder may then require the transferee company to purchase his shares on the terms of the offer, or on such other terms as may be agreed, or as the Court on either party's application may agree.

26

Mergers and the City Code on Takeovers and Mergers

Mergers

Under the Fair Trading Act 1973, as amended by the Competition Act 1980, the Secretary of State may refer large scale mergers and proposed mergers to the Monopolies and Mergers Commission for their consideration. The Commission will investigate the facts and if they consider that a merger operates or would operate against the public interest, the Secretary of State has the power to terminate or prevent the merger. The Fair Trading Act allows the Secretary of State to make a reference to the Commission in anticipation of a merger. Secretaries of State have preferred to use this power, as it is far easier to prevent a proposed merger, than to terminate an already completed merger. In the case of a referral of an existing merger the Secretary of State must refer it within six months of it taking place.

A merger arises when two or more enterprises of which one at least is carried on in the United Kingdom or by or under the control of a body corporate in the United Kingdom, have ceased to be distinct enterprises either by being brought under common ownership or control, or by one of them ceasing to function as a result of an arrangement to prevent competition between them.

The Fair Trading Act is concerned only with mergers which are of economic significance. The Secretary of State may refer a merger only if either the value of the assets taken over exceeds £15 000 000, or it produces a situation in which at least a quarter of all the goods or services of a particular description supplied in the United Kingdom, or a substantial part of the United Kingdom, will be supplied by or to the same person.

When a merger is referred to the Commission it must satisfy itself that the merger falls within the scope of the Act (i.e. the £15 000 000 assets or one-quarter market share) and it must decide whether the merger or proposed merger will operate against the public interest.

The Commission must take into account all matters which appear to them to be relevant, including the maintenance and promotion of effective competition in the United Kingdom, the protection of consumers with regards to goods and services, the reduction of costs by development and competition, the maintenance of a balanced industry and employment in the United Kingdom and the maintenance of a competitive market outside the United Kingdom.

The Commission in its report must give its conclusions on the matters raised in the reference, with reasons, and must also give a survey of the background to the merger. Any effects not in the public interest must be specified, together with any recommendations for remedying such effects. If the report states that there is nothing against the public interest, the merger will proceed. If there is an adverse report there are various courses open to the Secretary of State. He may request the Director General of Fair Trading to consult the parties, with a view to obtaining certain undertakings from them to remedy the harmful effects of the merger indicated in the report. If this proves impossible, the Secretary of State has wide powers which include the prevention of a proposed merger, the cancellation of an existing merger, or allowing the merger to proceed but subjecting the new enterprise to various regulations.

European Community law does not expressly provide for a system of merger control, although the aim of the third directive is the co-ordination of provisions regulating internal mergers within a member state. The Commission and the European Court of Justice have taken the view that Article 86 of the EEC Treaty can be applied, in certain circumstances, to a merger situation. Article 86 prohibits any abuse by one or more undertakings of a dominant position within the Common Market, or a substantial part of it, if this would affect trade between member states. The article contains four examples of abuse, but none of them refers to mergers.

The European Court applied Article 86 to a merger situation in *Europemballage Corporation and Continental Can Co. Inc. v. E.C. Commission*. An American company, through a subsidiary, obtained control of a German company which had a share of the German market in metal tins and containers. Two years later it obtained control of a Dutch company which was the largest manufacturer of metal containers in the Benelux countries. The Commission contended that the control of the German company gave the American company a dominant position in the German market. As this was a 'substantial part of the common market' within the meaning of Article 86, its subsequent acquisition of the Dutch company was an abuse of its dominant position, as it would eliminate possible future competition between the two companies and would in this way affect trade between member states. The European Court upheld the Commission's interpretation of Article 86, but allowed the company's appeal on the grounds that the Commission had not adequately analysed the product market. The merger was allowed to proceed.

The application of Article 86 to a merger situation has led to certain problems. So far Article 86 has only been applied to a merger situation where one of the parties has been in a dominant position before the merger, and as a result of the merger find themselves in a dominant situation. There are no provisions for allowing the Commission to hold up a merger pending investigation, or for submitting a proposed merger to the Commission for its consideration. Neither is there machinery for granting exemption on the grounds of efficiency or any grounds of public interest.

The City Code on takeovers and mergers

The 1948 Act makes no special provision as to the conduct of a takeover bid. This deficiency has largely been made good by the City Code on takeovers and mergers which was first published in 1968 and has been revised on several occasions (the latest revision appearing in 1981). It has no legal sanction, but is voluntarily observed by stockbrokers and merchant banks who are involved in takeover transactions. The Code is administered by the Takeover Panel which has its own permanent secretariat. Companies or individuals who act in breach of the Code face a private reprimand or public censure and in the most serious cases, withdrawal of Stock Exchange facilities. The Panel may refer certain aspects of a case to the Department of Trade or the Stock Exchange or to any other appropriate body.

The provisions of the Code are divided into two parts: the general principles and the rules.

The general principles
The general principles are concerned with the conduct to be observed in takeover and merger situations. The Code emphasises that the spirit as well as the precise wording of the general principles and rules must be observed.

Some of the most important general principles include the following:

Directors of both the offeror company (the company making the bid or offer) and the offeree company (the company whose shares are the object of a bid or offer), while owing a duty to their shareholders, must allow proceedings in a takeover bid to proceed fairly and regularly.

The directors of the offeree company must not, without the approval of the company in general meeting, take any action which could frustrate a genuine takeover bid which is imminent or which has been made. All shareholders must be given adequate information, advice, and sufficient time to allow them to make a reasoned judgment on a bid. The directors of the offeree company must seek competent, independent advice before expressing an opinion of an offer. If they recommend the rejection of a bid, or the acceptance of the lower of two bids, they must be prepared to justify such advice.

Any right of control which the offeror company already has in the offeree company must be exercised in good faith and no shareholder may be treated oppressively. If the offeror company makes a general bid following selective purchases of shares, the terms shall be at least as favourable as the selective purchase.

Both parties must make every effort to prevent the creation of a false market in their securities. All documents issued in connection with the takeover bid should be drafted with the same degree of care as if they were a prospectus under the Companies Act.

The directors of both the offeror and the offeree company must act in the best interests of the shareholders, creditors and employees. Their actions should not be motivated by self or family interest. The offeror should only announce an offer after careful and responsible consideration, and only if he has every reason to believe that he can implement the offer.

The rules
There are thirty-nine rules dealing with the standards of conduct required from the parties, and the procedures to be followed in the course of a takeover or merger.

The rules are wide ranging and flexible and are designed to deal with the variety of problems and situations which may arise in the course of a takeover or merger. This can be seen from a sample of the following rules:

An offer should first be made known to the board of directors of the offeree company or its advisers. If the offer is made by an intermediary, the identity of the bidder must be stated. The board of directors of the offeree company is entitled to be satisfied that in the event of the bid being successful, the necessary finance will be available.

The directors must immediately publish a press notice and circularise its shareholders informing them of the bid. It if it is not a firm bid, but negotiations are proceeding which could lead to a bid, the publication of the press notice and circular can be delayed. If, however, there is an 'untoward movement' in either company's shares, indicating a possible leak of information, an announcement must be released at once.

An announcement that talks are taking place and a request to the Stock Exchange to grant a temporary halt in dealings will be made when negotiations have reached an advanced stage, or negotiations are about to take place in which a wider circle of individuals will be consulted.

The Panel's consent is required for any partial offer; that is, an offer to purchase part only of the shareholding not already acquired by the offeror. In the case of a bid which would result in the offeror controlling less than 30 per cent of the voting rights, consent will normally be given. If a bid would result in a holding of 30 per cent, but less than 100 per cent of the voting rights, consent will not normally be given if the offeror has acquired selectively or in significant numbers shares of the offeree company in the previous twelve months.

An offer which would result in an offeror holding between 30 per cent and 50 per cent of a company's voting rights, will normally be conditional on its approval by holders of over 50 per cent of the voting rights not held by the offeror. (As many shareholders do not bother to vote at the meetings, a 30 per cent holding of the voting rights in a public company is regarded as effective control of that company.)

A person acquiring a 30 per cent control of a company's voting rights must make an offer for the remainder of the shares. A similar offer must be made if a person, in concert with another, already holding between 30 per cent and 50 per cent of a company's voting rights, acquires further shares (in a twelve month period) carrying more than 2 per cent of the voting rights. The price offered must represent the highest price paid, in the previous twelve months, by the offeror company for shares in the offeree company. The offer must be conditional upon the offeror obtaining sufficient acceptances to bring his holding to more than 50 per cent of the voting rights.

An offer must remain open for acceptance for at least twenty-one days. If it is revised, for example by offering an increased price, it must be kept open for a further fourteen days.

An offer document must state that the offer is conditional on its acceptance by a sufficient number of shareholders, so as to give the offeror control of over 50 per cent of the voting rights in the offeree company. If an offer is subsequently declared to be unconditional, it must be kept open for a further fourteen days, to allow individuals who have not previously accepted it an opportunity to accept.

An offer document must show the present shareholding of the

offeror company in the offeree company and also the shares owned or controlled by the directors of the offeror company in the offeree company.

A circular by the offeree company recommending acceptance or rejection of the bid must also give the shareholdings of its directors in the offeror company and in the offeree company, and must state whether such directors intend to accept the bid in respect of their holdings. The circular must also give details of the directors' service contracts and must indicate the effect of a successful bid on their emoluments.

Any person in possession of price-sensitive information regarding an offer or contemplated offer, must treat the information as confidential. No such person (except the offeror) may deal in the securities of the offeree company between the time when there is reason to suppose that an approach or offer is contemplated, and the announcement of the approach or offer or of the termination of the discussions. No such dealings may take place in the securities of the offeror company except where the proposed offer is not regarded as price-sensitive in relation to its securities.

During the offer period all the parties to a takeover or merger transaction are entitled to deal in these securities, subject to daily disclosure to the Stock Exchange, the Panel and the press.

When a company, in the course of a takeover, publishes profit forecasts, the basis of the forecast must be stated and the accounting policies and calculations for the forecast must be examined and reported on by the auditors or the consultant accountants. The basis of any valuation of assets must be given and these must have been valued by an independent valuer.

As can be seen the main object of the City Code is to secure fair and equal treatment for all shareholders when a takeover or merger is proposed, and to ensure adequate disclosure of information to all interested parties.

Appendix I

Index of Cases

Page references are given in bold type

Appendix II

The Companies Act 1980

The Companies Act 1980 is intended to amend and strengthen British company law in certain respects. It will be brought into force by regulation.

Part I: Classification and Registration of Companies, Etc.

The Directive is mainly concerned with the formation of public companies and the subscription and maintenance of their share capital. In order to ensure that its provisions are not applied to companies for which it would be inappropriate, the Act involves the redefinition of the terms 'public' and 'private' companies. The first part of the Act provides the necessary new definitions, and also the machinery for the registration and re-registration of companies.

Classification of companies (Sections 1 and 2)
> *Section 1* defines public and private companies.
>
> *Section 2* together with *Schedule 1*, sets out requirements as to the constitution of a public company in respect of the minimum number of its members, its name and its Memorandum of Association. It also introduces the designation 'Public Limited Company' for public companies. (*Section 78* provides that this may be abbreviated to 'plc', and also gives equivalents in Welsh).

Registration and re-registration of companies, etc. (Sections 3 to 13)
> *Section 3* makes provision for the registration of new public and private companies. It follows the existing Companies Acts' provisions but makes special provisions for public companies.
>
> *Section 4* prohibits a public company registered under Section 3 from doing business or exercising any borrowing powers until it obtains a certificate from the Registrar of Companies of compliance with requirements as to its allotted share capital.
>
> *Sections 5 to 12* provide for re-registration of private companies as public companies and *vice versa*. They also specify requirements that must be fulfilled for such re-registration and, in *Section 8* lay down transitional provisions for old public companies.

Section 13 amends the provisions of Part VIII of the Companies Act 1948. It permits a company not formed under the Companies Acts to be registered under the section as a public company provided certain conditions are satisfied.

Part II: The Capital of a Company

Part II deals with the share capital of public and, in some cases, private companies. It sets out requirements as to the issue of and payment for share capital, the maintenance of such share capital, the rights of existing shareholders on the issue of further shares and the variation and registration of class rights.

The issue of capital (Sections 14 to 16)

Section 14 prohibits directors of companies, whether public or private, from exercising any powers of a company to allot shares and certain other securities unless they are authorised to do so by the company in general meeting or by the Articles of the Company.

Section 15 prohibits private limited companies with a share capital from offering their shares or debentures to the public.

Section 16 provides that, where an increase in capital of a public company is not fully subscribed for, no share may be allotted unless the terms of the offer so provide.

Pre-emption rights (Sections 17 to 19)

Sections 17 to 19 deal with the rights of pre-emption of existing shareholders in public and private companies on the allotment of further shares for cash, how these rights may be altered and transitional provisions.

Payment for share capital (Sections 20 to 31)

Sections 20 to 25 and 28 and 29 specify the way in which shares may be allotted and paid up and prohibit the allotment of shares at a discount.

Sections 26 and 27 place conditions on a public company acquiring more than a certain value of assets from the subscribers to its Memorandum within its first two years of business, or from its members within two years of re-registration.

Section 28 empowers the courts to grant relief from civil liability for breach of these conditions.

Section 30 provides criminal penalties in the form of fines where a company fails to comply with the requirements of these sections.

Section 31 extends the provisions of Sections 20 to 30 (except Sections 26 and 27) as they apply to public companies and to other forms of companies which are in the process of becoming public companies.

Class rights (Sections 32 and 33)

Section 32 deals with the conditions under which rights attached to special classes of shares may be varied.

Section 33 provides for delivery to the Registrar of Companies of particulars of special rights attaching to a company's shares and of variations of those rights.

Maintenance of Capital (Sections 34 to 38)

Sections 34 to 38 deal with the maintenance of a company's capital. If the net assets of a public company fall to half of its called-up share capital an extraordinary general meeting must be called. A limited company cannot acquire its own shares for valuable consideration and the subscribers to the Memorandum or the directors can be held liable with any person who has failed to pay sums due on shares of the company bought by him as a nominee of that company. Shares forfeited or surrendered to a public company for failure to pay sums due must be disposed of by the company within three years, or they must be cancelled. A public company cannot (with certain exceptions) have any liens or other charges over its own shares.

Part III: Restrictions on Distributions of Profits and Assets (*Sections 39 to 45*)

Part III lays down rules restricting distributions to members of the company.

Sections 39, 40 and 44 and 45 prevent any company making a distribution except out of profits available for that purpose. There are detailed provisions for determining the amount available and restrictions on the purposes for which an unrealised profit can be applied.

A public company is permitted to make a distribution only when its net assets are not less than the aggregate of its called-up share capital and undistributable reserves and the distribution does not reduce the company's assets to an amount lower than the aggregate.

Section 41 lays down separate rules for investment companies, which it defines.

Section 42 makes special provision for the realised profits of insurance companies.

Section 43 defines the accounts which must be taken into consideration in determining whether a distribution can be made.

Part IV: Duties of Directors and Conflicts of Interests

Duty in relation to employees

Section 46 lays down that directors are, in the performance of their functions, to have regard to the interests of the company's employees as well as to the interests of its members.

Particular transactions giving rise to conflict of Interest (Sections 47–53)

Section 47 prevents directors granting themselves arrangements for long service employment with the company so that large sums of compensation may be claimed in the event of dismissal as director (e.g. on takeover of the company). Arrangements for employment for terms greater than five years will have to be affirmed by the shareholders in general meeting.

Section 48 prevents the transfer of property worth £50000 or more between directors and their companies unless sanctioned by a general meeting. Connected persons of directors are covered, as well as subsidiaries' dealings with holding company directors.

Section 49 defines the scope of the provisions contained in Sections 49–67 relating to the granting of loans or credit by companies to their directors and connected persons. It repeats the existing prohibition (in Section 190 of the 1948 Act) on loans and guarantees and securities on loans, by any company to its directors or to those of its holding company and it extends this prohibition principally to persons connected with directors of 'relevant' (in brief, public) companies and also for relevant companies, to quasi-loans. A quasi-loan to a person is, in substance, a loan: it consists of the payment to a third party (or agreement to make such a payment) on behalf of the director, rendering the director liable to reimburse the company.

Section 50 lists the exceptions to the prohibitions set out in Section 49. For example, Subsection (2) provides an exemption from the quasi-loan prohibition for up to £1000 per director if the quasi-loan is agreed to be repaid within two months. Payments or advances made for the purpose of defraying expenses incurred by directors acting as agents of the company are not, of course, caught by any of these provisions, as such payments do not call for reimbursement by the director, and therefore do not amount to a provision of credit. The exemption in subsection (3) allows all 'credit transactions' (e.g. HP, leases) between companies and directors if they are in the ordinary course of business and on normal commercial terms. Subsection (4)(d) permits moneylending companies to make loans and quasi-loans to directors on normal commercial terms (subject to a limit of £50000 for those money-lending companies which are not 'recognised banks'), and directors of moneylending companies are also allowed (by subsection (7)) to participate in subsidised house-loan schemes up to a limit of £50000.

Section 51: The object of this Section is to specify which arrangements or transactions are to be taken into account in determining whether the quantitative limits for relevant companies prescribed in Section 50 have been exceeded by directors and persons connected with them.

Section 52 sets out the civil consequences of contravening Section 49 and is based on the remedies available for a breach of duty by a director.

Section 53 makes it a criminal offence for relevant companies to lend to their directors in contravention of Section 49, and for directors deliberately to authorise transactions in breach of Section 49 to themselves, fellow directors, or connected persons of any of the directors. It will also be an offence for any person deliberately to procure any such transaction.

Section 54 describes the type of transactions which are to be disclosed, individually, in the annual accounts of companies and the group accounts of holding companies and, together with the other disclosure sections, replaces Section 197 of the 1948 Act and Section 16(1)(c) of the 1967 Act.

Section 55 provides a list of the particulars of each type of transaction required to be disclosed by Section 54.

Section 56 supplements the disclosure provisions in Section 54 and Section 55, providing for the aggregate disclosure both of transactions involving officers, and of transactions between recognised banks and their directors.

Section 57 requires recognised banks to keep an internal register containing details of all relevant transactions and to produce a statement available to shareholders at a specified time and place, containing all the details that other companies would be required to produce in their accounts.

Section 58 lays down various threshold limits for the disclosure provisions.

Section 59 places a duty on auditors to include in their report a statement giving the particulars (as far as possible) of any loans and other transactions of the kinds described in Sections 49 to 67 which have not been disclosed in the accounts. This replaces a similar provision in Section 197 of the 1948 Companies Act.

Section 60 supplements the disclosure provision in Section 199 of the 1948 Act so that directors will be required to disclose to the company their interest in all transactions or arrangements with the company.

Section 61 extends Section 26 of the 1967 Companies Act, which requires companies to keep a register of directors' contracts of service, to include contracts with subsidiary companies, and to require disclosure of the duration term in any contract requiring a director to work overseas.

Section 62 gives the Secretary of State power to increase all the financial limits specified in Sections 48–58 by order made by statutory instrument.

Section 63 extends the provisions of Part IV with certain exceptions to a 'shadow director', a person in accordance with whose directions or instructions the directors of a company are accustomed to act.

Section 64: This section defines 'connected persons' for the purposes of the previous prohibition and disclosure provisions. The circle of connected persons is to include the director's spouse, children and stepchildren (including illegitimate children but excluding children aged eighteen and above), trustees of any trust whose beneficiaries include the director or his connected persons, and companies with which the director is associated.

Section 65 provides definitions of various terms used in Sections 47–64: for example subsection (4) defines how the various transactions and arrangements are to be valued and subsection (7) exempts all transactions and arrangements entered into before the appointed day from the prohibitions, though any outstanding liabilities under them are to be included when calculating the 'relevant amounts' in Section 51.

Section 66 states those parts of the 1948 and 1967 Acts which will cease to have effect.

Section 67 applies the disclosure provisions of Part IV to unregistered companies.

Part V: Insider Dealing (*Sections 68 to 73*)

Part V defines insider information and insiders and makes insider dealing a criminal offence.

Section 68 sets out prohibitions relating to transactions in company securities on a recognised stock exchange, where a person connected with a company possesses information, by virtue of his connection with the company, which is such that it ought not to be disclosed except for the performance of his functions and which he knows is unpublished price-sensitive information. The prohibitions also bite on people who receive such information from outsiders. The prohibitions apply to dealing on a recognised stock exchange, counselling or procuring someone else to deal or passing on the information when subsequent dealing is likely. The prohibitions also apply in the case of information about takeover bids by an individual or group of individuals (which covers bodies without corporate status which are not covered by the earlier provisions).

There is an exception to the prohibitions if the thing is done otherwise than with a view to the making of a profit or avoidance of a loss by the use of the information. There are also various other defences including defences under certain circumstances for liquidators receivers trustees in bankruptcy and jobbers.

Section 69 lays down similar prohibitions in relation to information obtained by Crown Servants in their official capacity.

Section 70 applies the prohibitions in Section 68 and 69 to off-market deals in advertised securities through or by professional dealers making a market in the securities.

Section 71 excludes from the operation of Section 70 certain activities by issue managers of Eurobonds.

Section 72 lays down the penalties for contravening Sections 68 and 69: On conviction on indictment to imprisonment for a term not exceeding two years or an unlimited fine, or both; and on summary conviction to imprisonment for a term not exceeding six months or a fine not exceeding the statutory maximum, at present £1000 or both.

Section 73 interprets Sections 68 to 72. Connection with a company; Unpublished price-sensitive information are among the terms defined.

Part VI: Miscellaneous and General

Interests of employees and members (*Sections 74 and 75*)

Section 74 gives a company power to provide for employees when a business is being closed down or transferred, subject to proper approval by shareholders. The position of creditors is safeguarded as such a payment to employees will only be possible out of sums available for distribution.

Section 75 gives any member of a company or in certain cases the Secretary of State power to petition the Court on the ground that the affairs of the company are being or have been conducted in a manner which is unfairly prejudicial to some part of the members or that some proposed act or omission by the company would be prejudicial. The section gives the Court power if it thinks such a petition is justified to make such order as it thinks fit for giving relief.

Miscellaneous (Sections 76 to 83)

Section 76 makes it an offence for a person who is not a public company to use the title 'Public Limited Company'.

Section 77 and 78 allow abbreviations for public limited company, a Welsh alternative (but where one is used the fact that it is a public limited company must be publicised in English), and abbreviations for private companies.

Section 79 lays down the qualifications which company secretaries of public companies must have in future.

Section 80 lays down revised penalties and changes in mode or trial for offences under existing companies acts.

Section 81 amends the 1948 Act allowing additional information to be required in the directors' report.

Section 82 repeals various provisions of the 1948 Act.

Section 83 remedies an omission from the Banking Act 1979. It requires deposit-takers not licensed under the Banking Act to continue to make returns under the Protection of Depositors Act 1963 and continues the Department's powers in respect of such companies.

General (Sections 84 to 90)

Section 85 specifies the authorised minimum share capital of public companies as £50 000. This may be varied by an order approved by each House of Parliament.

Sections 86 to 90: Minor amendments, repeals and interpretations and corresponding provision for Northern Ireland.

Schedules

Schedule 1 lays down draft forms of Memorandum of Association of Public Companies.

Schedule 2 Increase of penalties and change in modes of trial.

Schedule 3 Minor and consequential amendments.

Schedule 4 Repeals.

Appendix III

The Companies Act 1981

Part I : Company Accounting and Disclosure

Part I implements the EC Fourth Directive on company accounts by laying down provisions for the form, content, filing, publication and audit of company accounts and reports.

Sections 1 and 2 and Schedule 1 implement the majority of the technical accounting provisions of the Directive and make corresponding provisions for group accounts. The Schedule prescribes formats for accounts; stipulates accounting principles to be followed by companies; lays down historical cost accounting rules and alternative rules (including provisions permitting current cost accounting) for arriving at the amounts to be stated in accounts; specifies the information to be given in the notes to the accounts; applies these rules generally to consolidated accounts; and makes certain special provisions for holding company, subsidiary company and investment company accounts.

All companies are required to prepare full accounts for shareholders but *Sections 5 to 10* confer exemptions in respect of accounts delivered to the Registrar of Companies by small and medium-sized companies which are not public companies, banking, insurance or certain shipping companies, or members of a group including a company of one of these kinds. By virtue of these provisions, small companies may file with the Registrar accounts consisting of an abbreviated balance sheet and notes only: no profit and loss account or directors' report are required. Medium-sized companies may file a modified profit and loss account and may omit from the notes to accounts certain information on turnover, but must submit a full balance sheet and directors' report. Each set of modified accounts sent to the Registrar must be accompanied by a special directors' statement and auditors' report.

Section 12 allows certain dormant companies not to appoint auditors and, subject to certain conditions, exempts them from the obligation to have an auditors' report.

Sections 13 to 16 make a number of changes to the contents of the directors' report, place a duty on auditors to consider whether the information given in a directors' report is consistent with the accounts and repeal Section 20 of the 1967 Act (particulars of exports to be given in directors' reports in certain cases).

Section 17, taken with Schedule 2, enables certain banking, insurance and shipping companies, and their holding companies, to continue to prepare individual and group accounts in compliance with the requirements of the 1948 Companies Act and with Schedule 8A to that Act (that is, the pre-1981 Act Schedule 8 as renumbered under Section 1 of the 1981 Act).

As an interim measure, individual and group accounts prepared by *any* company in respect of a financial year beginning before the appointed day (to be specified by Statutory Instrument) for the new accounting regime may comply with the pre-1981 Act requirements.

Other provisions of Part I deal with the publication of annual accounts, whether in full or in part, other than by delivering to the Registrar, for example by publication in a newspaper.

Part II : Company Names and Business Names

Company names

Part II of the Act simplifies the arrangements governing the approval of company names, whilst preventing the registration of names identical to those of certain existing organisations and retaining restrictions on the use of certain words and expressions. Names will also not be registered if they are considered to contravene other legislation or to be offensive, and may be refused registration if they give the impression of connection with Her Majesty's Government or a Local Authority (*Section 22*).

The Registrar is required to keep a statutory index containing the names of existing companies and other specified bodies which will be available for inspection free of charge (*Section 23*).

The Secretary of State has a power to direct a company to change its name if he considers that name to be the same as or 'too like' that of a body already shown on the index. A company can also be directed to change its name if it appears to have provided misleading information, or not to have fulfilled undertakings given for the purpose of registration (*Section 24*). The period within which a direction may be issued on the ground that a name is 'too like' another has been extended beyond the time allowed in existing legislation. Corresponding provisions are made for overseas companies trading here (*Section 27*).

A private company limited by guarantee which wishes to omit the word 'limited' from its name and which is able to make a statutory declaration that it fulfils certain specified conditions relating to its objects and profits will be able to omit that word under *Section 25* without obtaining the specific licence formerly required by Section 19 of the 1948 Act which will be repealed.

Business names

The new Act requires any business which is carried on under a name other than that of its owner, whether those owners are private individuals or companies capable of being wound up under the 1948 Act, to disclose information about that ownership at its business premises and on certain business documents. This information must also be given in writing to customers and suppliers when demanded (*Sections 28 and 29*). Any breach of these disclosure requirements is subject to penalties which are supplemented by a power to invoke a civil sanction against the offending business. (*Section 30*).

On the introduction of these requirements, early in 1982, the present Registry of Business Names will be abolished, although the Secretary of State will retain a power to control the use of certain words or expressions in business names on the same basis as in company names. Revised Notes of Guidance will be available to describe these new requirements.

Part III: Share Capital

Relief from section 56 of the 1948 Act

Sections 36 to 41 provide prospective and retrospective relief from Section 56 of the 1948 Act, which requires premiums on shares issued to be transferred to an undistributable share premium account.

Section 37 provides *prospective* relief in respect of broadly defined share-for-share arrangements whereby the acquiring company secures at least a 90 per cent equity holding in another company.

Section 38 offers slightly more restrictive *prospective* relief in respect of certain intra-group reconstructions.

Section 39 provides *retrospective* relief in respect of certain share-for-share arrangements effected in the past in which premiums have *not* been transferred to a share premium account.

The prospective and retrospective reliefs by these sections, which came into operation on Royal Assent, operate forwards and backwards respectively from the date of publication of the 1981 Companies (No. 2) Bill, 4 February 1981.

Section 41 provides the Secretary of State with a power, subject to affirmative resolution by both Houses, to give relief from Section 56 in relation to non-cash premiums and to restrict or otherwise modify the relief from Section 56 of the 1948 Act provided by these Sections.

Financial assistance for acquisition of shares

Sections 42 to 44 contain new provisions regulating the provision by a company of financial assistance for the purchase of its own shares or those of its holding company.

Section 42 redefines the basic prohibition (currently in Section 54 of the 1948 Act, which is now repealed), exempts transactions whose principal purpose is not to provide assistance and for the purpose of the acquisition also exempts certain specified transactions.

Section 43 exempts from the prohibition financial assistance given by private companies provided that certain requirements are met, including the making of a statutory declaration of solvency by the directors and in some cases authorisation by special resolution.

Section 44 contains supplementary provisions and enables a minority of members to apply to the Court for the cancellation of any special resolution authorising financial assistance by a private company.

Power of company to issue redeemable shares

Section 45 permits a company to issue redeemable shares. It replaces Section 58 of the Companies Act 1948, which permits a company to issue only preference shares as redeemable, and so widens the scope for companies to issue redeemable shares. The new provision lays down requirements for redeemable shares, most of which are derived from the existing law. One of the new requirements restricts the use of share premium account in paying up any premium on redemption, although the existing situation is maintained in Section 62 for preference shares already issued under Section 58 of the 1948 Act.

Purchase by a company of its own shares.

The power of a company to purchase its own shares is conferred by *Section 46*. Section 46 applies the requirements laid down in Section 45 for redemption of shares to purchase, and many of the subsequent Sections of the remainder of Part III apply both to redemption and purchase.

The provisions lay down precise conditions for a company purchasing its own shares. Purchases made on the Stock Exchange and Unlisted Securities Market are distinguished from others, and procedures for authorisation of market purchases (*Section 49*), of off-market contracts of purchases (Section 47), and of contingent purchase contracts such as options (*Section 48*), are prescribed. There must be disclosure of particulars of purchase (*Sections 14 and 52*).

Payment of the purchase or redemption price must normally, and any other payment associated with a purchase must always (*Section 51*), be found from a company's distributable profits, and a capital redemption reserve must be created equal to the nominal value of shares purchased or redeemed (*Section 53*). But a private company may have recourse to capital reserves to pay the price of a purchase after exhausting available profits if it complies with procedures set out in *Sections 54 to 57*.

Section 58 deals with the liability of a person receiving payment from capital and of a director of the company in the event of a winding up within one year after the payment.

Section 59 sets out the consequences of a failure of a company to meet a commitment to redeem or purchase shares.

A power is conferred on the Secretary of State to modify various aspects of the provisions by statutory instrument subject to affirmative resolution (*Section 61*).

Part IV : Disclosure of Interests in Shares

Part IV contains provisions obliging a person (i.e. a legal person, including a body corporate) having a substantial interest in a public company's shares to notify it of that fact, and conferring upon a public company a power to investigate beneficial interest in its shares.

Section 63 prescribes the main obligation to notify a public company of a known substantial interest in its shares, defined as 5 per cent of its voting power, and of changes in that interest.

Section 64 provides for the Secretary of State a power to vary this percentage subject to affirmative resolution.

Section 65 requires a person making a notification to include information about the identity of the registered holder of the shares in which he is interested.

Sections 66, 67 and 69 require a person to treat interests in shares of other persons as his own for the purposes of the obligation to notify a substantial interest.

Section 66 attributes to a person the interests of his or her spouse and child aged under eighteen. It also attributes interests of a body corporate which a person is deemed to control.

Section 67 attributes to a person who is a member of a 'concert party' (i.e. an agreement under which an interest in shares of a company is acquired and which includes using interests held by members of the party in any way involving mutual reliance on each other) all of the interests of the other members.

Section 68 imposes a consequential obligation on members of a concert party to keep each other informed so that they may comply with their obligation to make notification to the company when or if it arises.

Sections 70 and 71 respectively define when a person is to be regarded as having an interest in shares for the purposes of the obligation to notify a substantial interest and interests to be disregarded. The Secretary of State may add additional exemptions by statutory instrument.

Section 72 imposes an obligation upon a person who authorises an agent to deal on his behalf to ensure that his agent notifies him of any transaction likely to give rise to an obligation to notify, and also prescribes the penalties for failure to comply with this and earlier obligations.

Section 73 requires every public company to keep a register of notifications received under the preceding sections.

Section 74 is concerned with the second element of the disclosure of interests provisions. It provides for a company to investigate interests in its shares. Enquiries may be made of any person whom the company knows or has cause to believe to be interested in its share or to have been interested within the preceding three years.

Under *Section 75*, the company is required to record results of its inquiries in the register required to be kept under Section 73.

A minority having 10 per cent or more of the shares of a company may, under *Section 76*, require the company to use its power to investigate interests in its shares, if they can show reasonable grounds, and the company must provide interim reports at three monthly intervals until the investigation is complete and then a final report.

Section 77 prescribes penalties for failure to comply with a request for information from a company which include the possibility of the court placing restrictions on shares.

The remaining sections 78 to 83 ensure that information may be removed from the register only in prescribed cases, that the register is available for inspection by members and the public, and make supplementary provisions.

Part V : Miscellaneous and Supplemental

Distributions
Sections 84 and 85 supplement the distribution rules of the 1980 Act.

Investigations and inquiries
Sections 86 to 89 and 92 contain provisions to streamline company investigation procedures and strengthen the power of inspectors.

Section 86 changes the circumstances in which inspectors may be appointed at the request of the company.

Section 87 extends the classes of persons whom inspectors may examine on oath without application to the Court and provides for the production by past and present directors of particulars of their bank accounts in certain circumstances.

Section 88 revises the arrangements relating to the publication of inspectors' reports.

Section 89 widens the classes of persons placed under a duty to assist inspectors appointed under Section 172 of the 1948 Act.

Section 92 enables those conducting investigations on behalf of the Secretary of State under Section 334(3) of the Companies Act 1948 to exercise the powers given to inspectors appointed under Sections 164 or 165 of that Act.

Restrictions on participation in management of companies
Sections 93 and 94 strengthen the provisions which enable persons to be disqualified from taking part in the management of companies. The main changes are:

(a)   to empower courts of summary jurisdiction to disqualify, for up to five years, persons convicted summarily of an indictable offence in connection with the management, etc. of a company; and also persons with a history of default in making returns to the Registrar of Companies;

(b)   to extend the maximum period of disqualification which courts of higher jurisdiction may order in certain cases from five to fifteen years;

(c)   to widen the grounds on which a disqualification order may be made to include certain misconduct in connection with the promotion, formation, receivership or liquidation of a company (as well as in connection with its management);

(d) similarly, to extend the range of activities from which disqualified persons (including, under paragraph 9 of Schedule 3, those disqualified by virtue of being undischarged bankrupts) are debarred to include the additional ones mentioned in (c) above; and

(e) to bring directorships of overseas companies which carry on business within Great Britain within the coverage of the disqualification order.

Disclosure of directorships

Section 95 requires companies to keep details of past directorships held by their directors (other than directorships in any company which wholly owns them or in its or their wholly-owned subsidiaries, and in dormant companies), in addition to the details of other current directorships which they are at present required to keep by virtue of Section 200 of the Companies Act 1948. Such details will be available for inspection either at the company's registered office or at the Companies Registration Office.

Fraudulent trading

Section 96 extends the criminal sanction for fraudulent trading under Section 332(3) of the Companies Act 1948 so as to apply not only where the company is being wound up, as at present, but also where it is not in liquidation. It reverses the judgment in *DPP v. Schildkamp* (1971) and will in future enable prosecutions for fraudulent trading to be undertaken whether or not a company has been wound up.

Functions of the Registrar

Sections 97 to 100 make certain changes to the functions of the Registrar of Companies.

Section 97 requires him to allocate to every company a registered number and enables him, in addition, to allocate a letter.

Section 98 empowers him to provide copies of documents for public inspection, including microfiche copies, rather than the original documents themselves, except where the copies are illegible or unavailable.

Section 99 enables the Registrar when issuing certificates and copies of documents, either to certify them by hand or to authenticate by seal.

Section 100 enables him to destroy, after ten years, the original copies of companies' annual returns and accounts delivered to him, provided copies of the original documents are retained.

Registration of members' shareholdings and class rights

Section 101 requires that the register of members of a company limited by shares or by guarantee should disclose the class of share or membership held by each member.

Section 102 requires that details of rights of classes of a member of a company which does not have a share capital should be placed on public record with the Registrar of Companies, if these details are not already available in other documents delivered to the Registrar.

Disclosure of information

   Section 103 provides that legal professional privilege in investigations and inquiries extends to communications in the hands of the client as well as his legal advisers.

   Section 104 widens the circumstances in which information obtained under Section 109 of the Companies Act 1967 and certain other Acts can be disclosed under Section 111 of that Act.

Voluntary liquidations

   Section 105 relaxes the provisions of Section 283 of the 1948 Act concerning the voluntary winding up of companies by allowing more time for the delivery of a declaration of solvency to the Registrar and by providing a criminal penalty for failure to deliver, rather than the existing sanction which renders the winding up a creditors' voluntary winding up.

   Section 106 amends section 293(1) of the 1948 Act by requiring a minimum of seven days' notice to members of a meeting to put the company into creditors' voluntary liquidation: this restricts any power to hold meetings at short notice or without notice and does not reduce the normal notice requirements of the Act or the company's articles. Notice of a creditors' meeting, to be held on the same or the following day, is required to be sent out at the same time.

   Section 107 allows, subject to specified conditions, the voluntary winding up of a company to proceed as a members' voluntary winding up in circumstances where the required statutory declaration of solvency was posted, but not delivered, to the Registrar of Companies between 7 April and 1 August 1981.

Bona Vacantia

   Section 108 will entitle a person reviving a dissolved company to receive a cash payment equivalent to its assets, from the Crown, the Duchy of Lancaster or the Duchy of Cornwall (to which the assets of a company pass on its dissolution) where the Crown, the Duchy of Lancaster or the Duchy of Cornwall has already disposed of these assets.

Overseas Companies

   Section 109 defines and clarifies the requirements regarding the filing of documents by Channel Island and Isle of Man companies.

Amendment of Parts IV and V of the 1980 Act

   Sections 110 and 111 introduce certain relaxations and make technical adjustments to the provisions of Part IV of the Companies Act 1980 on directors' conflicts of interest.

   Section 110 introduces three exclusions from the requirement under Section 48 of the Companies Act 1980 that arrangements involving the acquisition of non-cash assets by a company from a director (or connected person) or *vice versa* should be approved by the general meeting:
   (a)   arrangements between a holding company and its wholly-owned subsidiaries, or between two wholly-owned subsidiaries of the same holding company;

(b)   arrangements entered into by a company in liquidation (other than a members' voluntary winding up); and

(c)   arrangements whereby directors are to receive assets from the company purely by virtue of being shareholders in it, for example, through rights or bonus issues of shares.

Section 111 enables a company to lend up to £2500 per director.

Section 112 makes certain technical amendments to Section 71 of the 1980 Act, which excludes certain dealings in international bonds from the prohibition on Insider Dealing. The Section also enables the Secretary of State to make further amendments to Section 71 by regulation, subject to the approval of both Houses of Parliament.

Supplemental

Sections 113 to 115 and 117 to 119 contain necessary supplemental, transitional and commencement provisions.

Section 116 will enable amendments of the Companies Acts and related legislation to be made by Order in Council provided that the amendments are recommended by the Law Commissions as desirable to permit a satisfactory consolidation of the Companies Acts.

Index

Index

MANAGEMENT SCIENCE

DENNIS WHITMORE

A major business objective today is to improve productivity, that is, to make better use of available resources, such as labour, materials and capital. However, the increasing specialisation of modern commerce and industry has meant that the contemporary manager often has to deal with a wide range of specialist functions in order to solve the problems with which he is faced.

The book is a compendium of the techniques available to help the manager both to recognize problems and formulate the most effective way of solving them. These techniques provide a tool kit of possible solutions from which the most appropriate method can be selected.

The fifteen chapters are grouped into two basic divisions, the first covering the fundamental concepts, such as problem solving and the science of control, and the second presenting a detailed analysis of the techniques, such as work study, ergonomics and operational research.

This is a book for all students whose studies include productivity or management sciences and for all personnel in line or function management.

Dennis Whitmore is a consultant in Management Sciences.

TEACH YOURSELF BOOKS

MANAGEMENT ACCOUNTING

BRIAN MURPHY

The role of the management accountant is to present management with the best possible financial information upon which they can base their decisions, and to establish control systems to ensure that the best use is being made of the concern's resources.

This book describes the main systems and techniques which are at present available to the management accountant. Topics covered include historical and standard costing, budgetary control, financial planning and marginal costing. Working examples are included throughout and a number of practical exercises are given in each chapter.

Brian Murphy is principal lecturer in management accounting at Huddersfield Polytechnic.

TEACH YOURSELF BOOKS

OFFICE MANAGEMENT

P. W. BETTS

The role of the office manager has completely changed in recent years, but the critical part he plays in determining the success of a concern still remains often unrecognised.

The on going business is dependent upon successful administrative operations at all organisation levels. Hence the generation of more and more paperwork and the ever increasing demand for administrative staff, but more paper and staff are not necessarily the answer. In this book the author gives a lucid account of the information and techniques essential to the departmental office manager. The text offers the business student an overall account of administrative management and explains the need for increased expertise in this practice. Executives responsible for organisational structure will also find this book invaluable.

P. W. Betts is Director of the Management Centre at Harrow College of Technology.

TEACH YOURSELF BOOKS

BANKING

STUART VALENTINE and STAN MASON

This comprehensive account of banking in the United Kingdom considers the functions and services of the major banking institutions and the role of banking in its wider economic context through the financing of industrial development and overseas trading.

A history of banking is followed by a detailed description of the different types of bank, the services they provide, their operation at home and abroad and their control by the Bank of England. The work of the Bank of England in implementing Government monetary policy and current legislation is also discussed in depth. The findings of the Wilson Committee on the practices of banks and other financial institutions are included, as are the Bank of England proposals for monetary control. Concluding chapters consider recent developments and future trends.

This book provides essential background reading for all those following business studies courses and is recommended by the Institute of Bankers to those studying 'Elements of Banking' in Stage 1 of the Institute of Banking examinations.

Stuart Valentine is Economic Adviser to the Stock Exchange and Stan Mason controls the Research and Information Section of the Corporate Finance Division of the Midland Bank.

TEACH YOURSELF BOOKS